LOYAL
DISSENT

Moral Traditions series
James F. Keenan, S.J., series editor

As of January 1, 2007, 13-digit ISBN numbers will replace the current 10-digit system. Paperback: 978-1-58901-087-1

Georgetown University Press, Washington, D.C.

Library of Congress Cataloging-in-Publication Data

    Curran, Charles E.
      Loyal dissent : memoir of a Catholic theologian / Charles E. Curran.
        p.   cm.—(Moral traditions series)
      Includes bibliographical references and index.
      ISBN-13: 978-1-58901-087-1 (pbk. : alk. paper)
      ISB-10: 1-58901-087-6 (pbk.: alk. paper)
      1. Curran, Charles E.   2. Catholic University of America—Faculty—Biography.
    3. Catholic Church—Biography.   I. Title.   II. Series.
    BX4705.C795A3   2006
    241′.042092—dc22

                                              2005027232

Printed in the United States of America

This book is printed on acid-free recycled paper meeting the requirements of the American National Standard for Permanence in Paper for Printed Library Materials.

13 12 11 10 09 08 07 06 9 8 7 6 5 4 3 2
First printing

LOYAL DISSENT

Memoir of a Catholic Theologian

CHARLES E. CURRAN

GEORGETOWN UNIVERSITY PRESS
Washington, D.C.

To my nieces and nephews,
Dan, Tom, Patty, Jim, Katie
Christa, Matt, Benita, Beth,
their spouses and children, especially Lauren Chase

Contents

Preface

THE ELECTION OF A POPE is a very important event in the life of the Catholic Church. The papal election in April 2005 was more significant than most, coming after the twenty-six-year papacy of Pope John Paul II. On April 18–19, attention focused on the 115 cardinals in the Sistine Chapel as they voted for the new pope.

During the conclave I realized that I was somewhat well acquainted with four of the electors, who had been schoolmates of mine in Rome. From 1955 to 1961 I did my seminary work in Rome, was ordained a priest there, and received two doctorates in theology. During those years I lived at the North American College, the seminary for students from dioceses in the United States, and later at the graduate house of the college for priests studying for advanced degrees. In those days I was well acquainted with the future cardinals but of course knew some better than others. With one of them I traveled extensively; we attended the Passion Play at Oberammergau in 1960 and visited the Holy Land together in 1961.

Our paths diverged in later years. We all had advanced degrees, but I made the academy my home, while the others became involved in church administration. My writings and life as a Catholic moral theologian have made some modest contribution to the theology and life of the Catholic Church. I have served as president of three national academic societies— the Catholic Theological Society of America (CTSA), the Society of Christian Ethics (SCE), and the American Theological Society (ATS). In addition, I have received the highest awards from both the CTSA and the College Theology Society (CTS) for outstanding contributions to theology.

I have written more than fifty books in the area of moral theology.[1] But I think I know my weaknesses and limitations in terms of whatever contributions I may have made.

I had even greater differences with the four future cardinals I knew while studying in Rome. In 1967 a strike at the Catholic University of America (CUA) succeeded in overturning the decision of the board of trustees not to renew my contract. All the archbishops in the United States, together with other bishops and a few laypeople, were members of the board at CUA. In 1968 I acted as the spokesperson for a group of Catholic scholars, ultimately numbering more than 600, who publicly recognized that one could disagree in theory and in practice with Pope Paul VI's 1968 encyclical *Humanae vitae,* which condemned artificial contraception, and still be a loyal Roman Catholic.

After Josef Ratzinger's election as pope, I realized that my disagreement with these former schoolmates went deeper than I had supposed. They were probably quite pleased with the election of the new pope. I was not. In 1986, after a seven-year investigation and a personal meeting at the Vatican, Cardinal Ratzinger, in his role as prefect of the Congregation for the Doctrine of the Faith (CDF) and with the approval of the pope, declared that I was neither suitable nor eligible to be a Catholic theologian. Now Ratzinger is Pope Benedict XVI.

Despite my differences with Josef Ratzinger and with the cardinal electors who had been my schoolmates in Rome, we share a common calling to the priesthood. Even more important, I share with them a strong commitment to the Catholic Church, despite what I consider its many shortcomings. When *Commonweal,* the lay-edited Catholic journal, asked me to do an article on my reaction to the new pope, I pointed out my major theological differences with Ratzinger and insisted on the need for a number of important reforms in the church today. I concluded, "As a Catholic Christian, I respect and love the office of the Bishop of Rome. I respect and love Pope Benedict XVI as he tries to carry out his most difficult office. Like all Catholics, I pray daily for the wisdom that he needs. But, while conscious of my own shortcomings, I will continue to offer what I believe are constructive criticisms for the good of the pilgrim church."[2]

Friends have urged me for years to write my memoirs. I began this project a year before the election of Pope Benedict XVI, but not without some hesitation. Some parts of the story have already appeared in print. I am not the most scintillating of writers, having spent my life writing primarily for an academic audience. Nor have I kept a diary or careful records, so I will have to rely heavily, at times, on memory, which as we all know can play tricks. There is a further problem. Memoirs tend to be very self-oriented. In all honesty, I am aware that my story is only a small part of a much bigger one. I am also very conscious of how much I have depended on others and their help along the way. Can I tell the story without succumbing to the danger of overemphasizing my own role and function? *Caveat lector.*

This book will try to explain how the church and moral theology have changed in the past fifty years and how I matured from an uncritical, dutiful, pre–Vatican II Catholic into a loyal dissenter who remains a committed Catholic.

Acknowledgments

M Y DEBTS ARE MANY. This volume mentions the many people who have influenced and helped me along my pilgrimage. I am particularly grateful to Southern Methodist University (SMU) for providing me a very hospitable and challenging academic environment for my teaching and research since 1991. In particular, my thanks go to the administration, faculty colleagues, students, and especially the librarians at the Bridwell Library. I am honored to hold the Elizabeth Scurlock University Professorship of Human Values, established by Jack and Laura Lee Blanton in memory of Laura Lee's mother. Laura Lee Blanton died in 1999, but because of the Blantons' significant benefactions to SMU, her memory and influence are strongly felt on this campus. I am indebted to Richard Brown, the director of Georgetown University Press, and James F. Keenan, the editor of its Moral Traditions series, together with the very efficient staff of the press, who have been both extremely helpful and encouraging. Richard Brown, Ann Early, Andrew Galligan, John Gargan, Kenneth Himes, and James Keenan painstakingly read the manuscript and made many helpful suggestions. My associate Carol Swartz has worked more closely with me than anyone else. She has greatly facilitated my work with her counsel, efficiency, and considerateness.

CHAPTER 1

Beginnings

I WAS BORN IN Rochester, New York, in 1934. My parents, John F. Curran and Gertrude Beisner Curran, both came from New York City, but my father moved to Rochester in 1926. They were married in 1927 and lived in Rochester the rest of their lives. I was the third of four children. My older brother, John (Jack), was born in 1929; my sister, Kathryn (Kay), in 1931; my younger brother, Ernest, in 1937. Most of us had nicknames generally given by my older brother: I was Chase. Friends who knew me as a youngster still call me Chase, but I am Charlie to those I met later in life. We all called my younger brother Diaper, a name that needs no explanation. Jack was eight years older than Diaper, and once he left Rochester for college he never returned. Until a few years ago, his children still referred to their Uncle Diaper. We called my father "D" after the D.A. in the radio program "Mr. District Attorney."

There is no doubt we were a Catholic family. My parents were quite close to Father John B. Sullivan, the pastor of the parish in which they first lived when they came to Rochester. Even after they moved, they continued to go to that church, but on Father Sullivan's advice they sent my older brother Jack to Nazareth Hall, a private school run by the Sisters of St. Joseph. In those days the tuition was $100 per year. Although my sister and younger brother went to St. Ambrose, the school of the parish in which we lived, my parents sent me to Nazareth Hall in 1939 to follow in my brother's footsteps. To this day I remember the names and person-alities of the sisters who taught me in the eight grades of grammar school.

My parents were both convinced Catholics, though they also had many other interests. My mother was a homemaker who took care of her husband, her children, and her house, but was also a daily communicant and very active in church and school organizations. She was the president of the mothers' club at Nazareth Hall and also at Aquinas Institute, the Catholic high school that my brother Jack attended. She was very energetic and had a wide network of friends. Growing up, we heard the story that her older brother had tried to teach her to drive, but she ran into a tree and never drove again. Her father, a German immigrant who married an Irish woman, was the only grandparent I ever knew.

My father, more of an introvert than my mother, came to Rochester to run the local one-person office of Utilities Mutual Insurance Company, which insured the workers of public utilities in New York State. Although never a candidate for public office, he had been interested in politics all his adult life. In Rochester he worked mostly behind the scenes as an advisor and speechwriter for the local Democratic Party, which was regionally the minority party despite its sometimes controlling the state and often the federal government. A 1957 book on Rochester, *Smugtown U.S.A.*, described my father as a "democratic stalwart . . . not only objective in his thinking but an able speech writer," and as "calm and phlegmatic," which was apt.[1]

Our family was middle class. As a kid, I used to take the monthly rent money ($40) to the man who built and owned our house. In the mid-forties, my father bought the house for $4,500.

We were a Catholic family but did not live in a Catholic ghetto; we thought of ourselves, first and foremost, as "Americans." My best friend in grammar school was a Christian Scientist. In the neighborhood, Catholics and Protestants (as far as I knew, there were no other religions) hung around together. Only later in life did I discover that my father and his family were strongly Irish and that his family was a magnet in New York City for many Irish immigrants. Years later I asked him why we never celebrated or even acknowledged our Irishness. My father told me that he was eighteen and the eldest child when his father died. All the Irish relatives, neighbors, and friends came to what they expected to be the usual interminable Irish wake, but he kicked them out at midnight. "They never talked to me since, and I have not had anything to do with them." That explains my lack of Irish consciousness!

The sisters at Nazareth Hall described me as bright and devout, but even as a child I showed an independent, questioning streak. Shortly after my first communion—May 5, 1940—the former principal of the school, Sister Aquinas, died, and we all attended her funeral at the motherhouse of the Sisters of St. Joseph. I asked my first-grade teacher, Sister Agnes Cecilia, why, if communion was so important, it was not part of funerals, for this was the custom at the time. Sr. Agnes Cecilia herself ultimately became the mother general of the Sisters of St. Joseph of Rochester, and led the community through a very difficult time in adjusting to the post–Vatican II church. We stayed in touch until her death in 2003. To her great credit, even after my ordination in the pre–Vatican II church, she still continued to call me Charles and I always called her sister, not mother.

In that very Catholic atmosphere and ethos, I was attracted to the church. As a family, we knew no priests (my parents' relationship to Father Sullivan waned after they moved away from the parish), but I was attracted to the priesthood. I had talked to a Paulist priest who came to the school to drum up vocations. In the eighth grade I asked my parents if I could go to St. Andrew's Seminary, the minor seminary of the Diocese of Rochester, which was a high school that also included two years of college. At St. Andrew's the seminarians lived at home during their school years, but they were not allowed to date and were committed to preparing for the priesthood. We were to go to daily Eucharist in our local parishes before taking the bus to school.

Looking back, I find I am quite defensive about my decision to attend St. Andrew's. I certainly would never recommend it to anyone today. But that was a different era, and by the age of thirteen I had discerned that I was called to be a Catholic priest. I am not a psychologist, but I am sure there were many factors that entered into that decision, some of them unconscious. But I have never regretted the decision, despite all the ups and downs of my life since then, many of them not of my own choosing.

As a youngster, I was a good and serious student but also a regular kid. I was interested in sports at an early age, thanks to the influence of my older brother, with whom I used to listen to sports reports and ball games on the radio each night. I especially liked to read sports books checked out of the local library. In 1942 I won a weekly contest, sponsored by a local radio station, by predicting the scores and winners of Saturday's college football games more accurately than any other contestant. I was invited to appear on the program the following Friday to predict the outcome of the following day's games. When my brother and I arrived at the radio station, the announcers were amazed to find out that the winner was eight years old. I had to stand on a chair in order to reach the microphone to make my predictions for the following day. As I recall, my predictions were way off.

My father usually drove my brother and me to grammar school on his way to work, but we took city buses home in the afternoon, changing buses downtown. Somehow or other my brother found out that the man who ran the newsstand where we changed buses was also a bookie who ran football pools. The bookie got a kick out of the ten-year-old kid who would put down his twenty-five cents each week in the hope of winning $1.25. I won more often than not, usually by picking the three strongest teams to defeat their opponents by more than the spread.

At the same time, I followed my older brother to Oak Hill Country Club to work as a caddy. I was the youngest, smallest kid there, but during the war they needed caddies and let me carry a single bag. Within a few years I had grown big enough to carry two bags. Because of wartime gas rationing, my brother and I usually hitchhiked to the course. Today I assume parents would be put in jail for allowing their children to hitchhike on a regular basis.

Even in grammar school I was interested in politics and world events, an interest I inherited from my father. I remember the day a football game on the radio was interrupted by news of the attack on Pearl Harbor. Jack and I called my father and got a map so that we could see exactly where Pearl Harbor was. As a freshman in the seminary, I organized and ran the campaign of my good friend Roger Switzer for vice president of the Mission Society, an unheard-of role for a lowly freshman. Many of the older students were quite impressed by our efforts, but in the end we fell short in the vote count.

My father also encouraged us to speak publicly. Jack and I took special elocution lessons at Nazareth Hall, and all four of us entered oratorical contests, most of them under Catholic school auspices. Our father coached us in the writing and delivery and we always did well, but our talks on the Marshall Plan or the Truman Doctrine often came in second to someone who spoke on the pope's peace plan!

Both parents urged us to excel in school and reminded us of the importance of an education. I think my mother was disappointed that I never really continued my piano lessons, but one can't have everything. After his father's death, my own father never went beyond high school. My mother did go to secretarial school for some time after high school. Like many parents of that generation, they were not warmly affectionate toward us, but they were very caring and encouraging in their own way.

Seminary in Rochester

I enjoyed life in the high school seminary. I found the classes interesting, liked my classmates, and was attracted to a deeper participation in the liturgical and sacramental life of the church. I still lived at home and worked on Saturdays selling women's shoes. After my sophomore year I worked as a kitchen cleanup person in a summer camp staffed by seminarians, and went on to serve as a counselor there for six summers. To the best of my knowledge, and I investigated this recently in light of the scandals that have rocked the Catholic Church, I do not think there was a single case of pedophilia at the camp in those years. I met people there who remain friends to this day, a good number of them men who left the active priesthood in the 1970s.

In 1953, at the close of my six years at St. Andrew's Seminary in Rochester, I was chosen class valedictorian and spoke at my graduation. The main speaker was Father Francis J. Connell, a Redemptorist priest and professor of moral theology at Catholic University of America, a person who would appear again when I took a teaching post at CUA. In fact, according to the rector of St. Andrew's, I could have had a scholarship to study at CUA for the next three years and earn an M.A. in philosophy. For a number of reasons, notably that I wanted to be a parish priest and not a teacher, I decided not to apply.

The next step was St. Bernard's Seminary, which covered the last two years of college and four years of theology in preparation for ordination to the priesthood. St. Bernard's had a reputation as a strict seminary and was called, not always affectionately, "The Rock." Our life there was regulated by the bell, and our days were essentially unvaried: early rising, meditation and mass, breakfast, a short break, classes, examination of conscience in church, lunch, recreation, more classes, rosary and spiritual reading in chapel, dinner, study time, night prayer in chapel, and lights out before ten. Grand silence was observed from night prayers until breakfast the following morning. We took three-hour walks off campus two afternoons a week, but some of us often went to play basketball at a distant gym. There was no gym in the seminary, but there were ball fields, an outside basketball court, handball courts, and even a few homemade golf holes. Seminarians were thus totally segregated from the world and led a quasi-monastic existence.

I was quite happy in this routine. I was devout, even adding additional devotional practices, such as the Way of the Cross during Lent. The classes followed a lecture method, often supplemented by a textbook. There was no requirement, or even any incentive, for outside reading. Again, I received high grades, but looking back I see that I was much too grade-conscious. I did enjoy my fellow students, though, and made many lasting friendships. There was a good camaraderie among the students, and we kidded one another and made wry comments about the idiosyncrasies of the faculty.

The only negative aspect of my life at St. Bernard's was an occasional doubt about celibacy. This question arose again when I was a seminarian in Rome, but I came to the conclusion that, despite attraction to sexual intimacy and marriage, I could be faithful to the promise of celibacy required of the priest.

Every year the Diocese of Rochester sent two seminarians who had completed their two years of college at St. Bernard's to the North American College in Rome to study theology for four years and prepare there for priesthood. It was no surprise to most of my classmates that I was one of those chosen.

Study in Rome

I went to Rome in September 1955 and returned for good in 1961. I left Rochester a very convinced, happy, and traditional pre–Vatican II Catholic. I came back, even before Vatican II, recognizing the need for change and reform in the church. What transpired in Rome? Looking back on it, there were no lightning strikes, but some significant events and people there changed my understanding.

The North American College is a college in the European sense—a house where students live. In this case, it was a seminary for students from the United States dedicated to the spiritual formation of those preparing for priesthood. Our theology classes were held at the Jesuit Gregorian University, where we earned a bachelor's degree in theology after two years and a licentiate after four. Seminary life at the North American College was similar to St. Bernard's in its emphasis on obedience and conformity, although it was not as strict as St. Bernard's had been.

With the exception of a lone seminar, the four years of theology at the Gregorian consisted of lectures given in Latin. Examinations in the major subjects were given orally in Latin at the end of the year. There were no papers and no outside reading. There was usually a textbook for each course, often written by the professor himself; in lieu of that, students distributed notes of the professors. It was only later that I heard Mortimer Adler's famous definition of the lecture system as the process whereby the notes of the professor become the notes of the pupil without passing through the mind of either! The American College authorities insisted on class attendance, but many Europeans did not feel this was necessary. In one course we kidded that the most unfair way to grade students would be to parade five Jesuits across the stage and ask them to point out the one who had taught the class.

Jesuit professors were admirable in their lifestyle and commitments. They lived in small rooms furnished only with a bed, a chair, a desk, and a washbasin. Most of those who taught me in the first year of theology had been teaching at the Gregorian since before World War II. Timothy Zapelena, a Basque, taught a course on the church, based on his own textbook, that emphasized that the Catholic Church was the kingdom of God founded by Jesus Christ on Peter and the Apostles. Sebastian Tromp, a Dutchman who was reputed to be the primary drafter of the 1943 encyclical of Pius XII on the mystical body of Christ, taught a course on revelation in which, in accord with the theology of the time, we proved from signs, miracles, and prophecies that the revelation of Jesus Christ was true.

The American Jesuit, Edwin Healy, who died suddenly in 1957, was one of the moral theology professors. Catholic moral theology in its pre–Vatican II mold used the Ten Commandments as a framework and was geared to training confessors for the sacrament of penance, so that they would know what was sinful and be able to evaluate the gravity of sins. Moral theology, so taught, did not consider the fullness of the Christian life but attended only to the legalistic aspects of what was sinful, and to what degree. The Americans liked Healy for his pragmatism and clarity, but many others had trouble with his less than fluent Latin and his flat midwestern American accent. Healy would occasionally use American idioms in his Latin lectures. Thus, for example, he occasionally refuted a position by claiming that it did not hold water. The Americans would all laugh loudly, while others frowned in confusion.

The German Jesuit Franz Hürth had come to the Gregorian to teach moral theology in the 1930s. He was reputed to have played an important role in drafting Pius XI's 1930 encyclical *Casti connubii,* which condemned artificial contraception. Even as seminarians we were aware that Hürth was the primary author of all of Pius XII's addresses and papal pronouncements on moral theology—and there were quite a few of them. Healy, with a twinkle in his eye, once said in class, "I hold this opinion, even though Father Hürth holds the opposite—although he writes occasionally under the name of Pius XII." Another story illustrates Hürth's significant role in preparing papal documents. On September 29, 1949, Pius XII gave an important address condemning artificial insemination even with the husband's seed. Hürth often published commentaries on Pius XII's moral addresses, but his commentary on this address appeared in the September 15 issue of the Gregorian publication *Periodica*—two weeks before the talk was given!

As a seminarian in the large lecture classes, I occasionally talked outside class with Hürth about moral issues. Later, when I had him for a doctoral seminar, we talked more often. Father Francis Furlong, the American who succeeded Healy after his death and was my dissertation director, approached me one day to ask a favor. Dr. Joseph Doyle, a Boston gynecologist, had designed and was promoting what he called the Doyle cervical spoon, which was supposed to remedy some infertility problems. The spoon was inserted into the woman's cervix to prevent harmful acids in the vagina from affecting the sperm and thus diminishing the possibility of conception. Furlong had heard a rumor that the Holy Office (Hürth played an important role at the Holy Office, precursor to the CDF, which was the watchdog for orthodox faith and morals) or even the pope might condemn the Doyle cervical spoon. He knew that I talked occasionally with Hürth and asked me to sound him out on whether the cervical spoon was going to be condemned. How could I turn down my dissertation director?

My conversation with Hürth—in Latin, of course—was fascinating. He was definitely opposed to the device, in accord with his understanding that the proper act of marital intercourse required the depositing of male semen in the female's vagina. But with the Doyle spoon the semen was deposited not in the vagina but in a *machinam Americanam,* as he called it. I tried to make a case for the cervical spoon but failed to convince him. A few years later I came to the conclusion that his approach was a good example of the problem of physicalism, whereby one "absolutized" the physical act of marital intercourse. At the end of our discussion Hürth smiled and said, "However, this is an American issue and I am not going to get involved in it." He had probably figured out the nature of my mission. I went back to Furlong with the good news that neither Hürth nor the Holy Office nor Pius XII was going to condemn the cervical spoon. It was a good lesson for me in the very human way in which papal documents were prepared.

The professors who taught me scripture were very strongly opposed to the historical critical method that was just then beginning to influence Catholic circles. At the Gregorian in the 1950s, we had none of the newer approaches to scripture that have now become fully acceptable in Catholic theology. The professors in systematic, or what was then called dogmatic, theology (theology dealing with matters of faith and belief) after the first year—Fathers Bernard Lonergan, Juan Alfaro, Maurizio Flick, and Zoltan Alzeghy—tried to move somewhat beyond the existing manuals of theology and open up some new horizons without departing from the general approach of the time. I learned from Lonergan the importance of historical consciousness and its effects on all of theology.

The German Josef Fuchs was the only professor of moral theology who brought a new approach to the discipline, one that emphasized its relationship to the whole Christian life and not just to the sacrament of penance. Some of my classmates at the American College got to know Fuchs much better than I did at the time, but later I became quite friendly with Fuchs.

Fuchs taught the course on sexuality and strongly supported existing Catholic teaching. In early 1968, when I was teaching at CUA, the Family Life Bureau of the U.S. Bishops' Conference brought Fuchs to Washington for a talk. (He had picked up English in the years since he'd taught me in Rome.) With three or four of my classmates from the North American College, I had lunch with Fuchs the following day. I commented that the substance of his talk suggested that he no longer opposed artificial contraception. He smiled and replied that perhaps he had changed but that I had changed much more than he. "I can remember when you were as rigid as a telephone pole," he said.

There is no doubt that in my first years in Rome I was the quintessence of the uncritical and unquestioning pre–Vatican II mentality. Needless to say, I earned high grades at the Gregorian, and at the beginning of my third year of study I was named the beadle of my class at the North American College. The head student was the prefect, who led the student body in prayers and in relationship with the faculty of the college. The beadle was in charge of the day-to-day relationship between the students at the college and Gregorian University—registration, picking up grades, handling routine inquiries. The "second beadle" came from the third theology class and assisted the "first beadle" from the fourth and final year of theology. In my fourth year I took over the role of first beadle. The beadle was one of six seminarians who were ordained to priesthood after the third year of theology in order to provide masses for various groups (sisters, workers) over the summer and into the next academic year. The beadles in my first two years at the American College ultimately became the Cardinal Archbishop of Baltimore and the Archbishop of Mobile.

I was ordained a priest in Rome on July 13, 1958, with my five classmates and many others in a ceremony at the Church of St. Alexis on the Aventine Hill in Rome. My parents, sister, and younger brother came to Rome for the occasion and we traveled in Europe for a couple of weeks afterward.

At the beginning of my fourth and final year of theology in Rome, I received a letter from Bishop Lawrence Casey, the auxiliary bishop of Rochester, who was basically in charge of personnel and for all practical purposes ran the diocese itself at that time. He told me that I was to go on to get a doctorate in moral theology at the Gregorian in order to teach at St. Bernard's Seminary. Now there is a good example of the pre–Vatican II church! There was no discussion, no consultation, and no questioning on my part—just a letter telling me what I was to do. And I was not in the least upset by this process! I simply obeyed and prepared for the future.

I had felt no calling to teach and had thus opted for the diocesan priesthood. But now I was told that I was to get a doctoral degree and prepare to teach in the diocesan seminary. I did not choose what was to become my life's work; I simply obeyed an order.

Another significant event occurred in the fall of 1958. Pope Pius XII died in early October at his summer residence at Castel Gandolfo. We were still at the North American summer villa in the same town, and the six of us who had been ordained served as a guard of honor around his body on the night of his death.

By the time of the conclave that would elect the next pope, we were back in Rome at the college. On the first day, the Gregorian University canceled classes in the late morning so that students could go to St. Peter's to see if a puff of white smoke had risen from the chimney of the Sistine Chapel, indicating that a new pope had been elected and would soon come out to the square. But no pope was chosen on the first day. The next day the Gregorian held all classes as usual. I went to the dean of theology and urged that we be free to go to St. Peter's Square, to which he responded that there were no police officers guarding the doors. When I explained that our rector, Archbishop Martin O'Connor, was very strict about class attendance, the dean confided that he had tried to have the Jesuit rector of the university follow the abbreviated schedule, but had failed. He encouraged me to talk directly to the rector, in spite of my protest that I was just a lowly beadle who did not carry on business with the rector. So, for the first and last time in my life, I went to the office of "the magnificent rector" (his proper title). The dean of theology had failed to move him, and so did I.

No sooner had I returned to the American College, however, than I got a message that Archbishop O'Connor wanted to see me. Archbishop O'Connor was a formal, even a pompous, individual who spent most of his time outside the college and left most day-to-day college matters to various vice-rectors. The students from that era still tell stories of O'Connor's many foibles and eccentricities. He dressed me down. "How dare you speak to the magnificent rector? That is my function. You have been totally insubordinate and you have embarrassed both the college and me. I am going to write your bishop about this whole matter." I replied that I hoped he would tell my bishop that I wanted to be in St. Peter's Square for the election of the pope! The archbishop looked away and said curtly, "Go to your room."

I was in St. Peter's Square the following evening when Angelo Giuseppe Roncalli was elected pope. Frankly, I was disappointed by my first glimpse of this new pope. Pius XII had been an austere, thin, autocratic figure whose blessings of the crowds in St. Peter's Square were solemn and formal. The new pope was a roly-poly smiling Italian who waved to the crowd at the same time he gave his blessing! But there will be much more to say about John XXIII later.

In my final semester at the seminary I prepared for the final general exam—an oral exam based on 100 theses and the last hurdle to clear before receiving my licentiate in theology degree. The Gregorian University awarded me the silver papal medal, called a *Pro pontifice* medal, from Pope John XXIII. This sounds more significant than it really was. Only one medal is actually given, but seventy-five students probably qualified for it. Apparently it was my reward for being the beadle of the biggest college going to the Gregorian. But my obituary can state that I received a papal medal!

I was thinking at this time about the order that I was to spend the next two years working for a doctorate in moral theology at the Gregorian. I read an Italian translation of Bernard Häring's groundbreaking book in moral theology, *The Law of Christ*. I also made inquiries about the Alfonsian Academy, a graduate school of moral theology run by the Redemptorist fathers in Rome where Häring was then teaching. The Alfonsian at that time was not empowered to grant doctoral degrees, but it did award a certificate.

I came home in July 1959 for the first time since leaving in 1955, celebrated my first mass with family and friends at home, and returned to Rome in the fall to begin my doctoral work. Now I lived at what was called the graduate house of the North American College, which housed priests who were studying at the various Roman universities for advanced degrees. Our life here was much freer. We could come and go as we pleased and had no schedule, but the doors were locked at ten at night. I soon learned, however, that a fifty-cent tip to one of the workers who lived there could get the door unlocked after ten!

I had already begun to move beyond the pre–Vatican II neoscholastic approaches of Catholicism. As a seminarian in Rome I had become quite conscious of the human side of the church, and had begun to recognize the significance of historical development in both theology and the life of the church. Pious Catholics visiting Rome would occasionally comment that it must be a great privilege to study in Rome and have such an opportunity to grow in faith. But in Rome I confronted the very human side of the church—the politics of any bureaucracy and of some priests who were trying to plot their careers in the life of the institution. By the time I finally left Rome, in 1961, I was conscious that the church was not only human but sinful. I was still a very committed Catholic, but I recognized the pilgrim nature of the church—that it is always in need of reform, an important concept that Vatican II brought to the fore.

My reading of Häring and my intellectual curiosity were pushing me to explore moral theology beyond the classroom manuals, with their narrow purpose of training confessors to understand the nature and gravity of sins. Because the licentiate already involved a comprehensive examination, the Gregorian required only five two-hour seminars, once a week for one semester, and a dissertation for the doctoral degree. I also enrolled in courses at the Alfonsian because they tried to cover all aspects of moral theology—biblical, patristic, historical, philosophical, systematic, pastoral, and so on. I learned quite a bit from these courses, but Bernard Häring had the most significant influence on my thought. Häring proposed a life-centered moral theology based on the covenant—the good news of God's gracious gift of love and life and our response to it. Continual conversion called for the Christian to grow in all aspects of moral living. Häring's holistic approach brought together morality, spirituality, scripture, and the sacraments. Even then, in the 1950s and early '60s, he strongly criticized the legalism and careerism too often found in the church. He was also a captivating lecturer—even in Latin. At my invitation and prodding, a few American graduate-student priests, some of whom were not even in moral theology, came to hear Häring lecture.

Even before starting my doctoral work, I had a dissertation topic—the prevention of conception after rape—thanks to Msgr. William Bachmann. Bachmann, my spiritual director at the American College, had taught moral theology at the seminary in Cleveland. The object of the thesis was to trace the development of the teaching in the manuals of moral theology from the sixteenth century to the present, and then to deal with contemporary medical and theological aspects of rape and conception. This was a conventional pre–Vatican II type of dissertation that did not really break new ground, but I did learn in the process how much of Catholic sexual and medical ethics was based on very dated biological information. For example, sexual teaching assumed that male semen was the only active element in procreation and that the woman provided only the nest (the Latin word *nidus*, or nest, was also used for the womb). Later this knowledge proved most helpful in my developing different approaches to sexual ethics.

In June 1960, at the end of the academic year, Domenico Capone, a Redemptorist systematic ethicist and historian of St. Alphonsus at the Alfonsian, asked to see me. Capone told me that starting in the new academic year (1960–61) the Alfonsian would be empowered to give the doctorate in moral theology. He urged me to enroll in the program and write a doctoral dissertation. I told him I was not interested because, as he knew, I was already getting my doctorate at the Gregorian. But he insisted that it would be good both for me and for the Alfonsian. I presented a number of problems and obstacles. For one thing, Roman libraries did not have open stacks and would not allow students to take books home. He then not only gave me a topic—"The Concept of Invincible Ignorance in Alphonsus Liguori"—but also said I could take home anything I needed from the library. To my objection that there might be a regulation in canon law preventing the awarding of degrees by two pontifical institutions at the same time, he responded, like any good Italian, *ci penso io,* which is loosely translated, "Don't worry about it. I'll take care of it." Since I planned to finish writing my Gregorian dissertation in August, I finally agreed to work with Capone in the 1960–61 academic year.

In the process of researching and writing the dissertation, I discovered how sharp were the controversies over theological issues. Alphonsus and his opponents often attacked one another with pseudonymous writings. I also learned that the subjective aspect of the human act can be more important than the objective aspect, so that one could be invincibly ignorant of the natural law.

The defense of my Alfonsian dissertation in June 1961 was fascinating. Capone, the director, and the Irish Redemptorist Sean O'Riordan praised the work very highly. The third reader, the American Redemptorist Francis X. Murphy, attacked me, the project itself, and even Alphonsus. According to Murphy, the first part of my work was mostly reporting, was highly repetitive, and could be reduced to a few pages. My analysis showed competency and theological insight, but my conclusions were quite limited and even supported the charge that Alphonsus was far from a clear and decisive thinker and in fact had only a second-rate mind. After Murphy finished talking, I did not say another word for the rest of the defense. He and Capone went at each other for well over half an hour.

According to the regulations, the grade for the dissertation was ultimately given only by the director and the first reader, so I received a *summa cum laude*. In fact, I was the first person officially to receive a doctorate from the Alfonsian.

Murphy was accurate in pointing out that the first half of my dissertation was basically only reporting and thus highly repetitive. I often tell this story to my doctoral students, because the tendency of most of them is simply to report what other people have said. It was obvious that I had not yet learned to speak in my own voice.

Afterward, to make sure there were no hard feelings, Murphy invited me to lunch before I left Rome for good, and we talked for most of the afternoon. Two things still stand out from that encounter. First, Murphy gave me some excellent advice. St. Bernard's Seminary was still known throughout the United States as being very conservative. "With your approach to moral theology," he said, "you will quickly run into trouble at the 'Rock.' Here is a suggestion. You speak Latin very well—much better than I do. St. Bernard's used to take great pride in the fact that until a few years ago the classes were taught in Latin. You should teach the first semester in Latin. That is the story that everyone will tell about your teaching, and they won't recognize and talk about the new approaches that you are taking to moral theology." I followed Murphy's wise advice and was able to last at St. Bernard's for four years before I was fired for my advanced positions.

That afternoon we also talked about church politics. Both of us were deeply disappointed by the Roman synod that had taken place in early 1960. In January 1959 Pope John XXIII publicly announced the three steps he was going to take to reform the life of the church—a synod of the Diocese of Rome, a revision of canon law, and an ecumenical council. The synod was a disaster both in its format (there was no real discussion of the issues; those present merely listened to documents that had already been written and approved them) and in its content (no real pastoral plan or insight but merely a bringing together of older church law). Murphy went on to tell me about some of the shenanigans in the Roman Curia, the technical name of the papal bureaucracy, and how its stewards were not going to promote any change in the church. Early in the fall of 1962, just as Vatican II was beginning, the *New Yorker* published an article titled "Letter from Vatican City" by the pseudonymous Xavier Rynne. Many people wondered about the identity of this Rynne, who pointed out the infighting taking place in the Curia to make sure there would be no great changes at the Vatican Council. I immediately realized that Rynne was Francis Xavier Murphy. Murphy had told me some of these stories a little more than a year earlier. I also knew that Murphy's mother's name was Rynne. Only much later did Murphy reveal that he was the principal author of the Xavier Rynne articles in the *New Yorker,* and of the books that were published at the end of each of the four sessions of the council.

Teaching at St. Bernard's

In July I went to the Holy Land, as well as to Egypt and Greece, and then returned to the States. In September 1961 I moved into St. Bernard's Seminary to teach special moral theology, which is concerned with the Ten Commandments and especially with the canonical aspects of the sacraments. The course was taught on a three-year cycle to about ninety or a hundred students in the second, third, and fourth or final year of theology. In addition, I had to teach the course in canon law on a two-year-cycle. In the pre–Vatican II church, moral theology and canon law were closely allied, as they both dealt with laws and obligations—precisely the approach I was trying to overcome. Even more ironically, I myself had had only two semesters of canon law as a seminarian in Rome. Half the students in the class I started to teach in 1961 had as much background in canon law as I had!

My six years in Rome, especially my last two in doctoral work, significantly colored my approach to moral theology. First, I rejected the narrow scope of the manuals of moral theology, with their focus on training confessors in the sacrament of penance. Moral theology has to deal with the whole of the Christian life, especially the call to continual conversion, as Bernard Häring insisted. A more holistic approach to moral theology embraces scriptural, liturgical, and systematic theological dimensions.

Second, the manuals of moral theology and the textbooks of the day followed a legal model in which law was the primary moral concept. These textbooks put heavy emphasis on church law, which tended to be reduced in the popular understanding to injunctions to attend mass on Sunday and refrain from eating meat on Friday. Grace was not the basis of the moral life but only a means of helping Catholics obey the laws. Third, the history I studied had opened my eyes to the reality of historical development and change in moral theology. The moral theology of the manuals was not the moral theology of the broad Catholic tradition. I had also become aware of historical consciousness, with its recognition of the importance of the particular, the individual, and the concrete, the need for a more inductive approach, and the recognition of the historical embeddedness of every human thinker and knower.

Fourth, my commitment to the renewal of moral theology brought me into contact with renewal movements in scripture, systematic theology, and liturgy. My ecclesiology was also changing. The church cannot be identified fully with the kingdom of God but is a pilgrim church always in need of conversion. The church is not just the pope and bishops but embraces all the baptized. Baptism is the greatest gift any Christian can receive.

My use of Latin in the classroom, on F. X. Murphy's advice, became the talk of the seminary and the talk of the diocese among the priests, but after a few months I dropped the Latin and began teaching in English. Since I objected to seeing moral theology as dealing only with the minimal or legalistic aspects of sin, I always began my course with a long introduction that portrayed the moral life as the loving response of the Christian to the gift of God in and through the risen Jesus and the Holy Spirit. One year these introductory lectures lasted into March! I also handed out notes (in Latin) so that the students could follow the lectures more easily.

I discovered that I enjoyed teaching, but it was hard work. For the first three years I had to prepare new courses for the first time, and for each one I put together my own long introduction. But there is no better way to learn than to teach. It was an exhausting but exhilarating experience. The students' education had been neoscholastic and pre–Vatican II. Many were receptive to the newer approaches, but others resisted strongly. Some reacted especially negatively when I added a fifth mark to the traditional four marks of the church—the church is one, holy, Catholic, apostolic, and *sinful*.

Perhaps the most heated discussion centered on the meaning of the Eucharist and what were called the fruits of the mass. Priestly devotion in the pre–Vatican II church insisted on the special fruit that accrues to the priest from each mass that is celebrated and therefore emphasizes the importance of even the private mass. I insisted that the mass is by nature social and that the role of the priest (now properly called the presider) is merely to facilitate the mass for the sake of the community. I replied to one student who disagreed that if he had been at the Last Supper he would have sawed the table into separate altars so they could have many private masses and more grace!

I also introduced outside reading and had the students meet me in small groups to discuss the assigned books. Although I was only five or six years older than the average student in the class, they received me very well and I enjoyed my teaching. When I was removed from the seminary, the ordination classes of 1964 and 1965 (both of which I had taught for the full three years of the cycle in moral theology) had a party for me and presented me with a plaque with a heading that read, "We have not here a permanent dwelling place." That year I had spent quite a bit of time in class on the virtue of hope as central for pilgrim Christians in a pilgrim church. I was glad to see that my students had a sense of humor!

The first three sessions of Vatican Council II (there were four all told) occurred while I was teaching at St. Bernard's. I had no role whatsoever in Vatican II but followed it from a distance. On the basis of my experience with the synod of Rome in 1960 and some very discouraging words from Rome about actions taken against certain professors at the Biblical Institute, as well as some restrictions on Josef Fuchs at the Gregorian, I was not hopeful about the council. In February 1962 Pope John XXIII decreed that all seminary theology classes were to be taught in Latin. Since I had empirical evidence that teaching in Latin did not work, I did not observe the new directive. I also knew that the preparatory documents for the council had been prepared primarily by conservative members of the Roman Curia, the papal bureaucracy. I was quite pleasantly surprised by John XXIII's opening address on October 11, 1962, which set a progressive tone by calling for an updating of the church, insisting that the council make no condemnations (previous councils and recent papal documents had been full of condemnations), and by disagreeing with the prophets of doom even among his own advisors.

Yes, I am most grateful for and a strong admirer of Pope John XXIII. But, in a lecture after he died in 1963, I pointed out that the greatness of John XXIII was his openness and his growth. Frankly, I do not think he had a clear vision of what he expected from the council. Before his papacy and even during the papacy itself, he had shown many signs of a very conservative mentality.

Vatican II rightly attacked the triumphalism in the church according to which the Catholic Church was holy, without spot, and in no need of reform. Ironically, it seems to me that to this day many liberal Catholics still suffer from a form of triumphalism. They want their heroines and heroes to be perfect, holy, and without spot. I thank God for John XXIII, but it is also much easier to inspire and start something than it is to complete it and put it into practice. In some ways, triumphalistic Catholics have tended to romanticize the papacy of John XXIII just as they have the presidency of John F. Kennedy.

The seminary faculty of about fifteen priests was most hospitable to me, the youngest among them. A few even encouraged me in my own newer approach. I was invited to join a group of five to seven that regularly got together for a drink before the main meal at noon. The rector Msgr. Wilfred T. Craugh was not too happy with us, but I found this a most congenial and convivial occasion. In fact, I brought this good custom with me when I went to Catholic University.

Despite the busy schedule, I began to write a bit. Father Robert McNamara, the professor of church history at St. Bernard's, who was himself on the conservative side, also encouraged me to write, and in fact read and helped me with most of the things I wrote during my time at St. Bernard's. In November 1961 Father Godfrey Diekmann, the editor of *Worship*, solicited a long letter from me in defense of Häring's *Law of Christ*. The reviewer in *Worship* had been quite negative about it, and Diekmann wanted the readers to have a more positive impression of the book. In the spring of 1962 I wrote a twenty-three-page pamphlet, "Morality and the Love of God," for the Paulist Press's doctrinal pamphlet series.

In the fall of 1962 Professor G. Ernest Wright of Harvard invited me to present a paper on conscience at the Roman Catholic–Protestant Colloquium to be sponsored by Harvard in the spring of 1963. This groundbreaking and historical conference was the first, and to this day probably the largest, ecumenical theological gathering of Protestants and Catholics in the United States. Cardinal Augustin Bea, the president of the Vatican Secretariat for Promoting Christian Unity, gave three plenary addresses. My first reaction to the invitation was negative. How could I, less than two years after receiving my doctorate, present a paper at such an august intellectual gathering? Professor Wright and Professor Frank Cross dismissed my hesitation. They definitely wanted someone to present a newer approach to moral theology, they said. They could get a good number of people to represent the older school, but they wanted someone representing the newer approach. They were convinced that I was the best person to do it.

And so, on my twenty-ninth birthday, shaking with fear and trepidation, I gave my paper, "The Problem of Conscience and the Twentieth-Century Christian."[2] Paul Lehmann, the noted Protestant ethicist, then at Princeton Seminary, gave the Protestant paper. My older peers were very supportive and did not try to take advantage of my lack of depth. Here for the first time I met many of the leading figures in Catholic intellectual life. About fifteen years later, the take-home exam for one of my courses in moral theology at CUA asked graduate students to write a ten-page critique of this paper. They never realized that the paper was my own, and they rightly pointed out its shortcomings. On the basis of having written one twenty-three-page pamphlet, I had been invited to give an address at perhaps the most significant ecumenical meeting held in the United States. What did that say about Harvard University, and also about the state of Catholic moral theology?

In December 1963 there appeared the first article by a Catholic theologian (Father Louis Janssens of Louvain, Belgium) to argue that the Catholic Church should accept the so-called birth control pill but not other forms of contraception.[3] At that time I was teaching every year the course on marriage and sexuality to fourth-year theology students. As a diocesan priest, I was also frequently asked questions about this issue and spoke at some forums in my early years defending the existing Catholic teaching opposing artificial contraception. I wrote three articles in more popular Catholic journals discussing some of the developments surrounding this issue. In the fall of 1964, in an address to the Catholic Club at Harvard that was published in their journal, I reversed myself and maintained that the Catholic Church should change its teaching on artificial contraception.[4]

In that address I admitted that I was not trying to develop a full-blown argument but rather pointed out four reasons for change. The first was the experience of Catholic married couples. I had met regularly with a group of young married couples in Rochester. In New York City, in June 1964, a few of us younger Catholic moral theologians met with some Catholic married couples loosely associated with the significant journal *Cross Currents.* The experience of many of these people, either in terms of the difficulty of practicing rhythm or of their recognition that artificial contraception was helpful and necessary for their married lives, made an impression on me. Second, I pointed out, on the basis of the research I had done for my doctoral dissertation, that Catholic theology originally based its sexual teaching on a totally inadequate knowledge of human biology that had long since been rectified by modern science. The erroneous belief that the male seed was the only active element in human procreation obviously influenced the Catholic teaching that each and every sexual act had to be open to procreation. Third, the moral judgment is the ultimate human judgment, bringing together all the different partial aspects—be they sociological, psychological, eugenic, hygienic, and so on. Seen in this light, the biological integrity of the marital act should not necessarily be morally normative, because other considerations must enter into the picture. I concluded by arguing that church teaching had changed on some issues in the past and could change here as well.

As the new kid on the block and with this newer approach to moral theology, I received a number of invitations to speak and teach. In the spring of 1964, through my good friend Frank Kett, Archbishop Richard

Cushing of Boston invited me to give eight lectures on moral theology in a series sponsored by him for the priests of the Archdiocese of Boston. I spoke in 1963 at the national convention of the Council of Catholic Men and at the 1964 annual convention of the Canon Law Society of America, where I argued that canon law should no longer require non-Catholics marrying Catholics to promise to raise their children in the Catholic Church. In 1965 I addressed the national convention of the Catholic College Teachers of Sacred Doctrine on freedom and responsibility, and the National Liturgical Conference on the relevance of moral theology today. These four addresses were published in the proceedings of these meetings.[5]

Father Gerard Sloyan invited me to teach moral theology for six weeks in the summer school of the department of religious education at CUA in 1964. Even before that, Father Walter Schmitz wanted me to come full-time to the School of Theology at CUA, a seminary for priests that also had a graduate program and awarded doctorates in moral theology. At that time the Bishop of Rochester, James E. Kearney, told CUA that I was unavailable because of the needs of St. Bernard's Seminary. Later in 1964 I received an invitation from Father Albert Schlitzer to join the faculty of the University of Notre Dame. In the summer of 1965 I gave theology institutes for U.S. Air Force chaplains, St. Francis Xavier University in Antigonish, Nova Scotia, the Carmelite Fathers in Niagara Falls, Canada, St. Mary's College in Winona, Minnesota, and the Benedictine Abbey at Canon City, Colorado.

During this period I also experienced my first "disinvitation," an event brought about by church authorities. In the fall I had spoken to the high school religion teachers in the Archdiocese of New York on a Friday afternoon at Fordham University, and had been invited to give another such talk in the spring. A month or so before the scheduled spring talk, the monsignor in charge of the program called to say that regrettably there was a scheduling problem and the spring date would have to be canceled. I took his message at face value, but about a month later I received a letter from a religious sister in New York saying she regretted that I could not be there for my scheduled talk because the substitute was not very interesting!

Meanwhile, tensions with the diocesan authorities continued to grow. Bishop Kearney, who did not go to the council for reasons of age and health, was the diocesan bishop, but he left much of the day-to-day operation to the auxiliary bishop, Lawrence Casey. Casey was not an intellectual but a hardworking, committed priest and bishop who had begun to open up a bit through his participation in Vatican II. He had approved my plan to bring some speakers in to the seminary occasionally for the continuing education of the priests. The first speaker was my professor, Father Bernard Häring. Later we had a workshop with Father Gus Weigel and Father John Sheerin, who were in Rochester as the first American Catholic observers for a meeting connected with the World Council of Churches. But later requests in 1964–65 to bring in speakers on the liturgy, and Father Roland Murphy on scripture, were rebuffed.

These developments indicated that tensions were deepening. I had been called on the carpet on a couple of occasions and told to be more careful; I was advised not to present the views of contemporary German theologians as the teaching of the church. In early 1965 I was called in again and warned about my teaching in general and especially about my call for a change in the church teaching on artificial contraception. I could publish in scholarly journals, but anything for a popular journal had to be sent beforehand to the chancery office for approval. I was also told that it would be better if I did not give talks in parishes. I had always sought (and received) Bishop Casey's permission before accepting any invitation that would keep me outside the diocese for some time. In the same letter in which I was given these instructions in early 1965, Casey gave me permission once again to teach at Catholic University during the summer of 1965. But Casey said I should tell Father Schlitzer at Notre Dame that I could not accept his invitation to teach there permanently because of the needs of the seminary.

Part, but only part, of the tension arose from a vituperative eight-page letter that a layman, Dr. Hugo Maria Kellner, wrote to Msgr. Wilfred T. Craugh, the rector of St. Bernard's, about my heretical preaching, teaching, and writing. He sent copies of this letter to every seminary rector and bishop in the United States. Kellner had previously sent three or four similar missives to bishops around the country in which he attacked what he called liberal and heretical developments in the Catholic Church. All agreed that Kellner was a "kook," but I think the diocesan officials were still somewhat fearful of what he was saying.

The other shoe finally dropped at the end of July 1965. When I returned from teaching at CUA, I found a message asking that I see Bishop Casey. He informed me that I could no longer teach at St. Bernard's but that the bishop would write a letter to Bishop William McDonald, the rector (president) of CUA, telling him that the Diocese of Rochester was now able and willing to release me to teach at CUA. Within a week Bishop McDonald wrote to express his gratitude that I could be released to teach at CUA beginning that semester.

What was the final straw? I had spoken earlier that summer at an institute sponsored by the Carmelite Fathers in Niagara Falls, Canada. The local press covered my talks and reported my support of artificial contraception for Catholic spouses. The bishop of Syracuse, who sent all his seminarians to St. Bernard's, was given a copy of the article and was very upset by it. He complained to the bishop of Rochester, who then made the final decision. I was never sure why the officials of the Diocese of Rochester reacted the way they did in releasing me to teach at CUA. I told Bishop Casey that I was very willing to leave the seminary and work in a parish, but he demurred. Were they just trying to get me out of the diocese? Or did they really think I belonged at CUA?

In August and September I was scheduled to give four institutes (the same series of talks in four places) for Catholic air force chaplains. Two incidents deserve mention. At the institute held near Notre Dame, I met with Eugene Geissler, the editor of Fides Press, a small, forward-looking Catholic press founded by Father Louis Putz, a pioneering proponent of the role of laity in the church. Geissler agreed to publish a book bringing together the articles I had written. *Christian Morality Today: The Renewal of Moral Theology* was published in 1966 with the imprimatur (literally, "let it be published") of the bishop of Fort Wayne-South Bend on the recommendation of Father Putz. The book went through at least seven printings and sold more than 50,000 copies. The articles were of a popular theological nature and were not intended for a scholarly audience. Apparently it was picked up as a textbook in a number of Catholic institutions.

None of my books published since then has sold even close to that number of copies.

At the air force chaplains' conference near Phoenix, the chancellor of the military ordinariate, a high-ranking official of the diocese who takes care of Catholic soldiers and their chaplains, took the microphone after hearing two of my talks to say that I could never speak to chaplains again and would never be given faculties or permission to celebrate liturgy, preach, or hear confessions for soldiers or chaplains. The Catholic chief of chaplains saw me later and apologized. He had earlier offered to play golf with the chancellor during my talks, but he had become confused about the schedule.

In August my father retired after working for forty-eight years for the same insurance company. He had always assumed that my being a priest guaranteed my job security, but now he was not so sure. In September I loaded all my books and belongings into a borrowed truck and moved to Caldwell Hall, a residence for priests at CUA, where I would begin teaching later that month.

CHAPTER 2

CUA: The Early Years

W HEN I ARRIVED at CUA in 1965, the university, which had opened in 1889, was both a pontifical university canonically erected by the Vatican and an American institution incorporated in the District of Columbia and accredited by American accrediting agencies. CUA was a charter member of the prestigious Association of American Universities, founded in 1909; unfortunately, a few years ago the university resigned from the group because of its inability to live up to the standards involved. The primary emphasis of the university from the start was on providing graduate education and degrees for Catholics, although an undergraduate college was added quite early. Before World War II, for all practical purposes, CUA was the only Catholic university in the United States to grant doctoral degrees.[1]

The university at that time was governed by the bishops of the United States through a board of trustees that included all the cardinals and residential archbishops in the United States, together with other elected bishops and a few laypeople. The university had the usual schools, although there was no medical school, but it also had schools of theology, canon law, and philosophy that granted pontifical degrees that were accredited by the Vatican. In my time there, the School of Theology also began to offer American accredited degrees such as the M.A. and Ph.D.

In 1965 CUA had a very conservative reputation by the lights of both the church and the academy. In 1963 university authorities had banned four progressive Catholic theologians from speaking on campus. In the 1960s Father Gerard Sloyan brought a more progressive theological tone to the department of religious education of the School of Arts and Sciences, which taught the undergraduate religion courses and also had an M.A. and Ph.D. program. Its large summer school (in which I had taught the two previous summers) attracted many priests and sisters working on master's degrees in the wake of Vatican II.

The School of Theology, in which all of the faculty members before 1968 were priests, had an especially conservative reputation. Two of the best-known faculty members, Joseph Clifford Fenton and Francis Connell, were well-known experts at Vatican II who espoused very conservative positions. Fenton edited the *American Ecclesiastical Review,* a journal geared to priests in ministry, which strenuously opposed any new developments in theology and pastoral practice. But there were also some outstanding scholars on the faculty, among them John Quasten in patristics and Roland Murphy in Old Testament.

Walter Schmitz, a Sulpician priest, became dean of theology in 1962 and ultimately succeeded in attracting new faculty and changing the image of the school. One source of new faculty came from priests who had recently received Roman doctorates. In 1964–65, Carl Peter of Omaha and Robert Hunt of Newark, both recent graduates of the Gregorian in Rome, joined the faculty. The first woman to be hired, in 1968, was Sr. Alexis Suelzer; only later did I realize what a very difficult time she had in that environment. Schmitz, on the advice of Bernard Häring and others, had contacted me in 1963 to see if I would be interested in coming on board. When I replied in the affirmative, he arranged for the rector (president), Bishop William McDonald, to contact my diocesan bishop to see if he would release me to teach at CUA. After I joined the faculty, Schmitz recruited David Tracy and Bernard McGinn, both of whom soon left to pursue illustrious careers at the University of Chicago. There were other new faculty appointments as well, and so the perspective of the school was changing dramatically.

When I began in 1965, the School of Theology had two basic programs—a seminary program that trained future priests from U.S. dioceses and from some religious orders, and a graduate program offering the licentiate (STL) and the doctorate (STD) in theology. In 1965 the first woman, Marie Egan, IHM, who later wrote her doctoral dissertation with me, was admitted to the program, along with one other woman religious. Some religious brothers had been admitted to the pontifical degree program earlier.

My Theological Development

Because of the late date of my appointment, I taught only two seminars in the first semester, and the light teaching load gave me a chance to get acclimated to my new surroundings. The university atmosphere, with its emphasis on scholarly publication, allowed me to write from a more in-depth, scholarly perspective. In the second semester of 1965–66 I directed a doctoral seminar on the issue of masturbation, as I was scheduled to deliver a paper on this subject at the June 1966 annual meeting of the Catholic Theological Society of America (CTSA). My paper challenged the universally accepted teaching in Catholic moral theology that masturbation always involves objectively grave matter, a teaching that, in practice, was often understood to mean that masturbation always involves mortal sin. A more moderate position, built on the important distinction between objectively grave matter and subjective culpability, claimed that grave subjective guilt is often lacking in this case. I defended my position that masturbation does not always involve grave or serious matter on the basis of our contemporary knowledge of masturbation, the Thomistic notion of grave sin, and the theory of fundamental option. I emphasized the importance of the pastoral aspect of this question.[2]

In my first years at CUA, I often focused on the basis in natural law theory for the Catholic teaching on morality, especially in the area of sexuality in light of changing contemporary views on sexual issues. At the same time, Protestant ethicists and others were discussing situation ethics and the so-called new morality. In two essays published in scholarly volumes in 1968, I developed a critique of the natural law approach used in the manuals of moral theology and in papal teaching.[3] The natural law maintains that human reason reflecting on human nature is able to arrive at moral wisdom and knowledge. There are two aspects to the question of natural law. From the theological point of view, natural law responds to the question of where the Christian and the moral theologian find moral wisdom and knowledge. Here I accept wholeheartedly the Catholic position that human reason can and should arrive at moral truth. The philosophical aspect of natural law concerns the meaning of human reason and of human nature. Here I proposed a number of criticisms of the existing approach.

First, on the basis of Bernard Lonergan's distinction between classicism and historical consciousness, Catholic natural law illustrates a classicist approach. Classicism emphasizes the eternal, immutable, and unchanging. Human nature is the same at all times and in all places. Historical consciousness, by contrast, emphasizes the particular, the historical, the individual, and the contingent. Historical consciousness opposes the one-sided emphasis that classicism places on continuity but also the one-sided emphasis that existentialism puts on discontinuity. Such existentialism fails to see any relationship between the present and the past or future and no binding relationships to others in the present. Classicism sees the human knower as completely free from historical and cultural conditioning; all human knowers have the same basic approach. Historical-mindedness sees the human knower as embedded in history and culture but still able to share some knowledge with all other human beings. Classicism, as seen in Catholic natural law, uses a deductive methodology that claims that its conclusions are as certain as its premises. Historical consciousness employs a more inductive method that strives not for absolute certitude but for the best possible explanation. Catholic natural law theory in general is characterized by a rigid and dogmatic self-certainty.

Second, the anthropology of natural law is inadequate. Thomas Aquinas himself accepted at times the Greek lawyer Ulpian's definition of the natural law as that which nature teaches man and all the animals. According to Aquinas, human anthropology comprises three layers—a bottom layer of what is common to all living things, a middle layer of what is common to all animals, and a top layer of what is proper to rational human beings. In the Thomistic understanding, the human being is a rational animal, but human rationality cannot interfere with the common-alities we share with other animals. In the area of sexuality, this commonality consists in the procreation and education of offspring. In matters of sexuality, Catholic natural law has traditionally identified human nature with animal nature; animal rather than human nature is normative.

Third, Catholic teaching has "absolutized" the biological or physical aspect of the sexual act. One can never interfere with the physical act of marital intercourse; hence, artificial contraception is always wrong. Many people have claimed that the problem with the Catholic condemnation of artificial contraception is the pronatalist Catholic position, but this is not the real problem. Hierarchical Catholic teaching also opposes artificial insemination even with the husband's semen, because the physical act of sexual intercourse between married people is the only acceptable means of achieving human procreation. In other areas, the Catholic approach has not identified the moral with the physical. Catholic teaching distinguishes between the physical act of killing, which may be acceptable in certain circumstances, and the moral act of murder, which is always wrong.

Fourth, the natural law basis for Catholic sexual ethics rests on a faulty faculty analysis. According to this theory, one looks at the sexual faculty (a technical Latin term) or power and sees there its God-given purpose of procreation and love union. Consequently, every sexual act coming from that faculty must be open to both procreation and love union. There are two problems here. Why does every sexual act have to illustrate the twofold finality of the sexual faculty? The totality of acts taken in their different contexts should illustrate the purpose of the faculty, but this does not mean that every sexual act must do so. Much more important, one should not absolutize the faculty, for the faculty should be seen in relationship to the person and to the various relationships in which the person is involved. The person is the basic criterion, because the faculty exists for the person. For the good of the person or the relationship of marriage, therefore, one can and should interfere with what was claimed to be the God-given purpose of the sexual faculty. Here the emphasis is on the human person and not on human nature.

Fifth, the manuals of moral theology of the time assumed that the theory of natural law proved the various Catholic positions in morality. But such an assumption was based on ahistorical considerations. Historically, one has to conclude that the natural law theory evolved in order to explain already existing teachings in a coherent and systematic way. These individual teachings came into existence long before Aquinas developed the theory of natural law.

The original teaching on a particular issue (e.g., contraception) came about as a result of a discernment of the whole community and was based on many different factors, but certainly the experience of Christian people played a role here. This understanding, together with the significance of historical consciousness, points out the important role of communal experience in arriving at moral truth. Obviously the experience of individuals and groups, and perhaps even of the whole community, can be wrong (consider, for example, the former Christian position on slavery), but the experience of the Christian community is an important source of moral wisdom and knowledge. In a sense, Catholic theology has always recognized this reality in its acceptance of the role of the *sensus fidelium*—the sense of the faithful. The church must always value the experience of people, even though that experience may sometimes be wrong.

I now had a solid threefold base from which to question certain Catholic sexual teachings—the philosophical critique of natural law, the realization that Catholic sexual teaching was influenced by outdated biological assumptions, and an emphasis on the experience of Christian people.

In 1966, as part of my endeavor to give a more in-depth defense of the call for change in Catholic approaches to moral theology, I decided to edit a book with other younger moral theologians further developing the rationale for change. I had been instrumental in getting Gerard Sloyan to appoint my friend Dan Maguire, a priest from Philadelphia, who was then teaching moral theology at St. Mary's Seminary in Baltimore, to a post teaching moral theology in the department of religious education at CUA beginning in September 1966. Dan enthusiastically agreed to write an essay for the proposed book and was most helpful in working with the other authors whom I recruited. The edited volume *Absolutes in Moral Theology?* was published in 1968.

We informed these authors that we were trying to influence Richard McCormick, the Jesuit priest who was then writing some of the "Notes on Moral Theology" for the Jesuit journal *Theological Studies*. McCormick was then beginning to change somewhat on the contraception issue but had not yet endorsed the need for a more thoroughgoing change in the approach to natural law. McCormick and I quickly became very good friends. A few years later, a conservative Catholic moral theologian, in an often biased and polemical article, criticized McCormick for, among other things, reversing his position on issues of moral theology, and specifically for endorsing the work of Charles E. Curran, which he had earlier opposed.[4]

Fired

On April 17, 1967, I was informed by Rector McDonald that the board of trustees, at their April 10 meeting in Chicago, had voted not to renew my contract—in other words, to fire me.[5] What had happened?

On September 7, 1965, Hugo Maria Kellner sent to all members of the CUA administration and faculty of theology a letter calling attention to my heretical positions and my support for artificial contraception. In response, my faculty colleagues were most warmly supportive, but the vice-rector, Joseph McAllister, warned me to be careful.

Msgr. McAllister called me in again on December 20, 1965, to discuss my participation in a White House conference on population held November 19. At this conference, as accurately reported by the National Catholic News Service, I pointed out the difference between Catholic moral teaching and public policy issues in a pluralistic society. McAllister was nervous about my being identified with CUA. He reminded me that article 67 of the university statutes states that faculty are not allowed to take part in public affairs, especially those of a political nature, without previous consultation with the rector.

The administration expressed more concern early in the fall of 1966. Rector McDonald called me to express his anxiety over an article that had appeared in the *National Catholic Reporter* about a theological institute I gave at St. Gregory's College in Oklahoma the previous summer, and about my membership on the board of directors of the Institute for Freedom in the Church. (Unfortunately, that group, like so many other liberal groups within the church, had neither staying power nor any visible success.) McAllister also met with me in the presence of the new vice-rector for academic affairs, Father Robert Trisco, and Dean Schmitz concerning the article. The faculty of theology questioned Dean Schmitz and me about this matter at their October meeting, then unanimously passed a resolution expressing confidence in my teaching and orthodoxy and objecting to my being harassed.

Despite these warnings and tensions with the administration, I enjoyed my teaching very much and continued to be affirmed by my faculty colleagues. Early in 1967 I applied for promotion to the rank of associate professor, as I had served the requisite number of years and had more than fulfilled the publishing requirements. In February 1967 the department of theology voted unanimously to promote me and in early March the academic senate voted for my associate professorship, which would take effect at the beginning of the 1967–68 academic year.

But other things were happening of which I had no knowledge. Later, an article by Roy Meachum in the *Washingtonian* would quote Archbishop Egidio Vagnozzi, the apostolic delegate (papal representative) to the United States, as saying he was responsible for my firing. The Vatican wanted to make an example out of a liberal Catholic priest, and I was to be the one. Just after my appointment was announced in late August, Archbishop Vagnozzi sent a letter to Rector McDonald about my orthodoxy on the basis of an article in the *Rochester Times Union* that discussed my liberal positions on artificial contraception. McDonald himself was very conservative, but such a letter from the apostolic delegate had to make him nervous and helps to explain why early on I was called on the carpet. Vagnozzi also asked Father Francis Connell, the former dean of theology and retired professor of moral theology, for an evaluation of my book, *Christian Morality Today*, published in 1966. Connell's reply to Vagnozzi was very negative. "It is incredible that a book like this could be published by a Catholic priest, especially by one who holds the important function of a teacher in the chief pontifical University of America. It is filled with errors. Unless something is done soon by ecclesiastical authority to remedy this situation, great harm will be done to the church."[6]

Archbishop Patrick A. O'Boyle, the archbishop of Washington and the chancellor of CUA, was also in communication with Father Connell about my writing. On April 16, 1966, Connell wrote O'Boyle on a number of matters but also enclosed the summary of the address on masturbation I was to give to the June 1966 meeting of the CTSA. This paper, Connell wrote, "without doubt . . . will induce thousands of young persons to masturbate without any qualms of conscience. Among these will be priests and clerics and nuns. And, of course, Father Curran will appear to be backed up by the Catholic University of America."[7]

Significant developments were also occurring within the board of trustees, undoubtedly heavily influenced by Vagnozzi and O'Boyle. Cardinal John Krol, archbishop of Philadelphia, first raised the possibility of dismissing me at a meeting of the executive committee of the trustees held on October 20, 1966. A committee of three—Krol, Archbishop Philip Hannan of New Orleans and the former auxiliary bishop of Washington, D.C., and Rector McDonald—was formed to investigate the matter. In the name of this committee, Krol made a report to the April 10, 1967, meeting of the board of trustees and proposed that my appointment should not be renewed. The board agreed that I should not be given any reason for the decision but simply informed of it. The resolution passed by a vote of 28-1. The lone dissenting vote came from Archbishop Paul Hallinan of Atlanta.

The Strike

Although I was unaware of all of this when called to the rector's quarters on Monday, April 17, I knew enough to be very suspicious. Before meeting with the rector I talked with some of my colleagues and friends, one of whom, George Kanoti, gave me a briefcase that, when opened, would record what was taking place. We laughed when we later listened to the recording, for the last thing on the tape was the voice of the vice rector saying, "Father Curran, you better close your briefcase because it is open." McDonald was joined at this meeting by his two closest assistants, Msgr. James Magner and Msgr. McAllister. Dean Schmitz had also been called in shortly before I arrived. After hearing McDonald out, I responded that the whole process was dishonest and that dishonesty in the church had to stop. I had a right to a full and fair hearing and had not received one. I threatened to make the whole situation public but finally agreed to do nothing for twenty-four hours. McDonald was apparently so flustered by my response that he never gave me the letter he had prepared.

I immediately gathered together some of my closest colleagues—Bob Hunt and Sean Quinlan from the School of Theology, Dean Schmitz, Dan Maguire, and others. We also brought in some of the priests who were studying theology because we knew they had close contact with both graduate and undergraduate students. These colleagues also talked with other faculty colleagues and friends in other schools of the university. My small group of advisors—mostly young Turks—decided that we had to fight for my reinstatement and that the best way to achieve this was to go public. On Tuesday morning, April 18, McDonald called to say he would arrange for me to meet with the administration and some of the trustees to discuss the matter the following week. I told him his offer was "too little and too late." It was full reinstatement or nothing.

On Tuesday afternoon the theology faculty met (I did not attend any meetings during the discussion of my case). All agreed that justice required that the decision against me be reversed, but the majority wanted to settle the issue without publicity. So the faculty unanimously agreed to send a telegram to all the members of the board. They told the trustees they wanted to avoid adverse publicity that could only further harm the university, but they strongly insisted that the decision be rescinded immediately.

Meanwhile, student leaders were briefed and decided to hold an informational meeting at 7:30 P.M. on Tuesday evening in the 450-seat McMahon Auditorium. The students, graduate and undergraduate together, formed a steering committee and leafleted the entire campus. By 7:20 the auditorium was filled to overflowing. Hunt, Quinlan, and Maguire spoke and roused the crowd, informing them of the trustees' action despite the approval I had from my own faculty and the academic senate. Dan Maguire said, "If there is no room for Charlie in the Catholic University *of* America, there is no room for the Catholic University *in* America." Later in the week two sisters in full religious garb put this message on a huge banner and carried it in the marches that followed. The following Sunday's "Week in Review" section in the *New York Times* printed this picture in its news story. The student steering committee also passed a resolution calling on the board to renew my contract.

On Wednesday morning, 2,000 students gathered in front of the rector's quarters and two of their leaders talked with the rector for more than an hour, but in vain. Meanwhile, outside, Al McBride, a faculty member in religious education, gave a rousing speech.

In this charged atmosphere the theology faculty met again the same morning. My closest friends were able to convince the others that they had to act firmly and publicly in light of all that was occurring on campus. The unanimous resolution of the faculty of theology ended, "Under these circumstances we cannot and will not function unless and until Father Curran is reinstated. We invite our colleagues in other schools of the university to join with us in our protest." The strike was on!

At 2:00 P.M. on Wednesday we held a press conference with three speakers—myself, Dean Schmitz, and Father Eugene Burke, who had been on the faculty for more than twenty-five years and had always strongly supported me. I tried to keep the focus on the narrow academic issue that the trustees had fired me without so much as a hearing, despite the recommendation of my faculty and the academic senate that I be promoted. The press, naturally, asked a lot of questions about my teaching, especially in the area of artificial contraception, but we tried to keep that issue from becoming the primary focus. We knew that on the narrow academic issue we could expect support from all corners of the campus.

The university faculty met in McMahon Auditorium on Thursday afternoon, while 3,000 students held a rally outside McMahon. The faculty, after many speeches (including a very impressive one by Bob Hunt) and much discussion, finally voted 400–18 to support the faculty of theology. Dr. Malcolm Henderson, chair of the assembly of ordinary professors, announced the resolution to the crowd and read the concluding sentence with a great flourish: "We cannot and will not function as members of our respective faculties unless and until Father Charles Curran is reinstated." Every school in the university, with the exception of the very small School of Education, joined officially in the strike.

The strike was national news, even front-page news in some cases, throughout the country. Telegrams of support poured in from academic and church institutions and societies and from many individuals. Beginning on Wednesday evening the informal leaders began meeting in my room to plan the tactics for the next day. We had press conferences, rallies, marches, picketing, and even a big liturgical celebration on Sunday afternoon at the large chapel of nearby Trinity College, thanks to the kindness of Sister Margaret Claydon, the president of Trinity. One of our concerns was how long we could hold out. After all, you can only have so many rallies and marches. But the trustees experienced much greater pressure than we.

As the strike wore on, the media continued to cover the story. Cardinals Lawrence Sheehan of Baltimore and Richard Cushing of Boston publicly criticized the action against me. Finally Dean Schmitz was informed that Chancellor O'Boyle and Rector McDonald would meet with the faculty of theology at 3:00 P.M. on Monday. They came with a prepared statement that fell short of committing themselves to a new contract and my promotion to associate professor. Meanwhile, a very large crowd had gathered in front of the library, but they were growing restless as the hours dragged on. When O'Boyle and McDonald finally emerged, well after 6:00 P.M., O'Boyle announced that the trustees had voted to reverse their decision. McDonald announced that my promotion to associate professor would become effective in September. Then I spoke to the crowd, reminding them that our achievement went beyond the fate of one university professor. We had acted responsibly in our protest and must continue to act responsibly to improve both our university and theological scholarship.

Why did the strike succeed? There had been a number of demonstrations on campuses throughout the country, and even at some Catholic colleges and universities, protesting actions taken by university administrators, but few of them had borne fruit, and seldom so quickly.

The strike at CUA was successful primarily because the conditions for it were ripe. Faculty grievances with the administration had been building over the years, among them the growing negative reputation of CUA in comparison to other Catholic universities, the declining number of graduate students, and Rector McDonald's interference in a number of academic aspects of the university. In 1963 the Graduate School of Arts and Sciences had issued a special committee report on departures from academic procedure that charged McDonald with interfering in the academic life and freedoms of the university in the name of church authority. The student body was also playing a more active role in the life of the university and challenged some of the administration's moves. The Second Vatican Council's call for a newer understanding of Catholic life had influenced faculty and students alike. The student newspaper, the *Tower,* had recently become more independent and was attracting capable, outspoken editors and writers. The attempt to silence me was the match that ignited a parched landscape.

The strike was also very well organized. Faculty from across schools and departments worked together. Graduate and undergraduate students formed a united coordinating committee. The group that gathered in my room every evening tried to keep all the parts together for the good of the whole. In a meeting two months later, Saul Alinsky, the well-known community organizer, congratulated me on our successful organization but also challenged me to keep the group working together in the future.

The way in which the strike was conducted was exemplary. Every effort was made to ensure that the talks, rallies, marches, and press conferences were very firm but always respectful. We did not want to be compared with the free speech movement in Berkeley. Student marshals made sure that those who were picketing and marching were properly dressed and even demanded that the young men wear ties! We also, as I've said, insisted on keeping the focus on the narrow academic issue at stake. The spirit of the demonstration was positive and upbeat, and not without its moments of levity. One sign seen frequently in the marches and rallies read, "Even my mother supports Father Curran."

Aftermath

The strike was the effort of many people working together, but Dean Schmitz put more on the line than anyone else. A generous and well-loved man and a respected churchman, Wally Schmitz was well-known to most of the bishops and had been associated with the seminary at CUA since the early 1930s. He was the master of liturgical ceremonies for Archbishop O'Boyle and was very friendly with him. Scholarship was not his primary interest, but he was determined as dean to create a strong Vatican II faculty for his school. Wally's background gave the strike instant credibility in the eyes of many bishops and others in the Catholic Church. He was not a wild-eyed radical who thought the church began with Vatican II. Sadly, in the end, Wally probably lost more than anyone else as a result of the strike. O'Boyle soon relieved him of his job of master of liturgical ceremonies and also broke off their relationship. Wally Schmitz, whose primary concern had been the ecclesiastical life of a cleric in the church, was willing to stand up for the principle of academic freedom and oppose hierarchical interference in the affairs of the university.

Wally and I did not become close friends until I'd been at CUA for a couple of years. One day in the early 1980s, he told me he was going to see his lawyer to change his will. I asked if he would leave me something in his will. His immediate response was typical. "Do you need money or something?" No, I said. I wanted him to leave me his academic robes, to remind me always of his courageous support of academic freedom. He put me in his will that day, he gave me the robes the next day, for he was retired and would not need them again. These are the academic robes I wear with pride and gratitude today. The headdress for a pontifical or Vatican doctorate in theology is not the usual mortarboard but a four-cornered biretta with a red pom-pom. I stand out whenever academic regalia is worn at Southern Methodist University.

The strike had a dramatic effect on CUA. Bishop McDonald resigned effective November 1968. A process began that completely revamped and reorganized the university and its governance. It is true that there were significant developments across the board in Catholic higher education in the United States during the late 1960s. The details of the change in general and at CUA in particular lie beyond the scope of this book. But a quick comparison of statutes makes the point very clearly. The 1937 statutes of the university, reprinted in 1964 and in effect at the time of the strike, stated that the university "venerates the Roman Pontiff as its supreme Ruler and Teacher and submits unreservedly to his Apostolic Authority as the only safe norm of truth" (par. 6). The statutes adopted in 1969 state that "the Catholic University . . . is essentially a free and autonomous center of study." It supports "an atmosphere of academic competence where freedom is fostered and where the only constraint upon truth is truth itself" (par. 1). Unfortunately, subsequent events would prove that these words did not mean what they said.

Needless to say, the strike also had a great effect on me. I came to CUA with little or no understanding of an American university. The Roman universities I had attended were really no more than theological schools. Even in my first two years at CUA I learned a lot about a university both in theory and in practice. But the strike focused my attention sharply on the whole question of the nature and structure of a Catholic university and of academic freedom. Thanks to the strike, I came into contact with the American Association of University Professors (AAUP), an organization founded in 1915 precisely to preserve, protect, and promote academic freedom. Again, considerations other than my own personal choice strongly influenced the directions and interests in my life.

The strike also catapulted me to prominence in Catholic theology and in the life of the church. Artificial contraception was the most contentious and well-publicized issue in the church at that time, and I was now identified publicly as the leading Catholic theologian opposing the existing teaching. Dan Maguire used to kid me that "the liberal thirty-three-year-old Catholic theologian" was now an official part of my name.

Bishop Sheen

The famous Fulton J. Sheen was appointed bishop of Rochester, my home diocese, to succeed Bishop Kearney and was installed in Rochester on December 15, 1966, and I flew up from Washington for the installation. On the plane I met the Vincentian father Frederick McGuire, whom I had known somewhat in Washington. Fred had actually been a hospital chaplain in Rochester for a year or two but had also served as a missionary in China, was the founder of the Center for Applied Research in the Apostolate, which is still functioning today at Georgetown University, and later worked for the United States Bishops' Conference on Latin American issues.

McGuire had also served as head of the group of religious orders with foreign missions. Much of his work consisted of fund-raising, and this put him in conflict with Fulton Sheen, who, as the director of the Society for the Propagation of the Faith, was responsible for raising money for the foreign missions. Sheen emphasized that donations to the Propagation of the Faith went to the pope, but did not help the individual religious orders directly. Given these circumstances, McGuire was not a fan of Sheen's and had a raft of anti-Sheen stories that he told me almost nonstop on the flight to Rochester. For example, a missionary priest came to see Sheen and described the difficult conditions in which he worked. As the missioner was leaving, Sheen took off his watch with a flourish and said, "Here Father, I wish I could give you more, but take my watch to help your work." Added McGuire, "Sheen used to buy those cheap watches by the gross!"

McGuire and I sat in the last pew in the cathedral. As the procession entered, everyone looked around, and there at the end was Fulton Sheen. As people saw him, you could hear many gasp, "He's so short!" As McGuire explained to me, Sheen was self-conscious about his short stature, which is why you never saw anybody else on the TV screen with him.

Sheen, like the rest of us, had his faults. His years in Rochester were not happy, but it was truly unfair to ask him to run a diocese at age seventy-one, when he had no previous experience in pastoral ministry in a diocese. All must acknowledge Sheen's extraordinary role on national TV in the 1950s, however, talking about spirituality and God. No spiritual leader since has ever done anything close to what Fulton Sheen did with his primetime TV show.

My relations with Sheen were few and formal but cordial before the strike. I called to inform him about my situation at the beginning of the strike. Dan Maguire, who was in my room at the time, remembers (I don't) that I told him I would be willing to return to Rochester to work as a priest in the diocese, but Sheen, who was cordial and noncommittal, told me to keep him informed about what was going on at CUA. After the strike I sent him further information. He thanked me in a letter and invited me to stop by when I was in Rochester and fill him in on what had happened at CUA. When I next saw him, he was friendly and urged me to help him think through the role of Catholic grammar schools in the church today. But we never mentioned CUA or the strike.

Again, however, I was in the dark about several things at the time of the strike. On the Monday morning before calling me, McDonald called Bishop Sheen to inform him that he was going to dismiss me from the university. Sheen apparently offered no objection but told McDonald he did not want me back in Rochester but would willingly allow me to teach elsewhere. This is a fascinating piece of information. It shows that the bishops, in accord with what Archbishop Vagnozzi said later, most definitely wanted to make a public example of me. They could very easily have gone to Bishop Sheen and persuaded him to call me back to Rochester for pastoral reasons. Frankly, this was the ordinary method of getting rid of a priest who was serving outside his diocese. But the bishops clearly wanted to send a signal to other liberal-minded priests. As it so often does in such circumstances, this course of action only backfired.

Further Developments

I thought that the matter of my tenure and "unorthodoxy" had been settled with the announcement, on April 24, 1967, that I had been reinstated and promoted. Just recently, however, I found out that this was not the case.[8] A few months later O'Boyle wrote to Bishop Alexander Zaleski of Lansing, Michigan, the chair of the bishops' committee on doctrine, that the executive committee of the board of trustees of CUA had unanimously endorsed his request to have the committee on doctrine examine my orthodoxy, especially as expressed in my essays collected in *Christian Morality Today*. O'Boyle's letter names those present at the meeting as Archbishop Krol, Bishop Bryan McEntegart of Brooklyn, a former rector of CUA, Bishop McDonald, and Lewis L. Guarnieri, a layman. Samuel J. Thomas, who has written an article on the real end of the Curran controversy with CUA, has not been allowed to see the minutes of the executive committee's meeting of June 13, 1967, to which O'Boyle referred, but has been told that the minutes do not mention any action of this type. O'Boyle wanted a final disposition of my case one way or the other before the bishops' annual meeting in November 1967 and thus sent Zaleski six copies of *Christian Morality Today* for the committee to review. (At least I earned some more royalties this way!)

Zaleski sent copies of O'Boyle's letter to the bishops on his committee, asking them to comment on the book and to suggest a procedure for a hearing. Three of the four bishops who responded found fault with my writings as superficial or as causing scandal or confusion in the church but not heresy—heresy being the denial of a dogma of faith—for no one would claim that the church's teaching on artificial contraception was a dogma of faith. John Fearns, the auxiliary bishop of New York and a former rector of St. Joseph's Seminary there, despite his problems with my superficial approach, wisely maintained that any further action by the bishops would only reignite the situation at CUA.

Zaleski sent his summary of the committee's response to O'Boyle but also suggested that three theologians be asked to comment on the book, a suggestion to which O'Boyle agreed. Thomas, in his article, maintains that this was a ploy on Zaleski's part designed to forestall any action against me before the November 1967 meeting of the U.S. bishops.

On September 14 Zaleski asked three theologians—John Ford, S.J., James Laubacher, a Sulpician priest, and Richard McCormick, S.J.—to review my book. John Ford was a member of the so-called papal birth control commission and a staunch opponent of artificial contraception. Nineteen sixty-five, my first year on the CUA faculty, was the last of his eight years. To his credit, at the first faculty meeting, having already received the Kellner letter, he greeted me warmly and said with a smile, "Welcome. It's good to have a heretical son-of-a-gun on the faculty!" In June 1967, at the CTSA convention, he told me in a friendly conversation that he disagreed with the process against me at CUA but that he would never have supported a strike. Ford told Zaleski that he was reluctant to criticize my book but would put on the hat of an ecclesiastical censor. He ended up charging that the book failed to recognize adequately the role of the hierarchical magisterium and that my approach would disturb the faithful.

James Laubacher, whom I knew only in passing, pointed out that he was a systematic rather than a moral theologian but characterized my book as neither heretical nor that much different from what some other scholars were saying, but said that it was unbalanced. Richard McCormick responded that he did not have time to read the book again but that he agreed with most of my positions, though he might express them differently; he described me as middle of the road and strongly advised against any ecclesiastical intervention. All of these people were pledged to secrecy on the subject, and McCormick never mentioned this episode to me.

Zaleski replied to O'Boyle that it was the consensus of the committee that my work displayed a lack of prudence, good pastoral judgment, and balanced scholarship, but that many things being said in the church were more extreme. In his response, O'Boyle realized that the matter was at an end. But a few months later, as the next chapter will make clear, he and I were again at loggerheads in a public way.

I had made three commitments to speak outside the university before the strike. I let all three institutions know that I would understand if they no longer wanted me and would keep the matter quiet, but all three reaffirmed the commitments. I spoke in Detroit under the auspices of the Institute of Continuing Education of the Archdiocese of Detroit run by Jane Wolford. Jane later invited me on three or four other occasions to speak in the Detroit Archdiocese. This time she arranged for her friend, Archbishop John Dearden, to introduce me. After the talk, I shared a taxi to the airport with the American Jesuit John Courtney Murray, who played such an important role in drafting the document on religious freedom at Vatican II. Murray congratulated me on the respectful way in which I had held my ground at CUA. He went on to tell me about his work on the Marshall Commission, to which he had been appointed by President Johnson, which was to advise the president on the subject of the draft. Murray himself was part of a small minority arguing that the government should accept selective conscientious objection to military service. This was interesting because Murray at the time was a strong supporter of the Vietnam War. Murray died later that summer.

At the June 1967 meeting of the CTSA in Chicago, I was nominated for vice president. The custom was for the person to serve one year as vice president and to succeed the next year as president. I cannot remember when I learned that I had been nominated, perhaps only at the meeting itself, but I do recall that some of my colleagues had been politicking for my nomination. The other nominee was Msgr. Austin Vaughan of St. Joseph's Seminary in New York. Then an older member nominated from the floor another older member, Msgr. James Rea. I was announced as the winner. That afternoon the president of the society called me; he was most embarrassed and apologetic. A mistake had been made. I had not received a majority of the votes, and they were going to vote again in the evening. On the second ballot, those who had voted for Msgr. Rea switched their ballots to Msgr. Vaughan, who won with ninety-four votes to my eighty-five.[9]

The 1967–68 academic year flew by. In early 1967 I signed a contract with Corpus Publications, and the edited volume *Absolutes in Moral Theology?*—which contained essays on moral absolutes from the perspective of conscience, the magisterium, natural law, Thomas Aquinas, the principle of double effect, the indissolubility of marriage, the principle of totality, and care for the dying—appeared in 1968. The same year, Fides published another volume of collected essays, *A New Look at Christian Morality*. The annual meeting of the CTSA was held that June in Washington, and I was again nominated for vice president, as was Father Thomas Clarke, S.J. Then an older, conservative member moved that the sitting officers remain in office for the coming year. The parliamentarian ruled the motion out of order, but another motion was made that the order of business be suspended so that the first motion could be voted on. In the ensuing discussion, Father Walter Burghardt, S.J., the president of the society, declared that he would not serve another year in any case. When the vote was finally taken, I was elected vice president of the Catholic Theological Society of America.[10]

I continued to enjoy the support of my colleagues on the faculty and the students at CUA, but there were occasional signs of strong opposition. On at least four occasions scurrilous fliers attacking me blanketed the campus. Two of them closed with the question, "WHERE WERE YOU, CHARLES CURRAN, BETWEEN THE HOURS OF 11 P.M. AND 3 A.M. ON APRIL 16 AND 17? THOSE OF US AT CU WHO KNOW ARE

ALLOWING YOU TO COME FORWARD AND EXPLAIN." The acting rector, John Whalen, apologized for the fliers and promised to try to find out who was behind them, but he was not successful.

Thus the 1967 strike had significant effects on both CUA and me, but there was more to come.

CHAPTER 3

The Uproar over Humanae Vitae

D URING THE STRIKE, we tried to keep the focus on the procedural issue that the trustees had overridden the votes of my colleagues and fired me without a hearing. But everyone knew I had been fired because of my position on artificial contraception, and this issue was not going to go away.

Humanae Vitae and the Response

In the mid-1960s Pope Paul VI announced that he had set up a commission to study the question of birth control. He had not allowed the Second Vatican Council to discuss the issue while this commission was at work. Ironically, during the April 1967 strike at CUA, the *National Catholic Reporter* published the commission's so-called majority report, which revealed that the commission's majority favored change on the question of birth control for married couples. Rumors circulated about how the pope would respond to this recommendation, and the issue became an increasingly hot topic. In the meantime, on June 27, 1968, the archbishops of Baltimore and Washington issued new guidelines for their priests and teachers, demanding that the church's condemnation of birth control be firmly asserted. The Association of Washington Priests sent these guidelines to all the officers of the Catholic Theological Society of America (CTSA), of which I was now vice president, for evaluation.

I had made plans in the spring of 1968 to spend the summer at St. Bonaventure's University in Olean, New York, where my friend Father Alcuin Coyle ran the summer theology program. I was to give six talks there over the course of the summer but would spend most of my time improving my German with the help of a tutor. In one of these talks, in late July, I explained why I thought the pope should change the teaching on contraception and what would happen if he did not. My comments received brief mention in the national press, and the *Washington Star* interviewed me on the new guidelines for the priests of Baltimore and Washington, many of whom opposed the new orders. My comments were part of a front-page story on Sunday, July 28, that centered on the opposition to these guidelines.

At the same time it was rumored that the pope's encyclical on the subject was about to be released. I consulted with some of my colleagues, and with others around the country, about how we should respond to the encyclical. It was my view that we theologians should issue a statement disagreeing with the encyclical if it proved to be as negative as we expected. On Sunday evening, July 28, I learned that *Time* magazine had obtained a copy of the encyclical and that it reaffirmed the condemnation of artificial contraception. The encyclical was to be released in Rome the following day. I quickly arranged to meet with Bob Hunt, Dan Maguire, and other CUA colleagues late Monday afternoon at my residence in CUA's Caldwell Hall. We were promised a copy of the encyclical by that time. I flew back to Washington on Monday morning and joined the nine others I had convened. Father James T. McHugh, who was then working for the Bishops' Conference in their Family Life Bureau, provided us with a copy of the encyclical. We read it, discussed it, and set to work on our response.[1]

Most of us agreed that we had to state clearly our disagreement with the encyclical and to assert that good Catholics could in theory and in practice reject its conclusion. My friend and former teacher, Francis X. Murphy, advised us to be more expedient and not declare our flat-out disagreement. But Murphy, who was older and more conservative than the rest of us, was a minority of one.

After hammering out a rough draft, Dan Maguire and I went to my room and typed up a final version that was acceptable to the others. John

Corrigan, a Washington priest on the summer school faculty and one of the group, told us that the Washington priests' association had reserved a room at the Mayflower Hotel for a press conference the following morning on the subject of the guidelines mentioned above. We could use this room for our own press conference. Then we went to work contacting other theologians throughout the country and soliciting their signatures on our statement.

I called Richard McBrien, who was then at Pope John XXIII Seminary in Boston, and he and other faculty members there agreed to sign. I also phoned Richard McCormick, who said he could not sign without first reading the encyclical. Finally I reached my teacher and mentor, Bernard Häring, who at that time was lecturing to the Immaculate Heart of Mary Sisters in Los Angeles. After listening to our statement, Häring said very quietly, but very firmly, that he would gladly sign and would do whatever he could to help. I was ecstatic. Häring's signature meant so much, both to me personally and to our cause. He was the leading Catholic moral theologian in the world at that time. At the press conference on Tuesday morning, we had eighty-seven signatures.

The statement consisted of ten paragraphs. There were many positive things in the encyclical, but our statement dealt primarily with the two central issues—the possibility of dissent from noninfallible teaching and the natural law defense of the teaching. We began by acknowledging a distinct role for the magisterium (the teaching authority in the church), but pointed out that theologians have a responsibility to evaluate the teaching of the magisterium. *Humanae vitae* was not an infallible teaching, we maintained. History showed that some noninfallible church teachings—for example, on religious liberty, interest taking, the right to silence, and the ends of marriage—were subsequently judged to be erroneous. The encyclical, we wrote, was deficient in its ahistorical approach to the question of contraception, its absolutism in making the biological morally normative, and its emphasis on the sexual act and faculty apart from the person. *Humanae vitae* added no new justifications for the Catholic teaching on birth control, and we asserted that Catholics could dissent from authoritative noninfallible teaching when there were sufficient reasons. Conscious of our duties and our limitations as Catholic theologians, we concluded that Catholics could responsibly decide to use birth control if it were necessary to preserve and foster the values and sacredness of their marriage.

In my prejudiced judgment, the statement has held up very well over the years. No one can deny that it is respectful and in no way impugns the role of authority in the church; but at the same time it is firm and clear. Critics claimed that we had issued our statement before reading the encyclical—very few bishops had yet seen it, after all—but any careful reader of our statement could only conclude that we had indeed read *Humanae vitae* carefully.

Jim McHugh became the bishop of Rockville Center, New York, but died of cancer in 2000. I often used to kid mutual friends, and even McHugh himself, that he never would have been made a bishop if it were known that he had supplied us with *Humanae vitae* and had shared our view of it at the time. He later became a staunch defender of *Humanae vitae* and ran the very strong (and in my opinion much too one-sided) pro-life office of the Bishops' Conference. We disagreed strongly on the issue of abortion and Catholic politicians' position on *Roe v. Wade*.

I had met McHugh, then a priest in Newark, through our mutual friend Bob Hunt and two other Newark priests on the CUA faculty. Over the years we drifted apart for less theological reasons as well. A few years ago, however, he called to say he was going to be in Dallas for a bishops' meeting and wondered if we could get together. He accepted an invitation to dinner at my house, only later to be invited to have dinner with Cardinal Bernard Law that evening. He told the cardinal he had another engagement—though he did not mention with whom!

Bob Hunt, who was married and living in Baltimore, stayed close to Jim. Hunt came down with a severe type of cancer himself and died, in August 1999, after a difficult year. McHugh was by then the Bishop of Camden, New Jersey, and he used to come to Baltimore every other week to visit Bob. McHugh presided at Bob's funeral, where a number of us from the old days got together, but he found out the next week that he too had cancer. Over the next two years we talked occasionally on the telephone. If nothing else, this shows that it is possible for people in the church to disagree strongly on specific issues but still share the common bond of faith and grace, and even friendship.

Some critics found our opposition to *Humanae Vitae* precipitous, but as we had read the encyclical carefully and crafted a thoughtful response, this charge was without merit. There is no virtue in delay; in fact, there is virtue in being timely. Our statement came at the moment that was most significant for Catholics, the day the encyclical was released.

Others, especially those within the church, claimed we had usurped the teaching and pastoral role of bishops. But we felt it was important, and a part of our service to the whole church, to express our view on the legitimate possibility of dissent from noninfallible teaching. One lay faculty member at CUA complained to me that he had been going to church every Sunday for fifty years and had never heard anyone maintain that this kind of dissent could be valid. This was hardly surprising, I replied. Protestants and others might attack the pope and the church, but no American Catholic before 1960 was going to say that the pope might be wrong—least of all in a sermon from a Catholic pulpit.

We strongly believed that our statement was for the good of the church, and subsequent events proved us right. Andrew Greeley pointed out in 1976 that the issuance of *Humanae vitae* had caused a great exodus from the Catholic Church in the United States. Sunday mass attendance dropped from 66 to 55 percent. One quarter of Catholics under thirty who attended Catholic colleges have left the church since 1965. Greeley considered and rejected the possibility that the reforms of Vatican II were behind this decline, or that it would have occurred anyway.[2] Our statement tried to make people aware that they could still be loyal Roman Catholics and disagree in theory and in practice with the encyclical.

Our statement was the first and the most publicized negative reaction to the encyclical. I thought it was important to obtain as many signatures as possible. Fortunately, there were many willing hands at CUA's summer school. On July 31 a large group helped send out 1,200 letters, with return postcards, soliciting signatures from other scholars. We copied addresses from the membership directories of the CTSA and the College Theology Society (CTS). Many people wanted to sign the statement, but we restricted it to scholars so as not to dilute its impact. Signers, we decided, should demonstrate special competence in the form of a degree, teaching role, or membership in a professional society in what we called the sacred sciences—theology, philosophy, and canon law. For the cover letter, I wanted to expand the base beyond the original signatories and the Washington geographical area. The two signers of the cover letter, in addition to myself, were John F. Cronin, S.S., of St. Mary's Seminary in Baltimore, who had worked for many years for the Bishops' Conference in Washington, and Edwin Falteisek, S.J., head of the department of pastoral ministry in the divinity school of Saint Louis University. Ultimately, more than 600 scholars signed the statement. The *National Catholic Reporter* published the names of all the original signers and also updated the list as it grew.

I tried to discourage one signer—James Mackey, an Irish priest who was teaching summer school at CUA. I told Jim that his signing might jeopardize his chances of an appointment at Maynooth, the national seminary in Ireland. He was not known in this country, I told him, and one name, more or less, was not going to affect our cause. But he insisted on signing. He never did get appointed to Maynooth, but he was appointed the first Roman Catholic since the Reformation to hold the chair of theology at the University of Edinburgh, Scotland.

In order to prolong the public discussion and publicity, I came up with a plan to hold a second press conference, on August 1, to announce that all the lay members of the papal birth control commission agreed in substance, according to their respective competencies, with our statement (I limited it to the lay members because Father John Ford strongly supported the encyclical). All readily agreed. The press conference was easy to arrange. I knew well three of the members who lived in Washington—André Hellegers and Thomas K. Burch of Georgetown, and John R. Cavanagh, a Washington psychiatrist. They all agreed to come to the press conference and make a short statement. John T. Noonan Jr., the special consultant to the commission on history, flew down from Boston. The news conference made the front page of the *New York Times* the next day.

But something else occurred at the August 1 press conference. On July 31, the day after we had issued our statement, Archbishop John F. Dearden of Detroit, the president of the Bishops' Conference, issued, in the name of the bishops of the United States, a statement on the encyclical that declared, "we, the Bishops of the Church in the United States, unite with him [Pope Paul VI] in calling upon our priests and people to receive with sincerity what he has taught, to study it carefully, and to form their consciences in its light."[3] At the press conference I was asked about Archbishop Dearden's comments and replied that our statement was in accord with his and not contradicted by it.[4] The next day Bishop Joseph L. Bernardin, the general secretary of the Bishops' Conference, responded in a public statement. "[T]he bishops in no way intended to imply there is any divergence between their statement and the teaching of the Holy Father."[5] Bernardin did not want us finding shade under the U.S. bishops' umbrella.

Once again I learned more about these events only years later—in this case from the late (and lamented) Bishop Kenneth Untener of Saginaw and another bishop, both of whom were working closely under Dearden in Detroit in 1968. Dearden had appointed Bernardin the first general secretary of the Bishops' Conference. In the course of our conversation, I ventured that the greatest disagreement between Dearden and Bernardin must have been over the 1976 Call-to-Action meeting that Dearden promoted but that Bernardin, then the president of the conference, totally derailed through stalling tactics. Many of the proposals of the conference called for change in Catholic teaching, and Bernardin obviously thought they would be unacceptable in Rome.

To my amazement, Ken Untener told me that, to the contrary, their most serious disagreement concerned me and the aftermath of *Humanae vitae*. Untener and his colleague had worked with Dearden on his statement and had purposely kept the statement somewhat vague so as not to condemn or even appear to acknowledge our statement. But once I had said publicly that the Dearden statement did not condemn ours, Bernardin issued his own press release without consulting Dearden. This action, according to Untener, had provoked the strongest disagreement between Dearden and Bernardin. What would have happened if Dearden's approach had prevailed? Who knows?

The "lively discussion" over *Humanae vitae*, to use Pope Paul VI's words, continued. In August, with the instigation and help of Justus

George Lawler, then an editor at Herder and Herder, I put together a group of essays titled *Contraception: Authority and Dissent,* which contained essays on authority from historical and contemporary perspectives by John Coulson, Brian Tierney, Joseph Komonchak, Noonan, and Maguire, and essays on the moral issue of contraception by Robert McAfee Brown, Häring, Hellegers, and myself. In my introduction to the volume I insisted that our position was not based on the general principle of freedom of conscience. Too often at that time, and even more so since, the problem has been reduced to one of conscience versus authority, but this is misplaced. Conscience can be wrong. Adolf Eichmann claimed he had followed his conscience, but he was rightly punished for his deeds. Sometimes it is one's own fault that conscience is wrong. The ultimate moral criterion is truth, and both authority and conscience strive for truth but neither can claim to achieve it all the time.

CUA and Our Dissent

Immediately after the *Humanae vitae* debates my focus turned to, or rather was turned to, CUA. Our statement on the encyclical had originated at CUA and twenty CUA professors had signed it. Many bishops, including Chancellor O'Boyle, were still unhappy about the previous year's strike. Even before our statement, O'Boyle, now a cardinal, released a public statement calling for absolute obedience to the encyclical "without equivocation, ambiguity, or simulation."[6] Father John Whalen, the acting rector of CUA after McDonald's resignation, was under heavy pressure.

Whalen suggested a meeting between dissenting theologians and some bishops to discuss our statement. I agreed, provided there was an equal number from both sides. The meeting took place at the Statler Hilton Hotel in New York, beginning with supper on Sunday, August 18, and closing after lunch on Monday. Not surprisingly, the meeting was strained and somewhat tense but always cordial. We theologians expressed our reasons for issuing a statement of dissent. We were helped in this discussion by a paper, given to me just before the meeting, by Joseph

Komonchak of St. Joseph's Seminary in New York, pointing out that a good number of the textbooks in theology used in seminaries in the late nineteenth and early twentieth centuries recognized that noninfallible church teachings might be wrong. Komonchak's essay later appeared in my edited book. Some bishops insisted that we theologians had usurped the teaching role of bishops and had confused the faithful. As expected, nobody changed positions, but the meeting did help to clarify the debate.

The CUA faculty members who attended this meeting returned immediately to Washington. Cardinal O'Boyle, through the acting rector, sent a special delivery letter dated August 9 to all faculty members of the School of Theology and the department of religious education announcing a special meeting with the chancellor on August 20.

The press referred to this meeting as a showdown, but this was inaccurate. O'Boyle brought the university's lawyers, a canon lawyer, and a court reporter and gave us the opportunity to defend the position we had taken in paragraphs eight and nine of the statement concerning the legitimacy of dissent in this case. Much of the meeting consisted of verbal jousting, primarily between Hunt, Maguire, and myself on one side and the university authorities on the other. I read into the record some of the reasons for our position, including references to the history of Vatican II and the approved authors (*auctores probati*) of the textbooks used in theology, among them Diekmann, Lercher, Palmieri, Straub, Pesch, Hervé, Van Noort, and Karrer, who directly or indirectly recognized the possibility of dissent from noninfallible church teaching. I also read into the record longer excerpts from the work of two of these authors. Jordan Kurland, the associate general secretary of the AAUP, attended the meeting at our request and pointed out that the professors from CUA had in no way claimed to speak for the university and had followed accepted academic norms. O'Boyle said he would have to refer the matter to the board of trustees, probably at a special meeting.

Near the end of the meeting, O'Boyle distributed a press release and asked for our comments. We said it was his press release, not ours. In off-the-record remarks, attested to by some who were not signatories, O'Boyle said he was going to release his statement to reporters who were waiting outside the room, and that we were free to do whatever we wanted. Bob

Hunt and I told reporters that no disciplinary action had been taken against us, and we presented the justification for our statement.

A brouhaha ensued. On August 22 O'Boyle issued a press release charging that two of the dissenting theologians, Rev. Charles Curran and Rev. Robert Hunt, had seriously misrepresented his position. The press release also noted that "false and misleading reports of the meeting suggested that my effort to be fair implied a vindication of the claimed 'right of dissent.' . . . Listening with patience does not imply agreement."[7] O'Boyle later claimed to the board of trustees that such "false and misleading reports" had been quoted in the *Washington Post*, the *Washington Star*, and the *Baltimore Sun*. In reality, those papers never reported any such statements from Hunt and me. I later discovered that a National Catholic News Service article, on the verge of publication, did report, though not as a direct quotation, that I felt vindicated. O'Boyle called the reporter, who told him that I had not used the word "vindicated" but that this was the reporter's own paraphrase. After that conversation, the story was "killed."[8] In those days, the national Catholic press was not free.

A special meeting of the CUA board of trustees was called for September 5 at the Madison Hotel in Washington. As a result of the strike, changes had already occurred with regard to both the governance of the university and the board of trustees. The chair of the board was a layman—Dr. Carroll A. Hochwalt of St. Louis. Faculty representatives were present at this meeting, and the board was obviously divided. O'Boyle and others were convinced we should be fired. But the trustees had learned that they could not fire tenured professors in an American university without a faculty hearing.

After the meeting opened with a reading of our statement, Cardinal James Francis McIntyre of Los Angeles introduced a long resolution that the board, having "seriously and penetratingly considered the utterances of Father Curran, his followers, and associates with regard to the encyclical *Humanae vitae*, . . . has come to the conclusion that these statements and other expressed opinions are in obvious conflict with known and practiced teachings of the Church as held for centuries and recently reiterated and confirmed by the Holy Father." The theologians had thus violated their profession of faith and their contract with the university and should be terminated. Much discussion followed. O'Boyle repeated his allegations (later judged by the faculty inquiry committee to be erroneous) that Hunt and I had told the press after the August 20 meeting that we felt vindicated. The bishops present, John Wright and Alexander Zaleski, alleged that there were tendencies in the dissenting theologians' approach that went beyond Vatican II in terms of authority in the church. But others spoke out on the need to follow accepted academic norms—namely, to allow faculty members a hearing by their peers, as guaranteed by AAUP guidelines. By afternoon McIntyre had withdrawn his resolution. A small committee of four, including Wright and Zaleski, were appointed to draft the final document and press release on the basis of the priorities agreed upon in the discussion.

At 9:00 P.M. Hochwalt read the board's statement to the press. He took no questions. The tension is evident in the first paragraph. "The Board of Trustees of the Catholic University of America recognizes the responsibility arising from its authority to grant Pontifical degrees in sacred sciences and adheres fully to the teaching authority of the Pope. . . . Further, the Board reaffirms the commitment of the Catholic University of America to accepted norms of academic freedom in the work of teaching and to the due process protective of such freedom." The twofold practical actions of the board mirrored this tension. First, the "Board recognizes that any final judgments concerning theological teachings and any canonical decisions involving teachers of sacred sciences belong properly to the bishops of the Church." Second, "The Board directs the acting-Rector of the University to institute through due academic process an immediate inquiry as to whether the teachers at this University who signed the recent statement of dissent have violated by their declarations or actions with respect to the Encyclical *Humanae vitae* their responsibilities to the University under its existing statutes and under their commitments as teachers in the University and specifically as teachers of theology and/or other sacred sciences."[9] Thus began a long and difficult year for us twenty "subject professors," as we were called.

Faculty Board of Inquiry

In one respect we were most fortunate. Bob Hunt's brother, John, who was the managing partner of the New York law firm of Cravath, Swaine, and Moore, told Bob he would defend us pro bono in any kind of academic or legal hearing. In the course of that year, I learned much from John Hunt and also came to know him as a friend. All twenty of us participated in drafting our written defense. But Bob Hunt and I, with help on occasion from Dan Maguire, John Smolko, and others, coordinated the work and often went to New York to work with the lawyers. Bob and I spent a good number of nights as guests in the home of John and his wife, Miriam. Terrence Connelly, an associate at Cravath and an alumnus of CUA, worked with John on the case. We, "the subject professors," can never adequately express our gratitude to Cravath and its lawyers for what they did for us. We have told the story of the inquiry in more detail elsewhere, but I shall summarize it here.[10]

Anyone associated with academic institutions knows that academic processes can proceed at a glacial pace. Acting rector Whalen asked the academic senate at its first meeting in September to work out the details of the inquiry. The senate first had to elect its "committee on committees," which then moved to appoint two committees to deal with aspects of the case and in particular the procedures to be followed by the inquiry. As the elected representative of the School of Theology to the academic senate, I pointed out that I would be present and would vote when we were considering procedures but would not be present or vote on any substantive issues.

On October 16 the procedures for the hearing were approved, and the members of the inquiry board, elected from all the schools of the university, chose Dean Donald Marlowe of the School of Engineering as the chair. Pre-inquiry conferences took place in December and early January. John Hunt insisted that the administration had to make its case and bring charges against us, that the burden of proof was on the university to prove our guilt, not on us to prove our innocence. In response, the new acting rector, Nivard Scheel, finally responded that the board of trustees would make no charges because it did not want to prejudice the result of the inquiry. The "focus of the present inquiry is on the style and method whereby some faculty members expressed personal dissent from Papal teaching, and apparently helped organize additional dissent to such teaching," he said. The board did not "question the right of the scholar to have or to hold private dissent on Papal teaching not defined as infallible."[11] This was a new approach. On August 20 O'Boyle had been concerned only with the part of our statement affirming the legitimacy of dissent. The September 5 statement of the trustees said the purpose of the inquiry was to determine whether the professors who had signed the statement had "violated by their declarations or actions" their responsibilities.

The broader context is important to understanding why the trustees shifted their focus. In the end, our dialogue with the bishops and our references to Vatican II and to older approved authors, together I am sure with other input, convinced the bishops that dissent from noninfallible teaching can be legitimate for Catholics. To my knowledge, the history of what occurred at this time among the bishops has not been written and may never be written, but Bishop Zaleski, as chair of the committee on doctrine, obviously played a significant role. Much later we learned that in September he presented to the executive committee of the Bishops' Conference a report acknowledging that a person in good faith might be unable to give internal assent to the encyclical. "Dissent can be expressed, but it must be done in a manner becoming to a docile believer and a loyal son of the church."[12]

Throughout the months following the release of the encyclical, various national conferences of bishops took somewhat different approaches to the encyclical. On November 15, 1968, the U.S. bishops issued their pastoral letter *Human Life in Our Day,* which read in part, "The expression of theological dissent from the magisterium is in order only if the reasons are serious and well-founded, if the manner of the dissent does not question or impugn the teaching authority of the Church, and is such as not to give scandal."[13] Our statement certainly met those criteria. In light of the restoration that has occurred in the Catholic Church since that time, however, the bishops as a whole no longer act in accord with that statement (about which more later).

Our hearing before the inquiry board began in January 1969. We were in frequent contact with the national AAUP office throughout the academic year, especially with Jordan Kurland and Herman Orentlicher. In addition, we subject professors were most fortunate that Professor Robert K. Webb, then at Columbia University and editor of the *American Histori-*

cal Review, served as our academic counsel and gave us his time, deep knowledge, and wise advice. His willingness to sacrifice his own scholarly work for the cause of the academy was most admirable. We also called in expert witnesses and received written testimony from twelve distinguished persons with expertise in different areas of the case.

The subject professors submitted about 250 pages explaining and justifying our original statement and the manner and mode of our dissent. We addressed the nature and function of the magisterium and the role of theologians in terms of interpretation that could, at times, take the form of dissent from noninfallible papal teaching as found in the *auctores probati* of the nineteenth and twentieth centuries. Noninfallible teaching does not involve matters of dogma but rather those things that are more peripheral and removed from the core of faith. History also shows that specific teachings of the papal magisterium have, in light of changing historical and cultural circumstances, later been judged wrong. Developments in the understanding of the church at Vatican II only reinforced the legitimacy of dissent in certain circumstances.

The one aspect of the issue that had not been discussed previously was the issue of *public* dissent. Here we appealed to church teaching on the right to be informed and the role of public opinion and free speech within the church. As theologians, we argued, we had a duty to communicate with the hierarchical magisterium, fellow theologians, the people intimately concerned with the issues, priests and other pastoral ministers, other churches, the news media, and the broader public. The decision to dissent publicly requires a balance of values and the exercise of prudence; when those conditions are met, it is decidedly responsible. The final section of our written defense dealt with the specific teaching of *Humanae vitae* and the reasons why we felt obligated to oppose its teaching on artificial contraception.

Our lawyers drafted a second document dealing with the propriety of our declarations and actions in light of accepted academic norms and procedures. This document developed in detail the history and meaning of academic freedom, the norms governing extramural expression by faculty members, academic freedom in church-related schools, recent developments in Catholic higher education in the United States in general and at

CUA in particular, and the basic compatibility between academic freedom and Catholic convictions. In light of all these considerations, the written testimony justified the academic propriety of our declarations and actions. In addition to the written submission, all of the subject professors, as well as our expert witnesses, testified at the hearing. We later incorporated the testimony of the expert witnesses into our presentation, and Sheed and Ward published two volumes dealing with our dissent from the viewpoint of both Catholic theology and academic norms and procedures.[14]

The board of inquiry submitted its final report to the academic senate of the university and to the subject professors, with the understanding that we would not make the report public until the meeting of the trustees. The board's report was 100 percent in our favor. The theologians' statement, it read, "represents a responsible theological dissent from the teaching of the Encyclical *Humanae Vitae,* and this dissent is reasonably supported as a tenable scholarly position. . . . [T]he release of this statement cannot be regarded as contrary to the accepted norms of academic procedure. Neither the timing, the content, nor the means of securing circulation and concurrence of colleagues are to be regarded as extraordinary or improper in the light of current academic practices. The alternatives of either repressing the statement or of adopting a policy of concerted silence would have been more truly improper."[15]

Needless to say, we were elated, and John Hunt, Terry Connelly, Bob Hunt, and I, along with maybe one or two others, went to a celebratory dinner before the lawyers took the shuttle back to New York. As we were eating, Bishop Bernardin, then the general secretary of the Bishops' Conference, came into the restaurant and asked what the report said; he knew that we were to receive the verdict that day. We felt that in light of his position we could tell him without violating our commitment not to make the report public. He congratulated us and later sent after-dinner drinks to our table.

The CUA Trustees' Reaction

The academic senate unanimously approved the inquiry board's report and sent it to the trustees, who were to meet in Houston on April 12–13.[16]

The chair of the board, Dr. Hochwalt, had retained a public relations counsel, who informed us that Hochwalt was going to stand for the principle of academic freedom even if he had to sacrifice unanimity on the board; but he also asked us not to flaunt our victory. Specifically, we were not to point out that dissent was a legitimate theological position for Catholics. We responded that we had acted responsibly in the past and would continue to act responsibly in the future, but we could not accept any further restriction. After all, our whole year-long struggle had been for the purpose of vindicating our academic freedom and our responsibility to act in accord with it.

The CUA trustees were meeting in Houston because the U.S. bishops as a whole were having a national meeting immediately thereafter. The bishops still exercised a great degree of influence at CUA for many reasons. They still constituted the largest group of trustees. The bishops had founded CUA, and they still supported it with annual collections and, in a certain sense, considered it their university. Obviously, many of the bishops were still upset with us. Tension between the academic and the church aspects of the university was certainly nothing new, but it was quite pronounced throughout the whole process of the hearing. O'Boyle, to his credit, continued to urge the bishops to support the university financially despite the strike in 1967 and the dissent in 1968.

The tensions within the board of trustees came through clearly in their response to the inquiry board's report. They "received" the report at the meeting in Houston and appointed a five-person committee headed by Cardinal Krol to examine it and make recommendations to the June 15 trustees' meeting in Washington, on the grounds that they needed more time to study the document. In one sense that was fair enough; but perhaps they also did not want to take action just before the national meeting of the bishops. They also declared that the faculty in its teaching of doctrine continued to be subject to the teaching authority of the church. Most observers pointed out that ultimately the trustees would have to accept the conclusions of the faculty inquiry board if they wanted to have any respect as an institution in good standing in American higher education. Krol's committee presented a six-page report to the June 15 meeting of the trustees, but we have never seen a copy of this report.

After the June 15 trustees' meeting, the trustees issued a press release announcing that they accepted the report of the faculty inquiry board insofar as it pertained to the academic propriety of the conduct of the dissenting faculty members. But they went on to say that they had directed an inquiry into the style, manner, and mode of the dissent and that, consequently, their acceptance of the report did not suggest that they approved our theological position. This assertion is contradicted by a number of facts, however. On September 5 the trustees had directed that the inquiry consider the declarations as well as actions of the professors. The December 23 letter sent in their names specifically requested that the inquiry board consider the responsibility of the professors' conduct in light of their profession of faith as well as accepted academic norms. Also, Bishop James P. Shannon, the trustees' representative to the inquiry, had approved the inquiry board's view that it would have to pass on the theological tenability of the dissent in light of the trustees' September 5 directions.

In addition, the inquiry report, approved by both the senate and the trustees, made no distinction between acceptance of the academic propriety of the dissent and approval of its theological tenability. The report had affirmed that, with respect to the expressions of Roman Catholic theologians, academic propriety requires theological tenability within the field of the Catholic faith commitment. But the report also made clear that the recognition of the academic freedom of the professors and the recognition that their position was theologically tenable did not imply university approval or disapproval of the opinions expressed in the exercise of that right.

After the meeting, it was widely reported in the Catholic press that the trustees had voted to "support the chancellor" in his decision to refer the orthodoxy of the professors' dissent to the committee on doctrine of the Bishops' Conference.[17] Cardinal John Dearden, the head of the Bishops' Conference, refused to allow that body to take up the matter but requested that Bishop Zaleski, the chair of the doctrinal committee, form a three-person committee to study the matter. (This action by Dearden is totally consistent with the earlier report that from the very beginning he did not want to condemn our dissent.) Zaleski's final report was in keeping with his earlier position: Theologians needed academic freedom, but it was the bishops' considered judgment that the dissent manifested by the theologians at CUA was not sufficiently sensitive to the pastoral implications of their actions. Chancellor O'Boyle, over some objections, submitted the report to the CUA trustees at their November 1969 meeting. The trustees voted to receive the report but not to approve it. The report from the doctrinal committee thus seems to have had no direct or immediate effect on the university, but it indicated the continuing strong opposition of a good number of bishops to what we had done.[18]

Cardinal O'Boyle and his supporters were obviously behind the attempt to distinguish between the academic propriety of our conduct and the nonapproval of our theological position. The broader historical context helps to explain why he did not want to recognize our dissent as theologically tenable.[19] O'Boyle had been involved in a very heated and divisive struggle with many of his priests in the Archdiocese of Washington over the encyclical. After we issued our statement on July 30, a group of Washington priests issued a "statement of conscience" expressing the pastoral approach they would take to the encyclical in light of our statement. The dispute was long and acrimonious. O'Boyle called in individually all the priests who had signed the statement and questioned them in a formal canonical hearing about their position. Then, on September 30, 1969, he imposed canonical penalties of various types on forty of his priests. One of the forty was Father Horace McKenna, S.J., who had been O'Boyle's confessor.

The dispute had a devastating effect on the Archdiocese of Washington and its priests. It was not settled until the spring of 1971 through the efforts of the Congregation for the Clergy in Rome. If the Washington priests accepted the somewhat ambiguous findings of the Congregation for the Clergy, they would not have to retract their original statement as O'Boyle had demanded. But by that time there were only nineteen active priests. Most of the others had left the priesthood because of the struggle. O'Boyle was the only bishop in the United States, and perhaps in the world, who imposed such canonical penalties on his priests in the aftermath of *Humanae vitae*. In the end, the Vatican itself did not support him.

In my judgment, O'Boyle's rigidity and stubbornness had dire effects on the church of Washington and even on himself. When O'Boyle died in

1987, the *London Independent* asked me to write his obituary, which I agreed to do. I mentioned these struggles, especially with his priests, but said that it would be unfair to remember O'Boyle only for these battles over *Humanae vitae.* To his credit, O'Boyle never forgot his roots in poverty, and he insisted on the church's mission to support social justice, religious freedom, Catholic-Jewish relations, workers, and the poor. Early in his tenure in Washington, he integrated the Catholic schools despite vocal opposition and financial boycotts. When President Richard Nixon started the custom of inviting prominent clergy to the White House for ecumenical Sunday services, O'Boyle refused to be among the Catholic cardinals and archbishops who led such services. His reaction to *Humanae vitae* made O'Boyle a tragic figure.

Dissent in and for the Church

Ever since *Humanae vitae* and its aftermath, I have been associated with the concept and the reality of dissent in the church. The core paragraph in our original statement on *Humanae vitae* maintains that "It is common teaching in the Church that Catholics may dissent from authoritative noninfallible teachings of the magisterium when sufficient reasons for so doing exist." We titled the book, based on the document we submitted to the inquiry board, *Dissent In and For the Church.* The CDF maintained, "One who dissents from the magisterium as you do is not suitable or eligible to teach Catholic theology."[20] Later I wrote *Faithful Dissent,* the title of which was suggested by Robert Heyer, my editor.

Some of my colleagues who share my basic approach to moral theology, beginning with my English friend, Kevin Kelly, and later Linda Hogan and Lisa Cahill, have objected to my using the term "dissent" on the grounds that it is a negative word associated with opposition and confrontation.[21] The term, in their view, risks obscuring all that is positive about what is involved in the position—its respect for tradition, concern for truth, love of the church, and recognition for shared responsibility within the church. Focusing on dissent can not only create a climate of confrontation but skewer the whole issue by deflecting attention from the fundamental questions of the respective roles of hierarchical teaching authority, theologians, and all believers in the service of truth in the church.

I acknowledged in the introduction to *Contraception: Authority and Dissent* that some of the contributors to the volume did not like the term because it connotes rebellion and disloyalty. We theologians at CUA were obviously aware of the negative connotations of the term, which is why we titled our book *Dissent In and For the Church;* the word *for* was important to us. In my view dissent is a positive force and need not carry negative connotations. In the political realm, this attitude has often been expressed as the highest form of patriotism, which consists in resisting one's country or one's government when it is in the wrong. In the context of the church, for me, dissent means speaking the truth in love, and that has always been my intention.

The events of 1967 and 1968 were both unique and historic. The successful strike at the national Catholic university and the acceptance by that university of the immediate, unprecedented, organized, and forceful dissent from a papal encyclical had a very significant effect on Catholic life in the United States. I would never have been involved in these events if not for circumstances completely beyond my control, but in these circumstances I tried to act responsibly and in the best interest of the church.

It goes without saying that not everyone shares my view of what I did. Msgr. George A. Kelly of New York has strenuously opposed the liberal direction of the post–Vatican II Catholic Church in the United States and has strongly criticized many bishops as well as theologians. He sees me as the main culprit in the liberalization of the church. "On a day that now seems long ago, April 24, 1967, a young priest, not ten years ordained, changed the course of Catholic development in the United States," Kelly has written. "He confronted American bishops and won. He challenged a pope and was promoted. . . . The U.S. hierarchy has not recovered since. . . . [Curran] undertook to redefine the Catholic Church and the authority of bishops as well. . . . Strangely, the national body of bishops did not see Curran's defiance as undermining the authority of all bishops. . . . At its November 1968 meeting, the National Conference of Catholic Bishops (NCCB) added to its own difficulties by publishing

'Norms for Licit Theological Dissent' in their pastoral *Human Life in Our Day*."[22]

I hope and pray that history will show that my interpretation of these events was correct and that it has served a positive role in the life of the church.

CHAPTER 4

Growing Tensions and Maturing Theology: The Seventies

WHAT WOULD HAPPEN in the Catholic Church after *Humanae vitae?* This encyclical clearly disappointed those of us who were expecting change after Vatican II. Would the encyclical usher in an era of increased tensions and polarization in the church?

As the 1970s began, I had the feeling that despite the brouhaha over *Humanae vitae,* the tensions in the church would abate rather than harden. The reaction to the encyclical showed that a strong majority of theologians supported the legitimacy of dissent. In their 1969 pastoral letter *Human Life in Our Day,* the U.S. bishops had explicitly recognized the legitimacy of dissent under three conditions—when there were serious reasons, when the teaching authority of the church was not impugned, and when no scandal was given. At CUA, the principle of academic freedom was firmly established, even if some bishops and trustees were not happy about it. All of these things were hopeful signs. The majority of Catholics in the pews disagreed with the encyclical, and some of them felt so strongly about this that they had left the church. Yes, there were tensions, but opposition, even between bishops and dissenting theologians, seemed far from irreversible. As the decade unfolded, however, these tensions became more severe and the various camps did indeed become polarized.

71

Throughout the 1970s and early '80s, I was also developing my own approach to the discipline of moral theology. My goal was ultimately to publish a systematic moral theology that would bring together all the various parts into a whole. I wanted to propose a holistic moral theology, one that would show that there was much more at stake than the discussion about absolute norms. For theoretical and pastoral reasons, however, I could not ignore controversies about these norms.

Other Controversial Issues

My detailed analysis and criticism of the teaching on artificial contraception provided me with the methodological approaches to challenge the inadequacies in other specific Catholic moral teachings. The principal aspects of my developing methodology were the importance of historical consciousness, the recognition of historical development in many teachings and the influence of outmoded biological understandings of human sexuality, the need for a critical evaluation of the experience of Christian people, and the problematic aspects of the neoscholastic understanding of natural law. Specific issues involving absolute prohibitory norms continued to be an area of great interest in the church and in theology. Here the pastoral and practical dimensions came to the fore, as many Catholics (and others) were grappling with such issues as homosexual relations, divorce, sterilization, and abortion. I pointed out early on that artificial contraception was not the only Catholic teaching open to challenge.

In 1970 Dr. John R. Cavanagh conducted a symposium on homosexuality at CUA and invited me to address the moral aspects of homosexual relations. Cavanagh, a lay Catholic psychiatrist in Washington, was a member of the papal birth control commission (he was the physician for Cardinal Cicognani when he was the apostolic delegate in Washington) and had served for a long time as a lecturer in pastoral counseling at CUA. Since my arrival in Washington we had been friendly, and he had joined the dissent from *Humanae vitae*. I later published my lecture in the *Thomist*, a scholarly journal of philosophy and theology published by the

Dominican Fathers. And I developed my argument on homosexuality in several later publications.[1]

As will become clear, I have generally agreed strongly with the broad fundamental aspects of the Catholic theological tradition, and I work primarily out of that tradition. Anyone working in a tradition first tries to justify something new in light of what has come before. But, on the other hand, the Catholic tradition is by its very nature a living tradition that does not simply repeat the past. I had come, through my earlier study of natural law, to appreciate the mutual relationship between theory and practice. Sometimes recognizing a new practice requires us to rethink our theory. Just the same, a theologian working in a living tradition definitely wants to strive for continuity, and to some extent is tempted to overlook the reality of change and discontinuity. Looking back, I can see the weaknesses and shortcomings in the position I proposed in the early 1970s with regard to homosexual unions and sexual relations.

I had come to accept the moral legitimacy of a union of two gay men or lesbians (in 1970 we used the word "homosexuals") striving for permanency. At that time, no Catholic theologian in this country had taken such a position publicly. I rejected, as not going far enough, the pastoral understanding of something being objectively wrong but not subjectively sinful. Likewise, the justification for homosexual relations as the lesser of two evils did not go far enough. Two of the people I criticized for not being radical enough at that time later changed their positions—as I hope we are all open to doing when convinced. At that time, I wanted to insist that homosexual actions between committed partners are in a true sense objectively good but still not on a par with heterosexual relationships.

A number of factors influenced my approach. I was then developing what I called the theory of compromise, a theory I no longer endorse completely. Sometimes the presence of sin and sinful structures can justify doing what we would not do in other circumstances. Think, for example, of the poor person who in order to get a job must pay a bribe. At that time, I also still accepted the natural law understanding of complementarity between male and female as the way things should be. Because of the sin of the world, but not personal sin, some people could not live out this complementarity. A committed homosexual relationship falls short of the ideal, I thought then, but for the homosexual a homosexual union striving for some permanency is the best and perhaps the only way to achieve some humanity. Such a relationship is good, but it is not the ideal.

In 1973 I addressed the issue of divorce and argued for a change in the Catholic Church's teaching to allow the legitimacy of divorce and remarriage in some circumstances.[2] The famous "except for the case of '*porneia*'" in Matthew 19 shows that the early church made some exceptions in what might have been Jesus' absolute pronouncement on divorce. Likewise, during the first thousand years of Christianity, divorce was allowed in certain circumstances. Arguments from reason or natural law—the commitment of the spouses, the well-being of the children, and the good of society—do not prove an absolute indissolubility. Nor do the theological arguments based on covenant love and Christian marriage as the symbol of the union of Christ and the church prove absolute indissolubility. We live in the eschatological tension between the now and the fullness of the reign of God in the future. Nothing in this world can ever perfectly mirror God's love. The Catholic Church in the 1970s was beginning to deal with this issue by increasing the possibility of marriages being declared null and void when spouses were judged incapable of committing themselves to a permanent relationship at the time of the marriage. I admire the ingenuity of the canon lawyers here, but existentially many people were convinced they did have a true marriage commitment from the beginning but unfortunately it broke down. The real issue in most cases of divorce is not whether true marital consent was there at the beginning but what happens when the marriage breaks down.

But, in keeping with the holistic approach of my mentor Bernard Häring, I later pointed out that recognizing the possibility of divorce was less important than the need for everyone in the church to work to strengthen existing marriage commitments, especially in light of modern American culture, which emphasizes individualism, absolute personal freedom, materialism, and consumerism, all of which tend to stand in the way of living out the Christian covenantal commitment of marriage. Consequently, I believed (and still believe), we must work to strengthen Christian marriage in our culture but at the same time recognize the need for divorce in certain circumstances.[3]

Abortion, in both its moral and legal aspects, was a burning issue in the early 1970s. In a 1973 article I pointed out that there were two aspects to the moral question of abortion—when truly individual human life begins, and how we solve conflicts involving human life.[4] On the first point, official Catholic teaching maintains that one has to act as if truly individual human life is present from the moment of conception. This teaching recognizes, although this is not generally known even among Catholics, the existence of theoretical doubt about when truly individual human life begins. Thomas Aquinas, for example, held that truly individual human life begins at forty days for males and eighty or ninety days for females. (I have no idea what the empirical basis for this was!) But in practice we must err on the side of caution, and the benefit of the doubt must be given to truly individual human life beginning at the moment of conception. On the second point, that of solving conflicts, Catholic teaching used the famous principle of the double effect. Direct abortion is always wrong, but indirect abortion can be accepted if there is a proportionate reason. I had some difficulties with the principle of double effect, but this is not the place to go into them. My colleague and good friend Richard McCormick started working on this issue in 1973, and over the years he developed his theory of proportionalism to deal with conflict situations.[5]

With regard to the beginning of human life, I argued in 1973 that truly individual human life is not present before the fourteenth day after conception precisely because there seems to be no individuality present. I have always been somewhat conservative on the moral issue of abortion and the question of the beginning of human life. I worry about the danger in American society of attributing dignity to people on the basis of what they do, make, or accomplish. In the last analysis, human dignity cannot be based on such criteria because they undermine the equal dignity of all human lives—rich and poor, healthy and sick, living and dying. At the same time, I also pointed out that Catholics could in good faith dissent on the issue of what was called in theological terms "ensoulment." Respect for human life is a basic principle on which we can all agree, but given the complexity of the question of when life begins, no one, not even the Catholic Church, can claim to have the definitive answer.

Even before the *Roe v. Wade* decision in January 1973, I was writing on the legal aspects of abortion.[6] I had taught some doctoral seminars on religious liberty and was familiar with John Courtney Murray's position, which was incorporated in Vatican II's Declaration on Religious Liberty. Murray saw religious freedom primarily as a juridical and constitutional issue. What is the role of law in a democracy? The Vatican II declaration and Murray maintain that the primary principle of law in our democratic society is as much freedom as possible and as little restraint as necessary. Civil law can and should intervene only when it is necessary to preserve and promote public order that involves social justice, public peace, and public morality.[7] After *Roe v. Wade* I also added the pragmatic aspects of law: Is it feasible? Is it enforceable? Can it pass? The Vatican II approach to the morality-law question differed from the traditionally accepted Thomistic approach found in Catholic teaching and theology. Aquinas, having no idea of a democratic society, began with the natural moral law. In his view, circumstances occasionally arise in which the legal system does not have to enforce natural law, but human law can never go against natural law. The Vatican II approach begins not with natural law but with human freedom.[8]

The Vatican II approach, however, opposes an assumption frequently held in our country—that one's religion should not affect one's political, public, or legal views. This assumption rests on the belief that religion is a private matter and should not have any cultural, political, or social influence. I do not see how a Christian can accept this proposition, though politicians often invoke it when they speak of their willingness to enforce the separation of church and state. Most of us would agree that there is a limit on the extent to which religion should affect the making or execution of law or public policy; that limit depends on the upholding of public order. If you believe that health care is a basic human right, then you have a right to work for the advancement of health care, whether the basis for your conviction is religious, philosophical, political, or anything else. The limit is not your motive for the position but its substance—the act, not the intention behind it. The proposed legislation must pertain to public order. Only then can it overcome the American presumption in favor of individual freedom.

I applied the Vatican II approach to abortion law in light of *Roe v. Wade*. If one believes that individual human life is truly present at conception, then one can work for a law to protect such life, regardless of motivation. Thus believers and even the churches can work for such a position. Pragmatically speaking, they would have to persuade a majority of people, perhaps even two-thirds, to accept their position and overturn the law. But Catholics who hold that individual human life is present from conception could also argue against opposing *Roe v. Wade*. Given the deep division of public opinion on the question of abortion, one could legitimately give the benefit of the doubt to individual freedom. One must also consider the feasibility of passing such a law and its enforceability. But the Catholic hierarchy in this country has failed to recognize the legitimacy of accepting *Roe v. Wade*, and there has been much public controversy concerning Catholic legislators and politicians as a result. Every presidential election since 1976 has witnessed these controversies.

In 1976, Archbishop Joseph Bernardin, then president of the National Conference of Catholic Bishops, met with the presidential candidates and indicated that the bishops could not support Jimmy Carter because of his position on abortion. A number of theologians contacted me and suggested that we issue a public statement disagreeing with this position similar to the one we released after *Humanae vitae*'s appearance in 1968. I decided to consult Father Thomas Kelly, the associate general secretary of the Bishops' Conference, to tell him that such a plan was afoot and that the statement in question would make three points. First, that Catholics should not vote for a candidate on the basis of one moral issue alone, given that there are always many issues at stake. Second, that we respect the rights of religious leaders and bishops to speak out for what they see as the national welfare. Third, that abortion is a serious problem in our society, but that Catholics can legitimately not support a constitutional amendment overturning the *Roe v. Wade* ruling. In short, that there is legitimate pluralism within the church.

Kelly told me there would be further comments from the bishops, and indeed Bernardin did make a clarification and the bishops themselves issued a document that has been issued in similar form in every presidential election year since then. This document states that the bishops are not supporting one candidate or another and urges people to vote on the basis of all the issues involved rather than just one. Unfortunately, however, neither then nor since have they been willing to recognize as legitimate the position that Catholics can in good conscience support *Roe v. Wade*. Two of the theologians who wanted me to organize a public statement at that time are now clearly identified as quite conservative in their theology.

In this connection, an amusing incident occurred in 1976. Father Geno Baroni, who had worked in inner-city Washington and with ethnic groups, talked to me about abortion laws in connection with his work for the Carter campaign. A few nights later I got a phone call from a man with a southern drawl identifying himself as Governor Jimmy Carter. At first I was sure someone was pulling my leg. But it was in fact Carter, and he wanted to talk about the Catholic Church and abortion. I told Carter that the bishops would never accept his position on abortion but that many of his other views were in line with Catholic social teaching. Later, Baroni and others arranged for Carter to address the national meeting of Catholic Charities.

In 1973 I wrote an article arguing for a change in the hierarchical teaching condemning sterilization. If one accepts contraception for spouses, one must logically accept the morality of sterilization. Contraception interferes with the sexual act; sterilization interferes with the sexual power or faculty, as it is called in moral theology. Since sterilization tends to be permanent, one needs a stronger and more permanent reason for its justification.[9]

Sexual ethics remained a contentious issue in the Catholic Church. In January 1976 the CDF issued a Declaration on Certain Questions Concerning Sexual Ethics.[10] I was still hoping such documents might result from a broad consultation within the church, but there was no such consultation for this document, which came directly from the Vatican. Unfortunately, its methodology rests on the purpose and structure of the sexual faculty and the sexual act. It fails to give primary importance to the person, suffers from the problem of physicalism mentioned earlier, and is pervaded by a deductive and classicist method. Specifically, I disagreed with its teaching on mortal sin, masturbation, and homosexuality, and an article I wrote on this was published in a French translation in *Le Supplé-*

ment, the French journal of moral theology that ultimately translated and published four more of my articles.[11]

On all of these issues I was on the cutting edge and was often the first Catholic moral theologian to call for change. The same methodological problems applied to most of these issues. I often pointed out that dissent on contraception logically entails dissent in other areas because of the same methodological problems. But positions were undoubtedly hardening, and the papal magisterium was not about to change its sexual teachings.

Methodological Aspects

While grappling with some of the important practical issues of the day, I also worked to develop my systematic moral theology. In the 1970s I elaborated my understanding of significant methodological and theoretical aspects of moral theology—stance, model, person as subject and agent, and conscience. In a 1980 article I put together an overview of my method and approach to fundamental moral theology.[12] I finally developed this method in a systematic way in *The Catholic Moral Tradition Today: A Synthesis* (1999).

Stance refers to the perspective or horizon from which the moral theologian looks at reality and what is happening in our world. Stance was not a traditional concept in Catholic moral theology, but I see it as the logical first step in systematic moral theology. I proposed as a stance the viewing of reality in terms of the fivefold Christians mysteries of creation, sin, incarnation, redemption, and resurrection destiny.[13]

Two developments of the early 1970s influenced my approach to stance. First, Vatican II called for more theological approaches to moral theology and brought in the roles of Christology, grace, and scripture. Pre–Vatican II natural law was theologically grounded in creation, but its specifically Christian aspects did not affect morality. Pope John XXIII's 1963 encyclical *Pacem in terris* illustrates such an approach, grounded in creation but failing to give any role to grace or sin. The Pastoral Constitution on the Church in the Modern World tries to follow a more integrated

Christian approach that brings in creation, sin, and Christology. But I criticized this constitution for being, like most theology of the era, too optimistic, for it failed to stress the importance of sin and the fact that the fullness of the reign of God will come only at the end of time.[14]

The second influence on my stance came from my study of the prominent Protestant ethicist Paul Ramsey. I was on sabbatical in 1972 and André Hellegers invited me to be among the first senior visiting scholars at the Kennedy Institute of Bioethics at Georgetown University, where I wrote my book on Ramsey, *Politics, Medicine, and Christian Ethics: A Dialogue with Paul Ramsey* (1973). Through reading Ramsey and other Protestants I had realized that the Catholic approach failed to give enough importance to the reality of human sinfulness, but in my judgment Ramsey put *too* much emphasis on sin.

How does this stance work? God created the world as good. Sin has damaged the goodness of creation but has not completely destroyed it. Through the incarnation, God joined God's self to the human, thus affirming the fundamental goodness of the human. Redemption in Christ Jesus has already occurred and brought with it the first fruits of the victory over sin and evil, but the fullness of resurrection destiny will come only at the end of time.

A few illustrations show how this stance works. Catholic natural law theory, based on the goodness of creation, recognizes that human reason, reflecting on what God created, can come to true moral wisdom and knowledge, a position I strongly support. The older Catholic approach, however, fails to incorporate the realities of sin and grace into its theory of natural law. Death for the Christian is a complex reality illumined by this stance. Creation tells us that a finite creature is going to die, so death in that sense is natural. But Genesis and the Scriptures see death as related to sin. We all experience death as loss and rupture; thus we fear death. Through the death and resurrection of Jesus, however, death becomes the way into eternal life. Thus death, short of the fullness of the reign of God, is a promise of entry into God's fullness. This stance also affected my approach to violence and war. In this imperfect and sinful world, which is not yet the fullness of the reign of God, it sometimes becomes necessary to use violence to prevent greater evil. Military intervention to prevent genocide is one example. The danger, of course, is that human beings and nations are always tempted to use violence too readily, and that the "greater evil" may be defined subjectively. Violence and war may be necessary to prevent a greater evil, but violence and war will never bring about true peace. I continue to see this stance as the logical first step in a systematic moral theology.

A basic criticism of Catholic theology at the time of Vatican II was its triumphalism: the church was totally identified with the reign of God. The primary failure in such an approach is eschatological; the fullness of the reign of God will come only at the end of time. The church, like all Christians and all people, lives out the tension between redemption as already present and the fullness of God's reign in the future. But immediately after Vatican II, and even today, many liberal Catholics still suffer from triumphalism, or what I used to call a chronic case of collapsed eschatology. They expect perfection to be just around the corner in both church and world. The stance I have outlined, with its eschatological tension, reminds us we are pilgrims of hope trying to do better but still falling short.

In light of this stance and especially the role of sin and sinful structures, I sketched out a theology or theory of compromise, mentioned briefly above in connection with homosexuality. The presence of sin can justify doing something we would not do otherwise. In 1968 I addressed some of the cases discussed in the situation ethics debate, such as concentration camps. Could one lie to the Gestapo in order to protect Jews hidden in one's house? The Catholic tradition itself recognized that if there were no sin there would be no need for private property or just-war theory.[15] And, as I noted, I used the theory of compromise to justify homosexual genital relationships between two persons in a committed relationship.[16]

I have since rejected that argument as a justification for homosexual relationships. The theory of compromise needed to be developed in a more ethical way to determine how, when, and where some compromises are morally acceptable and others are not. The theory of compromise was another way of pointing out the danger in Catholic sexual ethics of too narrowly identifying the object of the moral act with the physical structure of the act.

In the early 1970s I also developed a relationality-responsibility model for moral theology.[17] Classical ethics describes two different normative theories for ethics. The deontological theory sees morality in terms of duties, obligations, or laws. The teleological theory understands morality in terms of ends or goals and the means used to achieve them. Rather than speak of a normative theory, I used the broader term of "model" to describe how one should envision the moral life. The Christian lives in a web of fourfold relationships with God, neighbor, world, and self, and these relationships are spread out over time—past, present, and future.

Many factors contributed to this understanding. First was my opposition to physicalism and the faculty analysis of the reigning Catholic natural law theory. The faculty or power of sexuality must be seen in relation to the person and the person's relationships. Thus, for the good of the marriage, one can interfere with the sexual faculty or the sexual act. The relationality-responsibility model was also more consonant with a historically conscious approach.

Biblical and theological warrants also support a relationality-responsibility model. The primary ethical concept of the Hebrew Bible is the covenant, not the law. God promises to be our God and we promise to be God's people. Gift and response or call and response characterize the moral teaching of the New Testament. The doctrine of the Trinity reminds us that our God is not a monad but three persons in relationship.

I also learned much from Häring's approach and from H. Richard Niebuhr's development of the responsibility model.[18] I added the concept of relationality to Niebuhr's approach to give it a more metaphysical basis. Likewise, I wanted to emphasize that the person not only responds to the actions taken by others but can also initiate activity.

This model serves as the basis for a different approach to such issues as contraception, sterilization, divorce, homosexuality, and the solution of conflicts. I used this model early on to understand better the concept of sin, which in neoscholastic Catholicism was defined in deontological terms as an act against God's law. Mortal sin is the breaking of our multiple relationships with God, neighbor, world, and self, while venial sin is the weakening of these relationships. The understanding of sin in Genesis supports this relational approach. Thus, on the basis of observing just one act, one cannot be sure what effect this has had on the relationships. Such an approach also argues against an individualistic understanding of the person and relates the personal and social aspects more closely. In addition, the relationality-responsibility model recognizes the ecological dimension of all human existence. I still need to develop this model in greater depth, but its general approach and direction are clear.

Anthropology is the most important consideration in moral theology. The relationality-responsibility model sees the human person in terms of the multiple relationships with God, neighbor, world, and self. In moral theology the person is more important than the person's acts. The Bible reminds us that the good tree brings forth good fruit and the bad tree brings forth bad fruit. In moral theology, the person is both subject and agent. As agent, the person's acts affect others and the world, while as subject, the person through her own actions makes and shapes her own personal identity.

Not all acts of the person are of equal importance. The fundamental commitment or option is the most important act, for it directs, guides, and influences all the other particular choices. In my earliest writings I described this fundamental commitment in terms of Christian conversion as a call to continual conversion and growth in the Christian life.[19] I also understood this basic commitment as living out the baptismal commitment of the Paschal Mystery.[20] From the beginning I recognized the importance of the fundamental option for orienting the moral life of the person as both subject and agent.[21] Many Catholic theologians understood the fundamental option in light of Karl Rahner's theory of self-transcendence, but I opted for a relational understanding of the fundamental option because it gives more importance to the social and political dimensions of human existence.[22]

Only in 1985 did I develop in a more systematic way my understanding of the person as moral agent and subject.[23] Discipleship is the basic orientation and fundamental option of the Christian, but this must be seen in terms of multiple relationships. Virtues or good habits modify and guide these four relationships. General virtues, such as the theological virtues of faith, hope, and charity, as well as freedom and fidelity, affect all our relationships. Openness to receiving God's gift (poverty of spirit) and

thankfulness orient our relationship to God. Justice and a preferential option for the poor guide our relationships to others. Stewardship directs
our relationship to nature and the goods of this world. A proper love of
self orients our relationship to self. Thus the fundamental option and the
virtues of the moral person as subject and agent follow a relationality-
responsibility model.

In 1977 I proposed a systematic understanding of conscience, which is
a basic component of moral theology.[24] I had not defended my dissent
from *Humanae vitae* simply on the grounds of conscience. The statement
of the dilemma of conscience is quite simple—I must follow my conscience, but my conscience might be wrong. There is both a subjective
and an objective aspect of conscience: I must be true both to myself and
to the objective reality of the situation. I proposed the peace and joy of a
good conscience as the criterion for a good and true conscience. Many
people recognize the pangs and remorse of conscience as the criterion of
a bad conscience after the act has been done. I developed my criterion of
the peace and joy of a good conscience on the traditional spirituality of the
discernment of the Spirit as found in Catholic spirituality and on the basis
of the nature of moral judgment. The human person has a drive and a
thrust for value and the truth. We know we have made a good judgment
in general and a good judgment of conscience when that drive and thrust
have been fulfilled. The drive and thrust are quieted only when the value
is achieved. Yes, this approach puts more emphasis on the subjective aspect of conscience, but it affirms a radical identity between authentic subjectivity and true objectivity. I recognized the dangers of abuse arising out
of the person's failure to strive for a true authenticity, and I pointed out
some safeguards that could minimize this danger.

Thus, in 1980, I was in a position to propose a methodological overview of fundamental moral theology involving stance, model, anthropology (person as subject and agent), and decision making and norms. The
last part incorporated the work I had been doing on norms with my understanding of conscience.[25] But I never developed this outline in a monograph until my *The Catholic Moral Tradition Today: A Synthesis* (1999).

I also addressed significant methodological issues such as the role of
scripture in moral theology, the distinctiveness and uniqueness of Chris-

tian morality, the different levels of moral discourse, pluralism in moral theology, and the role of the sciences and empirical data in moral theology.

Most of my published work took the form of articles in periodicals and symposia that I later gathered into various collections of essays. Eleven such volumes were published, first by Fides and later by the University of Notre Dame Press, between 1970 and 1985. A friend once told me he had read my two books and my ten nonbooks! The need to address particular content or methodological issues was such that I never had the time to develop book-length monographs except on sabbatical. Because there were comparatively few people writing in moral theology, there was genuine interest in these collections of essays.

The Move to Social Ethics

In the 1970s I started teaching more courses in social ethics. The field of medical ethics and bioethics was developing rapidly. I decided to concentrate more closely on social and political ethics because few Catholic moral theologians were working in this area and because Catholic social teaching correctly criticized the one-sided individualism often present in the American ethos. My interest in fundamental and methodological issues in moral theology persisted, but from the late 1970s onward I moved away from writing and research in the areas of sexual and medical ethics, though I was sometimes asked to write or speak on these subjects because of my previous work.

My classes in social and political ethics included the study of the documents of the hierarchical magisterium. There had been a continuing series of such documents beginning with Pope Leo XIII in 1891, including Vatican II documents and papal documents down to the present day. I published articles showing the very significant changes and developments that had occurred within this tradition.[26]

From a methodological perspective, three significant changes took place. First, the early documents employed a pure natural law approach, whereas the later documents brought in more scriptural and theological aspects. Second, the documents gradually came to adopt a more personalist approach. Leo XIII opposed modern freedoms, equality, and the participation of citizens in government. In 1971 Pope Paul VI insisted on the primary importance, at that time, of the aspirations to equality and to civic participation as necessary for human dignity and freedom.[27] Thus the insistence on freedom, equality, and participation was rooted in the primacy of the person. Only in the mid-twentieth century did the papacy come to accept democracy as the best form of government.

Third, these official documents also move from a classicist to a more historically conscious method. Here we see how Catholicism is a living and growing tradition. As a result of these developments in official Catholic social teaching, there is now a significant difference between the methodology found in contemporary hierarchical social teaching and that found in hierarchical sexual teaching. If Catholic sexual teaching used a more personalistic and historically conscious method, it would have to change some of its existing particular teachings. I pointed out this significant difference between the method used in these two different areas of hierarchical teaching.[28]

In 1982 the University of Notre Dame Press published my *American Catholic Social Ethics,* on which I had worked during my 1979 sabbatical. The book explored new territory in analyzing and criticizing the approach of five different theorists or movements in the Catholic community in the twentieth-century United States: John A. Ryan; *The Central-Verein* and William J. Engelen; the Catholic Worker Movement and Paul Hanly Furfey; John Courtney Murray; and the Catholic Peace Movement and James W. Douglass. In a final chapter I developed my own approach in light of my analysis and criticism of the others. This book is a good illustration of my interest in history, methodology, and social ethics.

In 1985, at the suggestion of my editor and friend John Ehmann, Notre Dame Press published a collection of my previously published articles on social ethics under the title *Directions in Catholic Social Ethics.* A companion volume, *Directions in Fundamental Moral Theology,* brought together articles dealing with that topic.

In the late 1970s Dick McCormick and I, with help and encouragement from Paulist Press, began to edit a series of books under the title Readings in Moral Theology; there are fourteen volumes in this series to date. The series brings together previously published articles on specific subjects (moral norms, dissent, Catholic social teaching, sexuality, the moral theology of John Paul II, conscience, and so on) and is generally aimed at M.A. and Ph.D. students as well as at professors of moral theology. In the early volumes we tried to translate into English a few important articles written in other languages, but this became too difficult and time consuming. The series tries to represent the full spectrum of opinion in Catholic moral theology, not just the positions we espoused. We wanted to create a full-fledged dialogue from which no point of view would be excluded. Our commitment to the church, we thought, was such that all positions and beliefs deserved a hearing. There is still a great need today for Catholics of different positions to talk to one another.

My schedule during these years was quite busy; I gave many speeches and addresses and held many summer sessions. But I saved most of the summer for my own reading and writing. Dick McBrien, who was then running the Boston College summer school, agreed to hire me for just one week, but he told me that my name would be mud if he ever saw me scheduled elsewhere for longer than that. Whenever anyone asked me to teach summer school for more than a one-week session, I replied that I could not because McBrien would denounce me!

Life at CUA

I continued to enjoy my teaching, usually courses in fundamental moral theology and, after the mid-1970s, social ethics for M.A. and M.Div. students, most of whom were seminarians. I liked teaching and received high evaluations from the students; negative criticisms charged that I required too much work of students and tried to cover too much material. For doctoral students I developed a different type of seminar. Every student had to read the same book each week, write a two-page evaluation, stressing what they agreed and disagreed with, and hand it in ahead of time. Discussions took off from there. Recalling my own weaknesses as a doctoral student, I wanted to develop their critical skills and their ability to speak in their own voice, so I followed this format rather than assigning long term papers.

One group of students composed an ode that they sang at the end of the last class and then handed down to future seminar groups. The chorus went as follows:

> Now working on the Charlie papers
> Working on the Charlie course
> Reading those Charlie books and getting
> That mental Charlie horse.
> Now that it's all over, though,
> There's one thing more to say:
> Given a chance to do it all again—
> NO WAY!

Beneath the levity, I think they appreciated what they got out of the course, despite all the work involved.

I enjoyed the atmosphere at CUA in those days. Above all I appreciated the many faculty members who had been so supportive in 1967 and 1968. They stood up not for one person but for their ideal of what a Catholic university should be. They firmly asserted the need for CUA to be both truly Catholic and truly an American university at once. Many of us committed ourselves to this vision. I began to take a greater interest in the life of the university as a whole. After 1967 CUA changed dramatically, adopting new statutes and new structures; it seemed to be putting into practice our vision of being both a Catholic and an American institution. In many ways I was the symbol of this vision, but I realized that I was only a symbol and was most appreciative of the many faculty members who had committed themselves to work in the same direction. For many years I represented the School of Theology on the academic senate of the university.

Ironically, despite all the tensions with the church, the faculty at CUA had a much larger role in university administration than was the case at 99 percent of American institutions of higher learning. CUA was founded on the German model of universities, in which the faculty really governed the institution. In 1971 I was promoted to the rank of full professor—the highest grade of professor, though at CUA the title was "ordinary professor." Many of my friends from other institutions used to kid me about what it meant to be an ordinary professor. They said I deserved the title! The term means nothing to most American academics, but at CUA an "ordinary" professor has the power to run the institution. In Catholic canon law in those days, the diocesan bishop was called the Ordinary because he had the power to govern the diocese.

American universities are run primarily by the administration, the faculty playing only an advisory role. German and in fact European universities had no separate category called the administration before 1968. Instead, the president or rector of the institution was a faculty member who usually served a limited term. At CUA, if the president went against the academic senate, the senate had a right to bring the matter to the board of trustees. But of course CUA had the neuralgic problem of balancing church teaching and academic freedom. We had hoped, after the strike, the dissent from *Humanae vitae* in 1968–69, and the new statutes, that the problem of academic freedom had been solved—but we were wrong. During this period a number of institutions put out feelers to see if I would be interested in leaving CUA, but I turned them all down. I felt a commitment to many of my colleagues and friends at CUA and to our shared vision.

I lived on campus, in two rooms in Caldwell Hall. Most of the priests on the faculty lived in Curley Hall, and we had our meals there. I had brought with me the custom of getting folks together for a drink before dinner. Anywhere from five to ten people belonged to this group, and we met every night in a different room before dinner. At some point we tried to form a prayer group, but this idea never got off the ground. What did work very well was a noonday liturgy that involved some faculty priests, some lay faculty from around the university, student sisters and priests, and others. Early on, we discouraged priests from concelebrating because such a practice did not make theological sense. There was one presider of the eucharistic liturgy, and the rest of us celebrated together. I remember that one Holy Thursday I was given the difficult task of telling a very distinguished priest on the faculty, who came to the celebration with his alb and stole, that we would prefer that he join the rest of us celebrating around the table. He graciously acquiesced. Even in the '70s, we began to have women preach the homily. We had a similar, but larger, Eucharist on Sunday morning. Somewhat later I found out that I had been dubbed the pastor of Caldwell Hall. That was not exactly accurate, but it is true that I organized the liturgies and provided the continuity of the whole operation. We were a community of university people, united in our study, our research, and our liturgical life together.

I also developed new friendships. I became quite friendly with Jim Coriden, a canon lawyer on our faculty who had been a year ahead of me at both the seminary and graduate school in Rome. Coriden had begun running groundbreaking symposia on significant issues for the Canon Law Society of America, which became a leading progressive force in the Catholic Church at that time. Unfortunately, the academic senate committee rejected Coriden's application for tenure on a 3-3 vote. Some said his relationship with me had been a factor. His loss hurt us, but he began a most successful career as dean and professor at the Washington Theological Union and has been acknowledged for the past twenty-five years as one of the leading canonists in this country. Coriden has a finely tuned sense of justice and has given himself unstintingly to those who have been victims of injustice in the church.

Despite the events of 1967 and 1968, the new statutes, and even the appointment of a lay president in September 1969, tensions between the church and the academy continued to fester. Walter Schmitz announced in 1968 that he was retiring as dean. The faculty unanimously elected Roland Murphy, a well-respected biblical scholar, the new dean. But Clarence Walton, the new lay president, told Murphy in August 1969 that he could not appoint him dean because he had signed the *Humanae vitae* statement. Roland replied that if he was not orthodox enough to be dean, he could not stay on the faculty, either, and left CUA for a distinguished career at Duke University. For one reason or another, CUA lost a number of very good scholars who had been among the subject professors. Bill Bassett, Dan Maguire, and Warren Reich ultimately decided to resign the priesthood and had to leave CUA. Dave Tracy and Bernie McGinn went off to the University of Chicago, where both have had illustrious careers.

Tensions between the church and the academy, the trustees and the faculty, worsened in the 1970s and early '80s. John Dedek, a priest and moral theologian from Chicago, joined our faculty in the mid-1970s. He had published in the pastoral journal *Chicago Studies* on many of the hot issues of the day, and at CUA he published a series of very scholarly articles on absolute norms and intrinsic evil in the medieval period, often using unpublished manuscripts as sources. He cleared all of the hurdles for tenure, but some bishop trustees were upset by his positions on moral issues. At their January 1979 meeting, the trustees went into executive session to discuss his tenure; they were to announce their decision on Dedek at the March meeting. A few weeks before that meeting Dedek came to my room with an impish smile on his face. "I have just taken the bribe. Cardinal Cody called and offered me a parish in Chicago, which I accepted." Thus the problem for CUA was solved.[29]

In the early 1980s, similar investigations by special committees of bishop trustees took place in the tenure cases of James H. Provost in canon law and Elizabeth Johnson in theology. In the end, both were given tenure, but they, together with most of us on the faculty, rightly resented the humiliating process they had to endure. My good friend Beth Johnson left CUA for Fordham and is now the foremost Catholic feminist theologian in the country.

In spite of the growing tensions at CUA, and the unhappiness of a number of people with my presence there, I found the atmosphere most congenial and stimulating in those days. There was one further benefit of being at CUA. Our faculty got along quite well and we had a critical mass of people doing serious work in theology and other aspects of religious studies. Thanks to faculty colleagues, CUA was a stimulating place even though it was no longer the only Catholic university in the United States granting doctoral degrees in theology. Scholars and church people from other countries would often drop by for visits with one or another of the theology faculty. In this and other ways our Washington location was a great plus. The Bishops' Conference was headquartered in Washington, and I got on very well with many of the staff there. So the doings on campus and in the Washington area more broadly contributed to making CUA a very stimulating environment for anyone interested in the life of the church in its American context.

Life Outside CUA

Outside the university, in the broader theological and academic world, I had assumed a very visible leadership role in Catholic moral theology. The truth is, I was too young to assume such a role. I had only been teaching moral theology since 1961. Leadership in an academic field usually comes only after years of study, teaching, and research. But the events of 1967–68 put the public spotlight on me. And because leading Catholic moral theologians in this country resisted the new approaches to moral theology brought about by Vatican II, it fell to younger people to pick up the banner of change. Dick McCormick, my senior by fourteen years, took over writing the influential "Notes on Moral Theology" for *Theological Studies* in 1965 and, with his deep knowledge of the Catholic tradition and his penetrating mind, became a major voice in Catholic moral theology throughout the world. I have no doubt that I would have developed greater depth and breadth in my own discipline had I not been thrown into a position of leadership at such a tender age.

I served as president of the Catholic Theological Society of America during its anniversary year of 1969–70. Because my goal was to keep the society together despite the differences between the older, pre–Vatican II generation and the new thinkers, I invited all the founding members of the society to attend a special celebration at the convention in Detroit. In 1970–71 I was elected president of what is now called the Society of Christian Ethics (SCE), which began as an organization of Protestant seminary professors of social ethics in 1959 and was joined by Catholics in the mid-1960s. I was the first Roman Catholic president of this organization, and today Roman Catholics make up about one-third of its membership.[30] I was the youngest person ever elected president of both organizations.

Every year the CTSA recognizes a theologian for outstanding accomplishment in theology. When the society was founded, Cardinal Francis Spellman of New York offered a small monetary prize to the recipient of this honor, and the award, accordingly, was named for Spellman. When Cardinal Terence Cooke succeeded Spellman as archbishop of New York, he willingly agreed to continue funding the Cardinal Spellman Award. In 1972 my colleagues on the committee named me the winner of the award. As a matter of courtesy, they called to inform Cardinal Cooke of their choice before it was announced. They spoke to Cooke's secretary, Msgr. Theodore McCarrick (today the cardinal archbishop of Washington, D.C.), and McCarrick, after consulting with the cardinal, informed the committee that Cardinal Cooke could not accept the committee's decision. To their great credit, the board of directors of the CTSA decided to change the name of the award, which explains why I was the first recipient of the John Courtney Murray Award for distinguished achievement in Catholic theology. I knew nothing of all this at the time, but I shall always be grateful for their action and for the moving citation written for the occasion by Dick McCormick.[31]

Within the broader life of the Catholic Church in the United States, I was often the center of controversy. Although there were a good number of dioceses where I was not welcome, I received many invitations to speak at colleges and universities, national and regional meetings of various Catholic groups, summer institutes, and groups of religious and priests. In these talks I often addressed the issues of pluralism and dissent in the church and the specific issues of sterilization, divorce, homosexuality, and abortion, especially in terms of the legal issue after the 1973 *Roe v. Wade* decision. Pickets and protestors often appeared at these talks. I usually offered to decline the invitation if a sponsoring group feared the kind of controversy I tended to generate. Most of them insisted that I come, but sometimes they had to acquiesce in the interest of self-protection.

In short, I had become a symbol. To more liberal Catholics, I was a saint, to more conservative Catholics, the devil. The reality seems to me to fall somewhere between the two extremes, but my symbolic role created quite a bit of controversy in those days. The right-wing Catholic press— *Our Sunday Visitor, National Catholic Register, Twin Circle, Pro-Ecclesia*— often depicted me as the epitome of all that had gone wrong in the church. Many of these publications also attacked other theologians, as well as some U.S. bishops, for their support of me at CUA, among other things.

The *Wanderer* was the most critical and unreasonable of them all. Its writers often urged their readers to write to the authorities at CUA, to the Bishops' Conference, and to the Vatican to protest my teaching at CUA and urge that I be removed. I was by no means the only target. Other theologians, among them Fathers Raymond Brown, Avery Dulles, Richard McCormick, and Richard McBrien, were also the victims of scurrilous attacks. Dick McCormick loved to quote an article that referred to me as "that aging *'enfant terrible'* who issues outrageous moral pronouncements."[32]

I had been invited to address the 1974 meeting of the Canon Law Society on the issue of divorce and why I thought the church should accept it. At a press conference after the talk, I got into a conversation with Frank Morriss, a columnist for the *Wanderer* and the *National Catholic Register*. In a pleasant way I asked him to at least admit that I was a responsible person. He wrote later: "He asked that I put in print my remark. I believe him to be responsible. Yes, alas, I do. I am convinced that he fully appreciates that he is a thorough going relativist and subjectivist."[33] Once I threatened a lawsuit against a columnist who mistakenly identified me as the person he was describing in his column. He issued a written apology that went something like this: "In my column I mistakenly identified the person I talked to as Father Charles Curran, but I think Father Curran is even worse than the person I described."

The role of the right-wing Catholic press has often been discussed in Catholic circles. Most recognize that it speaks to a very small but determined number of Catholics who have little or no credibility outside their small circle. They have attacked not only liberal theologians but the Bishops' Conference in general and individual bishops in particular. Unfortunately, they have had an unwarranted influence in some circles within the Vatican.

One anecdote illustrates the attitude even of many bishops toward the *Wanderer*. In 1978 I gave a talk to a group in Detroit in the church where Auxiliary Bishop Arthur Krawczak was pastor, though his church had nothing to do with sponsoring the talk. The *Wanderer* sent reporters. After the talk, the bishop came in to shut off the lights and close up the building. The *Wanderer* folk accosted him. Did he know that Father Curran had just called for dissent in his church? The bishop replied that he had not been there but did not know why the *Wanderer* was so worried. "I am not worried," he said. "Father Curran is spending the night in my rectory, and we are going to have a drink and a good conversation." The next edition of the *Wanderer* had a front-page headline: "Curran calls for more dissent; Bishop not worried." I wrote Bishop Krawczak to apologize for causing him a problem. He wrote back immediately to say there was no need to apologize. Cardinal Dearden and Bishop Tom Gumbleton had often made the front page in the *Wanderer,* and he was very happy to join them!

Archbishop Robert Joseph Dwyer also called for my ouster from CUA. Dwyer had retired as archbishop of Portland, Oregon, in 1974 and become editor of the conservative *National Catholic Register* and a columnist for *Twin Circle.* In a 1975 column he attacked me and criticized CUA for keeping me on the faculty after I had publicly defied the supreme magisterium.[34] Before he died, in 1976, he tried twice to hand-deliver to Pope Paul VI a long letter describing the problems of the church in the United States at that time. He attacked the Bishops' Conference in general and some of their staff, but he specifically attacked me by name for creating a schism within the Catholic Church.[35]

Further Tensions

In the spring semester of 1968 I went to Peru under the auspices of the Maryknoll Fathers to give a week-long institute for English-speaking missioners. I then agreed to go to the Far East for four or five weeks in the early summer of 1969 for Maryknoll, but the bishops of South Korea blocked this plan. In 1981 I agreed with the Columban missioners in the Philippines to spend four or five weeks in different places with their community and other missionaries, but Cardinal Jaime Sin of Manila intervened and quashed the tour. I was fortunate, however, to give talks overseas on a number of occasions. I was able to undertake these journeys not just as a tourist but to get a real feel for the countries and what was going on there.

A fascinating change and "disinvitation" happened at the *Linacre Quarterly,* the journal of what was then called the National Federation of Catholic Physicians' Guilds. John Cavanagh had been a leading member of that group and urged me to publish in their journal. In the early 1970s Dr. John Mullooly, a comparatively new editor, wanted to bring in newer perspectives on moral theology, and he appointed Dick McCormick and me to the editorial advisory board. I published four progressive articles in that journal in the early and mid-1970s—one on sterilization, one on cooperating with those who disagree with one's position, one a sharp critique of the CDF's document on sexual ethics, and the fourth on the role of the ethical and religious directives for Catholic hospitals in a pluralistic society.

In March 1978 Mullooly informed me that the board was going to replace some members of the editorial board of the *Linacre,* including me, with new blood. I knew Mullooly well enough to probe him about what was really going on, and he finally admitted that the board had instructed him to get me off the *Linacre.* As a proponent of compromise in theology and in the life of the church, I proposed that I stay on the board for a predetermined term and then resign. The board was unwilling to accept such an arrangement. Dick McCormick, who was aware of the situation, tried in vain to intervene on my behalf and then resigned in protest. Since then the *Linacre Quarterly* has been unwilling to publish any articles that even hinted of disagreement with the Vatican—yet another sign of a pullback to pre–Vatican II positions.

A similar situation, but one with a different outcome, occurred a few years later. The *London Tablet* is an old, established English Catholic weekly recognized by many people as the most authoritative Catholic journal in the English-speaking world. The *Tablet* strongly supported the reforms of Vatican II. To ensure its future, the trustees established the *Tablet* trust in England to receive donations to fund an endowment. In 1985 another trust was incorporated in the United States for the same purpose, and I was asked, along with Father Theodore Hesburgh of Notre Dame and J. Peter Grace, a wealthy Catholic, to serve on that board.

After my condemnation by the Vatican became public in 1986, I wrote Marcus Murphy, the vice chair of the trust's directors, that I did not want to be a problem for the *Tablet* and would resign quietly if and when they thought best. Murphy thanked me for my attitude but asked me not to resign. In 1987 I received an official notice that J. Peter Grace had resigned from the trust's board. Murphy then sent me a handwritten note explaining that Grace had objected to my being a director. "The UK Trustees were well aware of your repeated offer to withdraw if your association became controversial," Murphy wrote. "All the trustees unanimously want you to continue and would feel it quite inappropriate if the attitude of Peter Grace came to be accepted as the only stance."

Sometimes I found myself caught in the middle of a local crossfire. In 1970 the priests' continuing education committee of the Diocese of St. John, New Brunswick, Canada, invited me to give a study week in January 1971. Later they asked if I would give a public lecture on change in the church on the evening of my arrival. When I arrived at the local Catholic high school on a cold winter night for the public talk, I immediately smelled a rat. The auditorium was jam-packed and there were TV cameras there. When I finished the talk, one gentleman rose and began reading from a prepared text, quoting isolated statements from my various books. After he had gone on for about five minutes, protests from the audience forced him to stop, but he spontaneously rose to question me two more times in the course of the short question-and-answer period. Near the end of the event, another gentleman stood up and demanded that the bishop, who was present, come to the stage and tell the audience whether they should accept what they had just heard.

I had seen Bishop Joseph MacNeil sitting in the auditorium. He had been my gracious host when I first talked in the Diocese of Antigonish, Nova Scotia, in 1965, but I had not seen him since he'd become bishop of St. John. The bishop came to the stage and told the audience that I was a priest in good standing and a recognized Catholic theologian. Yes, he said, some of my statements were controversial, but that was not all bad; controversy could be good for the church. He added that the greatest theologians in the history of the church were neither popes nor bishops.

Someone told me later that the two men in the audience had been engaged in an ongoing dispute with the bishop. The episode created a ruckus in St. John; the lecture and the controversy were reported in the daily press and in the Catholic diocesan newspaper. In fact, two weeks later the diocesan paper ran a story under the front-page headline, "Father Curran's Books to Be at City Library."[36]

I was of course well aware of my public persona as a radical dissenter. My readers and students did not share that evaluation, however. In class and in my writing I continued to insist that moral theology deals not only with the minimal but also with the call of all Christians to holiness. I did dissent on specific issues, but these were comparatively few and not at the center of my teaching. In my public addresses I remained firm in my convictions but always tried to put dissent in proper perspective. Even after they had heard me speak in public, a good number of people concluded that I was not so radical after all. I got a good chuckle from the headline in the campus paper of Louisiana State University the morning after I gave a talk that had been highly contested—"Curran Doesn't Live Up to Radical Expectations."[37]

Without doubt, there continued to be problems with the negative connotations of the word "dissent." I never wanted to deceive, or to camouflage the fact that I thought some specific church teachings were wrong and should be challenged. As time passed and in retrospect, I was able to put this kind of dissent into a broader context, but this was not always easy when I gave a talk on a particular issue. Then, too, controversy sells, and so the controversial aspects of my talks received the most public exposure.

For reasons not only political but ecclesial, I deliberately endeavored to show that I was not just a dissenter. It was very important to me that people understood, insofar as I could make them understand, that I was deeply committed to the church and to the unity of the church. No message I sought to convey was more important than the message that we must learn to live in communion with one another in the church, however strongly we may disagree on particular issues. After the *Roe v. Wade* decision, I wrote a public statement, for which I obtained the signatures of sixty "liberal" Catholic theologians, affirming our opposition to the Supreme Court's reasoning that individual human life is not present in the fetus before the time of viability. Since there was disagreement among us as to when truly individual human life did begin, the statement simply expressed our disagreement with the moral reasoning of the court decision and said nothing about the legal aspects. I, and some other signers, hoped to convey by this statement that our purpose in life was not only to disagree with the teachings of the church.[38]

In 1973 Father John Harvey proposed that I work with him to establish a retreat center for gay priests. Harvey and I disagreed on the moral issue of homosexuality in general, but we agreed that the priest's commitment to celibacy was important. He thought it would be helpful, and would give a broader platform for what he was trying to do, if I agreed to become vice president of Renewal, Rest, and Recreation, Inc., the organization he had founded for this purpose. After a while, however, it became clear that my name was more of a hindrance than a help, so I resigned.

Relationship with the Hierarchical Church

The 1970s were also marked by some contacts with church authorities. One was with Archbishop Bernardin in his capacity as president of the Bishops' Conference in March 1975. Bernardin wanted to confer with me before going to Rome on business. He had received some communications from the CDF and also from a number of bishops about certain problems connected with my writings on divorce, remarriage, and homosexuality. Bernardin sought the meeting on his own, with no mandate from others, in order to express his concern to me and hear my side of the story. Thomas Kelly, then the associate secretary of the conference, called me to arrange the details.

I admit to being somewhat suspicious and perhaps a little paranoid about such meetings. I had determined that never would I face five or six inquisitors on my own. Tom and I finally agreed that the meeting would take place between Bernardin and myself, with Kelly there to take notes. Kelly would draw up a summary of the meeting that we would both approve and that Bernardin could share informally with others. Bernardin expressed concern over the impact of my writings in the pastoral sphere, and said that the proper role of theology was speculative rather than pastoral. I pointed out that moral theology has always played a pastoral role precisely because it deals with human life and actions. I never heard from Bernardin about that meeting or what happened after it.

A little earlier I had had a call from Raymond Powers, who worked for the apostolic delegate, Jean Jadot. The apostolic delegate is the papal representative to the church in the United States, serves as a liaison between the Vatican and individual bishops, and is instrumental in the appointment of new bishops. Some have even called him, unkindly, the official Vatican spy. Ray, whom I knew, asked if I would be willing to meet with the archbishop. I agreed but added that if he planned to bring advisors, then I would have the same number with me. I also asked about the purpose, format, and agenda of the meeting.

About an hour later the archbishop called and apologized for not calling himself in the first place. He explained that he wanted to meet with me three or four times a year in an informal way and off the record in order to hear what I was thinking and writing. He emphasized that he would not agree with everything I said but that he thought it was important for him to know what I was saying and why. If the CDF had been in correspondence with Bernardin, I was sure they must also have been in contact with Jadot about me. But I accepted his invitation gladly, and we continued to meet on a regular basis until he was "promoted to Rome" in 1980.

We would meet upstairs in the delegation in his personal study, where I would often find him smoking a Belgian cigar. From the very beginning he reiterated his intentions for these meetings and urged that we be perfectly frank with one another. I was never invited to any formal or public dinners or receptions at the delegation, as were other theologians in the Washington area, but we met regularly in this informal and open manner. Over time we got to know each other fairly well, and our conversations were as open, honest, and frank as any I have ever had.

I think it was at our second meeting that he told me he had finally met my former bishop, Fulton Sheen. Jadot's comment about Sheen was that he was a marvelous combination of the gospel and Hollywood! On one early occasion, he asked my opinion about five new bishops who had been appointed to the CUA board of trustees. I replied that one was excellent, three were not very good, and one was so-so. When he agreed with my evaluation of the one as excellent, I told him I did not think that he should tell me his opinion of American bishops. He responded that I was always open and frank with him, and he would always be that way with me. When I told him the name of the bishop I thought was "so-so," he replied that I was too generous in my estimation of that man.

All agreed that Jadot had a great influence on the Catholic Church in the United States, moving it in a pastoral and progressive dimension. The rigid traditionalists, of course, blamed him for this. Early in John Paul II's pontificate, Jadot was appointed the pro-president of the Secretariat for Non-Christians in Rome. This position put one in line for receiving the red hat of the cardinalate, but Jadot was never made a cardinal; his approach and vision were not that of John Paul II. He retired to Belgium in 1984.

A curious incident occurred at a one-week summer course I taught at the University of San Diego in the early 1980s. The class met five mornings for three hours, and midway through the first session I suggested that we introduce ourselves, but one man declined to do so. When I mentioned this to the director of the summer session, he arranged to come to the second meeting to ascertain whether everyone there had in fact registered for the course. The gentleman in question said that his registration had been paid by a Father Sullivan in Los Angeles, but he still would not identify himself. After the third session, a young woman, the only undergraduate in the class, as I recall, approached me to ask what a papal nuncio was. The unidentified man had apparently told her that this was his position. On Thursday the office of the apostolic delegate in Washington, Archbishop Laghi, phoned for Archbishop William Aquin Carew, the apostolic delegate to Jerusalem and Palestine, a position Laghi himself had previously held. Carew did not come to the Friday class.

During these years, because of my notoriety and dissenting positions, I was never appointed to any official position in the church—for example, as a member of the many theological dialogue teams that were taking place with individual Protestant churches. But I did have good relationships with many of the staff people who worked for the Bishops' Conference. These relationships were even stronger when George Higgins, who had worked for the conference for forty years, retired. At that time my colleague and dean, Carl Peter, and I worked together, despite the fact that our theologies were moving further apart, to pressure both CUA officials and George to move to CUA, live on campus, and teach one course a semester as a special lecturer. This would allow George to stay in Washington, where he was well known and had many friends. He could also continue his long-running column for the Catholic press.

George was a prodigious reader, but, at the end of the day, he loved to party and at times to needle people in a good-natured way. When I first met him in the mid-1960s, it was usually with some other CUA faculty, and we frequently indulged ourselves in complaints about Rector McDonald. George would inevitably respond by asking how many articles McDonald had prevented us from writing that week! In one discussion, George bated Hans Küng on the church tax that all Germans had to pay, which also paid Küng's salary. "How can you, Hans, with all your support for freedom, defend that compulsory church tax?"

When we approached George about coming to CUA, he was a bit reluctant. He said he had never taught in his life, had great respect for professionals, and did not think he could begin teaching at age sixty-five. He finally overcame these reservations, and things worked out very well. It is true that George was not the best teacher in the world, but he inspired some of our better students with his deep knowledge and broad interests. George was free of egoism and seldom if ever talked about himself and all that he was doing. He had been the church's bridge to the labor movement, to Jewish relations, and to many politicians.

Even before George came to CUA, I received a call in early 1974 from John Cosgrove, a layman working for the bishops in the area of justice. Cosgrove was to oversee the preparation of a draft of a pastoral statement condemning capital punishment that the bishops would issue in November. He obviously could not ask me to write the draft but wondered if I had any suggestions for who might. I suggested Germain Grisez, and Cosgrove was elated. Grisez was a staunch defender of *Humanae vitae* and of all Catholic hierarchical sexual and medical moral teachings and had developed his own revised theory of natural law, but I knew he also was a strong opponent of capital punishment. Grisez was perfect. He could appeal to both conservative and liberal bishops. Occasionally John would call to keep me informed and again express his gratitude. He called at the end of the summer, however, in a different tone of voice. Grisez had sent him a very long paper, a deep philosophical analysis with more than 100 footnotes. Cosgrove lamented that the bishops could not use this as a draft for their more pastoral statement. My good idea had gone up in smoke! In November the bishops issued a thirteen-word statement declaring their opposition to capital punishment.[39]

Through the bishops' staff, I was able to make presentations to the drafting committees of the two pastoral letters on peace (first draft in 1982, final document in 1985) and the economy (first draft in 1984, final document in 1986). J. Bryan Hehir, the leading staff person for the bishops in political and international affairs, was a good friend of mine and the leading staffer for the pastoral letter on peace; we talked frequently about the project. Since Hehir and George Higgins were close friends, the three of us got together on occasion. Bryan had been attacked over the years by right-wing Catholics for his positions on Latin America and his criticism of American foreign policy, but he had the strong support of both the liberal and conservative wings of the American bishops. Cardinal John Dearden of Detroit and Cardinal John Krol of Philadelphia, the first two presidents of the Bishops' Conference, had great respect for Bryan and depended heavily on him. Later, Joseph Bernardin relied on Bryan even more heavily. It was Bryan who coined the phrase and developed the theory of the "consistent ethic of life," a concept about which I have expressed some reservations. Bryan said, in front of others, that I was the theological source he most relied on in working on the peace pastoral. I was much less involved in the economic pastoral but followed the process closely, as George Higgins was a member of the drafting committee. During that period I wrote about eight articles dealing with the pastoral letters and related topics. One of them was translated into French and another into Italian in the primary journals of moral theology in those countries.

Meanwhile, public opposition to my lecturing to Catholic audiences became much stronger in 1979–80. The most significant episode involved Bishop Joseph V. Sullivan of Baton Rouge. Daniel Drinan, a former student of mine, was the pastor of the Catholic campus ministry at LSU and had asked me as early as the spring of 1977 to give a talk there. I was trying to limit my outside speaking engagements but told him I would be willing to give a talk early in 1979 during a sabbatical. We later agreed that I would speak on American Catholic social ethics in the twentieth century on February 19, 1979. But the bishop of Baton Rouge objected to my coming, so Drinan asked if I would agree to speak under the auspices of the united campus ministry rather than the Catholic campus ministry. I told him I would do whatever he thought best. On February 15 Sullivan released a statement and held a press conference comparing my positions with hierarchical teaching on a number of issues—abortion, fornication, sterilization, divorce, and *Humanae vitae*. The quotations taken from my books on all but one of these subjects were identical to the quotations given in an earlier series of articles in the *Wanderer* comparing my positions with official church teaching.[40]

This was the first time a bishop had used a public press conference to attack me, and it created quite a stir. Conservative Catholics were gleeful and congratulated Sullivan for standing up for the truth. They also urged their readers to write to church authorities demanding that I be disciplined.[41] The *National Catholic Reporter* ran a long article on continuing tensions in the Diocese of Baton Rouge.[42] Conservative Catholic publications reported a letter from Archbishop Jerome Hamer, the secretary of the CDF, to Bishop Sullivan, commenting on his statements and actions in reference to me. Archbishop Hamer wrote, "Please accept my personal thanks for providing public clarification of some of the ambiguous and erroneous teachings of Father Curran." Someone sent me the letter, but only later did I realize that the Vatican protocol number on the letter was not Sullivan's but mine!

Sullivan's actions mobilized others. On two subsequent occasions, people took out ads in the secular press quoting Sullivan and protesting my speaking. I had accepted an invitation to give one lecture in the sexuality institute sponsored by the Office of Religious Education of the Archdiocese of Milwaukee in June 1979. On May 12 a group called the St. Thomas More Educational Foundation took out quarter-page ads in the two Milwaukee dailies quoting Sullivan's comparison of my teaching with official Catholic teaching and protesting my coming to Milwaukee. On June 2 they ran an even larger ad, reprinting the *Wanderer*'s editorial of May 17,

1979, urging readers to pressure authorities at both CUA and the Vatican to silence me and remove me from the university. The lecture was held at Marquette University, and campus security was out in force. Only those who had signed up for the entire workshop were allowed inside. As I recall, things seemed quite normal within the lecture room itself.

Father Matthew Lamb, a theologian then in Marquette, published a very ironic op-ed piece in the *Milwaukee Journal.* Lamb wanted to bring to the attention of the St. Thomas More Educational Foundation the writings of a Catholic author who advocated communism and euthanasia and toyed with the idea of women priests and of priests being elected by the community, a book, he wrote, available in practically every Catholic library. Lamb wrote that he could almost hear this author—Thomas More—having a hearty laugh at the pretensions of the foundation, and that perhaps in 400 or 500 years some Catholics of a similar mind to the foundation would start a similar crusade under the banner of a Father Charles Curran Educational Foundation![43]

A bizarre incident occurred in 1980 at Saint Louis University. I was to give two lectures in a one-week summer school institute. A conservative activist, John O. Shields, organized a small committee and took out a full-page ad in the April 10, 1980, *St. Louis Globe Democrat* to protest my coming. This ad, too, repeated much of Bishop Sullivan's statement about my unorthodox teaching. Saint Louis University stayed the course, but I delivered the two lectures to a class of fewer than twenty students!

Building on the opposition of Bishop Sullivan, conservative opponents were now even more vocal and more public in their opposition to me. These tensions with the hierarchical church culminated in the CDF's investigation and condemnation of me as a Catholic theologian—a process that began in 1979 and concluded in 1986.

CHAPTER 5

Investigation and Condemnation

O N AUGUST 2, 1979, Cardinal William Wakefield Baum, then the archbishop of Washington and the chancellor, ex officio, of CUA, handed me a letter signed by Cardinal Franjo Seper, the prefect of the Congregation for the Doctrine of the Faith, informing me that I was under investigation. In accordance with their procedures, in the first step of the investigation the CDF had found "errors and ambiguities" in my writings and was sending me the enclosed sixteen pages of "Observations," to which I was to respond.[1]

The "fundamental observation" was my "misconception of the specific competence of the authentic magisterium of the Church in matters *de fide et moribus*" (of faith and morals). I had minimized and even denied the value of the noninfallible magisterium that, thanks to the Holy Spirit, enjoys the presumption of truth. In exceptional cases, the document said, a theologian could withhold assent from a noninfallible teaching, but this did not justify public dissent. With regard to my specific errors and ambiguities, the observations listed the following items and included quotations from my articles and books as supporting evidence: fundamental option, theory of compromise, charge of physicalism against Aquinas and Catholic moral theology, understanding of the indissolubility of marriage in scripture as an ideal, cooperation, the indissolubility of marriage, abortion, and issues of sexual morality, including masturbation, homosexuality, premarital sexuality, contraception, and sterilization.

That afternoon Archbishop Jadot called and we arranged a meeting. He apologized for not having told me that the letter was coming. I replied that I fully understood that he could not and should not have told me about it. Jadot's only surprise was that the letter had not come six months earlier. I pointed out that the CDF was probably waiting for the new bishop, Matthew Clark, to be installed in Rochester, which did not take place until May 27, 1979. The former bishop, Joseph L. Hogan, had been my teacher, a supportive colleague at St. Bernard's Seminary, and my staunch defender. Hogan had succeeded Sheen in Rochester and encouraged a progressive Vatican II church, even encouraging women religious to preach. The women's ordination conference in this country was founded and first headquartered in Rochester, New York! Jadot agreed with my analysis, and we talked about how I should proceed. I do not want to convey the impression that Jadot agreed with everything I said; he did not. In fact, he strongly urged me not to publicly dispute the final action taken against me by the CDF.

I had had no specific warning that such a document was coming, but the public protests against me had been growing, and one had to assume that the CDF was looking at me. About a year before, I had received an enigmatic aerogram from Joe Fuchs in Rome that consisted of one long sentence, in Italian, saying that someone in the Vatican might have an interest in me. After I later shared the sixteen-page document with him in person, he explained that he had sent the aerogram after the librarian of the Gregorian University asked him to return all books of mine that he had checked out of the library because the CDF was looking for them.

The Early Correspondence

I wrote Seper on August 29 that I would respond despite the fact that the process itself in many ways violated the basic principles of justice. I also asked for more than the month the CDF had given me to prepare my response, for my father had just died on August 9. I complained that the CDF itself had already publicly condemned me in the April 24, 1979, letter of Archbishop Hamer, the secretary, or second person, in the CDF, to

Bishop Sullivan, which had my protocol number and which was pub-lished in two Catholic publications in the United States. I appended to this letter a copy of Hamer's letter. My protocol number from the congre-gation is 48/66, which means that I was the forty-eighth file opened in 1966. I was not surprised that the file had been started that early.

In the same letter of August 29, I pointed out that nowhere in the six-teen pages of observations did the CDF mention the book *Dissent In and For the Church,* a systematic treatment of our public dissent at CUA from *Humanae vitae.* I sent the CDF a list of all my books and offered to send copies of whatever they did not have. On October 4 Hamer replied, in typical Vatican diplomatic language, "The congregation has at its disposi-tion the books you included on your publications list. Nevertheless, I would be pleased to accept your offer to send us a copy of *Dissent In and For the Church.*" When I mentioned this later to Joe Fuchs, he responded with a twinkle in his eye, "They do not have that book because I did not have that book. I did not have that book because, unlike all your other books, you never sent me a copy!"

In my first full response to the CDF, on October 26, I pointed out the serious flaws in the process described in "New Procedure in Doctrinal Examination," which was issued in 1971 and a copy of which was enclosed in the letter to me. This procedure violates basic principles of justice in that it does not recognize the right of the accused to hear specific charges, to know who are the accusers, to have a copy of all the files against one, and to have representation of one's own choice. The congregation is pros-ecutor, judge, and jury. On March 20, 1980, Seper replied to my com-plaint. The CDF's procedure was not a trial, he said, but rather a procedure designed to guarantee a careful and accurate evaluation of my writings. It was thus inappropriate to speak of "accusers" and "charges," and "representation" was to be furnished by the author himself. The truth, however, is that the procedure denies basic rights to the accused.

In all this correspondence I used the diplomatic pouch of the apostolic delegation in Washington and addressed myself directly to the CDF. I began my first response by pointing out that if the observations were in-tended to serve the purpose of true dialogue, of discovering the points of disagreement, if any, between us, then it had some problems. The observations quoted my books out of context, often failing to quote balancing statements. In addition, they did not clearly state what was erroneous and what was ambiguous in my writings. To facilitate a true dialogue on the "fundamental flaw" of my understanding of the hierarchical magisterium, I formulated five questions, gave my response to these questions, indicated that many other theologians held positions similar to mine, and asked the CDF to clarify its position. The five questions concerned the possibility of noninfallible teachings being wrong and the proper response of the theologian if he thought such a teaching was wrong. Must the theologian simply be silent, or should the theologian express dissent?

I sought the advice of a few trusted friends and colleagues in theology on my new situation. I was in immediate contact with John Hunt, who from the beginning said he would defend me in any process that might take place. I also wrote to a few moral theologians I knew in Europe to see if they knew of any similar investigations. Since I was on sabbatical leave that year, I went to Rome in November to consult with Häring, Fuchs, and others. Häring advised me to respond thoroughly to the CDF and said he doubted that any action would ultimately be taken against me.

Was the CDF just firing a warning shot across the bow, or were they more serious than that? On the one hand, other theologians around the world had taken positions similar to mine for at least five years. On the other hand, thanks to my many writings, the strike at CUA, and my dissent from *Humanae vitae,* I was a very public and symbolic figure. If they wanted to make an example of someone, I was an obvious choice.

There was another interesting aspect of the investigation. At CUA, in relation to *Humanae vitae,* the trustees and bishops had tried to focus belatedly on the public and organized mode of our dissent, whereas initially they had objected to the content of the dissent itself. The CDF, by contrast, said nothing about the mode and manner of my dissent but only about the content of my writings.

At the outset, I did not want the CDF's charges against me to become public, but somehow or other there was a leak. I wondered if one of the colleagues I had contacted was the source, but one archbishop was convinced that the leak had come from Rome. It certainly came from Europe. *Le Monde,* the French daily, in an article on October 25, 1979, stated among other things that Edward Schillebeeckx and I had been called to Rome. In London, first the *Tablet,* the Catholic publication, and later the *Times* and the *Economist* reported the same story.[2] I responded that I had not been called to Rome but was in correspondence with Rome and that I knew some other theologians in the United States were also in correspondence with Rome. I did not mention publicly that the correspondence with other theologians did not involve the formal process that I was going through.

The CDF's response to my October 1979 letter arrived only fifteen months later, in February 1981, and was less than two pages long. Its substance was that my comments on *Dissent In and For the Church* did not change the original observations and that I should complete my response. I resolved then that I would take as long to respond to them as they had taken to respond to me. In June 1981 I sent Seper a short letter pointing out that I had never claimed that there were substantial differences between *Dissent In and For the Church* and my other writings. I also asked why the CDF had not responded to my questions.

In January 1982, James A. Hickey, the recently named archbishop of Washington and now also the chancellor of CUA, wrote me that the CDF had asked him to inquire when they might expect my response. I wrote Hickey in March indicating my problem with the whole process and reporting the CDF's long delay in responding to me, adding that I would most certainly reply. On June 21, 1982, I sent to Cardinal Josef Ratzinger, the new prefect of the CDF, a long second response dealing with all the particular issues that had been raised in the original observations. Here again I stressed that many other theologians held positions similar to my own. I received an acknowledgment of my response in a July 16 letter from Hamer.

In February 1983 Ratzinger informed me that my answers were not satisfactory and that I would soon receive a fuller report. In May he sent me observations dated April 1983 that discussed three areas. First, on the subject of dissent, I was told that I failed to recognize the proper role of the magisterium. The second section listed four areas in which my dissent was clear—artificial contraception, indissolubility of marriage, abortion and euthanasia, and sexual ethics, including masturbation, premarital sexuality, homosexual acts, and direct sterilization. A third section addressed issues that were still unclear—how could I be certain the magisterium is wrong, theory of compromise, New Testament ideals, frequency of dissent, and physicalism or biologism. The cover letter was ominous. I was asked to respond to the issues that were unclear and invited "to indicate . . . whether or not you would like to revise those positions in clear public dissent from the Magisterium."

On August 10, 1983, I sent Ratzinger a sixteen-page response dealing only with magisterial teaching, because the CDF had never responded to my earlier questions. Did the CDF, I asked, accept the norms proposed by the U.S. bishops in 1968: "The expression of theological dissent from the magisterium is in order only if the reasons are serious and well-founded, if the manner of dissent does not question or impugn the teaching authority of the church, and is such as not to give scandal"?[3] I pointed out that fairness and justice required that the CDF do three things: (1) indicate the norms governing dissent, (2) point out how I had violated these norms, and (3) indicate how my positions differed from those of others who had dissented. I was frustrated by the CDF's continued unwillingness to enter truly into a dialogue that would point out exactly how and why we disagreed. But the February 1983 letter from Ratzinger left me more convinced than ever that the CDF was going to take some action against me.

In December 1983 Ratzinger wrote, again asking me to complete my response. I complained again about the lack of justice and fairness in the CDF's procedures and in the substance of the correspondence. On April 13 Ratzinger wrote again, saying that the CDF's position on public dissent was clear and insisting that I respond by September 1 or be judged unwilling to respond. I responded on August 24 but again objected to the process as a means of guaranteeing "a careful and accurate examination" (their words) of my writings.

My Reactions

By August 1984, on the basis of both the correspondence and what had been happening in the church, I was convinced that the CDF was determined to take some action against me. The restoration movement of Pope John Paul II was already taking place. Early in his pontificate the pope had issued the apostolic constitution *Sapientia Christiana,* saying that all those who teach disciplines concerning faith or morals in pontifical schools need a mandate from the chancellor.[4] In 1979 the CDF declared that Hans Küng was not a Catholic theologian. In response, Leonard Swidler of Temple University, David Tracy of the University of Chicago, and I quickly released a statement signed by more than sixty Catholic theologians publicly recognizing that Küng was a responsible Catholic theologian.[5] Canon 812 of the new code of canon law (1983) called for Catholic theologians in all Catholic institutions of whatever type to have a mandate from church authorities.[6] Also, canon 1371 declared that those who dissented from noninfallible teaching, even after a warning, were to be punished with a just penalty. These two canonical requirements were entirely new. In the meantime, the Vatican was appointing more conservative bishops throughout the world.

At the same time, the U.S. church was also moving in a more conservative direction. The Vatican investigated some religious women and even two bishops. Also, the CDF forced the removal of the imprimatur from Philip Keane's *Sexual Morality* and pointed out the errors in John Mc-Neill's *The Church and the Homosexual,* as well as the errors in the book *Human Sexuality,* which was a report from a committee appointed by the CTSA. The primary author of the book, Father Anthony Kosnik, was forced out of his seminary teaching position.[7]

At his weekly general audience on July 18, 1984, Pope John Paul II began a long series of reflections on the encyclical *Humanae vitae* that reaffirmed its teachings. After the first of these, the Vatican press office held a briefing for reporters given by Msgr. Carlo Caffara, a consultant for the CDF and president of the Pontifical Institute for Studies in Marriage and Family, which was established by Pope John Paul II in 1982. Caffara accused four theologians—Hans Küng, Franz Böckle (both of whom were Swiss but teaching in German universities), Marc Oraison of France, and me of robbing the encyclical of its intended effect by our dissent.[8] How could Caffara really believe that four theologians had caused so many Catholics to reject the teaching of the encyclical? His remark was also in very bad taste because Marc Oraison was deceased. In my view, however, the primary question was whether Caffara was speaking on his own or for a higher authority. Some friends in Rome told me they thought he was speaking entirely on his own, but in any case the message was loud and clear.

What was I to do in these circumstances? In my prejudiced judgment, any action against me would have severe negative consequences. First, it would be wrong theologically. By definition, noninfallible church teachings are fallible, as the U.S. bishops recognized in 1968. At CUA, after *Humanae vitae,* the trustees had tried to change their focus and consider only the manner and mode of dissent rather than its content. The CDF could not do this because they examined only my writings themselves. From their perspective, public dissent was what was found in my writings. Pastorally, any action against me would create a clear chasm between many theologians and the hierarchical magisterium. Many theologians dissent on one or another noninfallible church teaching. Personally, any action against me would be unjust given that many other Catholic theologians had taken similar positions and in light of the procedural and substantive shortcomings in the CDF's process and investigation. Academically, action against me would be a blow to academic freedom in Catholic higher education in general and would have especially negative consequences for the academic reputation of CUA.

As the author of a theory of compromise and a pragmatist aware of the political realities, I decided to float a compromise. I could not and would not change my positions, for these were a matter of personal integrity, but some compromises were possible. I did not want to compromise simply to retain my academic position; I was fighting for important theological and academic principles. I resolved that I would be willing to move quietly from the department of theology at CUA to the department of religion and religious education, which does not have pontifical status—that is, it is not a Vatican-accredited department and does not teach seminarians. In return for my move, the Vatican would quietly drop its investigation. If the compromise were to work, I had to convince the two principal actors on the church scene in the United States—Hickey, the chancellor of CUA, and Bernardin, the chair of the board of trustees. A good friend working with the Bishops' Conference agreed to present my proposal to Hickey, Bernardin, and other leading U.S. bishops. I also wrote a formal declaration of intent, spelling out this compromise to Father William J. Byron, S.J., the president of CUA, and urged him also to use his good offices to advance the compromise.

I had been keeping my faculty in the department of theology abreast of the situation all along, provided they promised to keep my reports confidential. Five faculty colleagues—John Ford, Elizabeth Johnson, Brian Johnstone, David Power, and Francis Schüssler Fiorenza—ultimately became the steering committee for this group. In late August 1984, about twenty graduate students in the department of theology formed a group called FACT—Friends of American Catholic Theology. They studied the issue of dissent, sponsored three public forums on doing theology in the United States in the 1984–85 school year, and discussed possible ways to support me if the Vatican took action against me. I contacted a number of colleagues who were past presidents of the CTSA. Under the leadership of Richard McBrien, Richard McCormick, and David Tracy, they privately wrote a strong letter to Ratzinger urging that no action be taken against me.

But my friend at the Bishops' Conference who had volunteered to prepare my compromise to the bishops reported in late 1984 that the bishops would not accept the compromise. They had not rejected it but simply were not going to act on it. I concluded that they were biding their time because there was no immediate fire burning. Like many busy people, they had enough pressing problems to deal with.

A more threatening sign appeared in December 1984. A friend sent me the November issue of the Italian publication *Jesus,* which contained excerpts from an interview that Cardinal Ratzinger had given to the Italian journalist Vittorio Messori. This interview later appeared in published volumes in many different languages, but the language on moral theology in the United States, in the English version, differed quite a bit from the original Italian in *Jesus.* Ratzinger's original comments deserve to be quoted in full:

> Looking at North America, we see a world where riches are the measure and where the values and style of life proposed by Catholicism appear more

than ever as a scandal. The moral teaching of the church is seen as a remote and extraneous body which contrasts not only with the concrete practices of life but also with the basic way of thinking. It becomes difficult, if not impossible, to present the authentic Catholic ethics as reasonable since it is so far distant from what is considered normal and obvious. Consequently, many moralists (it is above all in the field of ethics that North Americans are involved, whereas in the fields of theology and exegesis they are dependent upon Europe) believe that they are forced to choose between dissent from the society or dissent from the magisterium. Many choose this latter dissent, adapting themselves to compromises with the secular ethic that ends up by denying men and women the most profound aspect of their nature, leading them to a new slavery while claiming to free them.[9]

The gross oversimplification of this passage profoundly saddened me. I have always criticized the dangers of individualism, materialism, and consumerism in American culture and society, but history reminds us that at the same time the church has learned important lessons from American and other cultures and societies. In these comments Ratzinger followed his interpretation of Augustine, not shared by all Augustine scholars, which sees the church as the city of God opposed to the present culture, which is the human city. I have often pointed out that the primary difference between Ratzinger and me, from a theological perspective, is that I am a theological Thomist whereas he is a theological Augustinian. A theological Thomist recognizes the basic goodness of the human being and believes that on the basis of human reason and experience the Christian can arrive at moral wisdom and knowledge. Some theological Augustinians tend to see opposition between the present sinful reality and the reign of God.

Many people have argued that Ratzinger changed his positions considerably, especially after he became the prefect of the CDF.[10] But I think there is more continuity than they allow, and that it lies in Ratzinger's consistently Augustinian approach. There is no doubt that Ratzinger was a leading theological light in the reforms of Vatican II. In retrospect, it seems to me that there were two approaches to renewal at Vatican II. The first insisted on the *aggiornamento,* or throwing open the windows of the church and bringing it up to date. The second insisted on *ressourcement,* which called for going back to the sources, especially the early church tradition. Ratzinger belonged to the second school. After the Second Vatican Council, the division between these two approaches became more apparent. People from the *ressourcement* school, such as Von Balthasar, Danielou, De Lubac, Bouyer, and Ratzinger, opposed much of the post–Vatican II movement toward a more progressive theology. The theological Thomists, by contrast, such as Rahner, Schillebeeckx, Congar, Chenu, and Küng, continued to pursue a more progressive path.

When I read this Italian article, I became aware of exactly where Ratzinger stood and felt that his comments were directed primarily at me. (The interview also gave me an occasion to kid some of my colleagues in biblical studies and systematic theology that, according to Ratzinger, their work was mostly derivative from Europe.)

I resolved that I would respond publicly to whatever action the Vatican took against me, and four arguments supported this decision. First, the role of the theologian calls for us to communicate with all people in the church, and even those outside the church, an argument developed in our 1968–69 testimony after the *Humanae vitae* episode at CUA. Second, the issues were so significant that they affected many people and many different publics. Third, the unfair process used by the CDF needed to be publicly exposed and criticized. Fourth, to me it was a matter of truth and the good of the church.

In October 1984 Ratzinger acknowledged my response of August 1, but I had no further word from him for another twelve months. All this time I had never discussed the issue with my own bishop, Matthew Clark. I knew that Clark had been receiving copies of the Vatican letters, and he later told me that shortly after he was appointed bishop of Rochester, the CDF informed him of the process against me. From a church perspective, one easy solution to the whole problem would have been for my bishop to call me back to Rochester. Since that approach had not been taken, I could only conclude that the Vatican wanted to make a public example of me. But I thought it important to be in dialogue with my own bishop.

In June 1985, while I was in Moraga, California, for some lectures, Bryan Hehir arranged for me to meet with Archbishop John Quinn of San Francisco, who was recognized as an important leader among the

American hierarchy. I knew John and arranged to meet him in San Francisco. As we walked into his dining room, I could not help noticing a huge portrait of Bishop McDonald, the former rector of CUA. When Quinn saw me looking at the picture, he immediately explained that McDonald had lived in this place and that he had never bothered to remove his portrait. Quinn was somewhat sympathetic to my situation but said that he was on the outside and could only advise me. He did, however, urge me not to fight the pope or the church publicly. I mentioned that I was a bit uneasy talking to him because I had not yet talked to my own bishop.

When I returned to Washington, I called Bishop Clark and asked if I could fly up to Rochester to talk with him. He was very accommodating on the phone and apologized for not having been in contact with me. He said he would clear his schedule so that he would be free any time I could make it. When I saw him a few weeks later, I was greatly heartened by his strong support for me and my work. He disagreed with the approach taken by the CDF and thought it unjust. In the future, Clark was to play a very courageous role in supporting me and my work in a public manner.

Further Negotiations

Finally, on October 8, 1985, Hickey called me to say he had a response from Ratzinger for me and wanted to set up a meeting for October 10 that would also include Cardinal Bernardin. Ratzinger's letter of September 17, 1985, stated that the CDF was now "in a position to bring this inquiry to a conclusion. The results of the Congregation's inquiry were presented to the Sovereign Pontiff in an audience granted to the undersigned Cardinal Prefect on June 28, 1985 and were confirmed by him." I was asked to reconsider and retract my positions on contraception and sterilization, abortion and euthanasia, masturbation, premarital sexuality, and the indissolubility of marriage. If I did not retract, I could no longer be called a Catholic theologian and could not teach in the name of the church.

I met with Hickey and Bernardin on October 10 and three subsequent occasions. The meetings were both honest and cordial. I again went into my compromise mode. Joe Bernardin was well known as an ecclesiastical fixer who always tried to work out some kind of compromise. From the beginning, I indicated that a substantive compromise was impossible. In conscience, I could not and would not change my positions. By now I felt certain that the CDF was not going to change its position, either. I reminded them that in the cases of Edward Schillebeeckx and Leonardo Boff it appeared that some compromise had been reached. Bernardin and especially Hickey were obviously hoping that I would be willing to go further, but I could not. My procedural compromise involved three points. I had not taught sexual ethics—the area in which the disputed points centered—for more than ten years, and I was willing not to teach that subject in the future. Second, the congregation could issue a statement pointing out the problems with my writings but not condemning me. Third, I was to be on sabbatical in the 1986 calendar year and that would mean I would not be teaching that year anyway.

I pointed out in the strongest possible terms the negative consequences that would result if the Vatican were to say that I was no longer a Catholic theologian. For emphasis, McBrien, McCormick, and Tracy wrote strong personal letters to Hickey and Bernardin. Likewise, Francis Schussler Fiorenza, then the president of the CTSA, and William Shea, the president of the CTS, also wrote personal letters underscoring the harm that would occur if the CDF declared I was not a Catholic theologian. The group of five faculty members in my department sent a magisterial eight-page letter to Hickey touching on all the bases but pointing out especially the harm that would come to CUA. Hickey and Bernardin agreed to take the compromise to the Vatican, but Bernardin had already indicated to me that he was the junior partner here and that Hickey, as chancellor of CUA, had to play the primary role. Hickey was scheduled to go to Rome in December, but because of illness the trip was postponed until early January.

Upon his return from Rome Hickey arranged a meeting with Bernardin and me for January 16. His message was that the Vatican could not continue to allow me to teach in the name of the church while holding the positions I held. I had two options. Cardinal Ratzinger would receive me for an informal meeting to discuss the issues, but I had to request the meeting, agree to a joint press release afterward, and recognize that such a meeting was not part of the CDF's official procedure. The official procedure called for a colloquy only if the CDF thought it necessary because of a lack of clarity on the issues, but my positions were very clear. Friends had often pointed out that I might not have the most scintillating writing style but I was always crystal clear. At least now I had confirmation of this from the Vatican! If I did not ask for the colloquy, I was to give the CDF my final response to their request that I reconsider and retract my positions. I had until February 15.

I later concluded that the compromise had never really been discussed in Rome. Bernardin told me that Hickey met first with the pope for thirty-five minutes; only after that did he meet with Ratzinger. There was no doubt then that the pope himself played a central role in this whole question. Anthony Kosnik, a moral theologian friend of mine who was the primary author of the book *Human Sexuality,* had told me that the pope was a reader of a dissertation in Krakow that had spent a good part of a chapter disagreeing with my positions in moral theology. A priest friend in Rochester later told me that a Vatican official reported to him that Cardinal Ratzinger said that my case was the most difficult he had to deal with but that, in the end, it had been taken out of his hands. I have no firsthand information about this remark by Ratzinger, and it might have been only a rumor. But it does seem to fit in with what I now know.

I have never been able to figure out why Ratzinger offered me this informal meeting. His letter to me of February 8, 1986, setting up the details of the meeting, described it as outside the procedures of the CDF and not necessary according to their regulations, given that the substance of my positions was clear. He offered the meeting "with a view to clarifying the decision we have reached and which has already been communicated to you." It seemed clear that the outcome was a foregone conclusion and that the meeting was not going to change anything. Perhaps it was merely a public relations ploy.

I requested the meeting just to show my own willingness to go the extra mile and leave no stone unturned, but I expected nothing new to come of it. According to the arrangements, I could bring one person with me as my counsel. Long before this, I had asked Bernard Häring to play this role if the need ever arose, and he willingly accepted it. In fact, Häring asked for and was given a meeting with Ratzinger just before our meeting on March 8 in order to discuss the case with him. It was only later that I discovered that Häring had gone through a rather painful experience with the CDF earlier and had resolved that he would never set foot in that building again.[11] But, for my sake, he was now willing to do so.

The few weeks before my going to Rome in March provided the opportunity to think through what I was trying to accomplish. I tend to be realistic, if not pessimistic, about what might happen in general. In this case, I was convinced that I would lose in the short term, but I wanted to make this a teaching moment for the good of the church and theology. The tendency for some would be to write me off as an angry rebel or an arrogant intellectual, but I am neither of these. Most commentators have always recognized that I am a progressively moderate Catholic theologian. I knew that I would need to avoid all expressions of anger, name calling, and derogatory remarks of any kind. My argument was theological and I would conduct myself as a teacher, not an ideologue. The idea of a teaching moment became the leitmotif for all that I would do.

I was well aware of the criticism from some people in the church that I was too quick to use the media as a public arena. It is true that I had been willing to make things public because I thought it was ultimately for the good of the church. In many instances, however, I was only responding to what had already been done to me. I often used to paraphrase the Bible and say that they who live by the media will die by the media. I knew that the media would be basically sympathetic to me as the underdog against church authority. But there was also the danger, inherent in modern American journalism, that the media tend to sensationalize events, to cast things in stark black and white, to lose sight of the subtleties and complexities that do not make for good sound bites. I was determined to make every effort to show that I was not an angry rebel opposed to everything in the Catholic Church. And I would not go to the media first. The CDF had insisted on a joint press release from both of us after the meeting in the Vatican. I would hold my peace until questioned by the media in the wake of that press release.

My goal of making the Vatican meeting a teaching moment was clear, but how was I to achieve this goal? Again I consulted with my friends, faculty colleagues, and the student organization FACT, which had been meeting since August 1984, with my colleague and friend David Power as faculty liaison. After October 1985, I began to meet regularly with the coordinating group of FACT—Johann Klodzen, Mary Zelinski Hellwig, and Sally Ann McReynolds, who all had been students in a good number of my classes. They came up with the idea of obtaining signatures on a statement of support for me and urging people to write letters on my behalf to church authorities. I again contacted McBrien, McCormick, and Tracy, who agreed to draft a letter that would be sent for signatures to Catholic theologians in the United States. FACT was willing to do all the work connected with these endeavors.

The Vatican Meeting

Bishop Clark had told me to feel free to ask him to do anything on my behalf, although he might have to decline. I did not ask him to come to Rome with me. The issues involved moral theology, and Bernard Häring was the ideal choice, because of both his international reputation and his personal relationship with me. I told Clark that as bishop he had different responsibilities, especially the role of leadership and preserving the unity of the church in Rochester. I suggested that instead he write a personal letter to Ratzinger before the meeting, and he willingly accepted this suggestion.

George Higgins wanted to accompany me to the meeting, but I did not think that George should bother to go and did not respond to him. Our mutual friend, Bryan Hehir, called to say that George was hurt by my silence. George had been a loyal and creative staff person for the bishops for forty years and was perhaps the best-known priest in the United States. When I finally talked directly to him, George explained that he wanted everybody in the church to know exactly where he stood on this issue, so I acquiesced.

I left Washington on March 5 for the March 8 meeting with Ratzinger accompanied by George Higgins and William Cenkner, the dean of the School of Religious Studies, who generously insisted on accompanying me as a sign of his personal support and the support of my school. I appreciated this deeply, and I was also extremely grateful for George's presence with me in Rome. Among other things, he could be very serious but also added a light touch to things.

On Saturday morning, outside the Holy Office building in the Vatican, Häring, Higgins, Cenkner, and I were given the letter of Bishop Clark to Ratzinger by the vicar for religious in Rochester, Sr. Muriel Curran (no relation). She was in Rome for a meeting and had hand-delivered the letter earlier in the week. We were greatly heartened by what we read in the letter, which was echoed by a public statement that Clark later issued and that read in part:

> I speak now as Father Curran's bishop and friend. . . . Father Curran is a priest whose personal life could well be called exemplary. He lives simply and has a remarkable ability to combine a life of serious scholarship with a generous availability to a great variety of persons. My personal observations, supported by the testimony of many, is that Father Curran is a man deeply committed to the spiritual life. . . .
>
> As a theologian, Father Curran enjoys considerable respect, not only in our diocese, but also across the country. He is unfailingly thorough and respectful in his exposition of the teaching of the church. Indeed, I have heard it said that few theologians have a better grasp of or express more clearly the fullness of the Catholic moral tradition. In instances when Father Curran offers theological views that appear to be at variance to the current official statements of the church, he always does so in a responsible manner. He is respectful of authority in the church in a most Christian manner.
>
> Some members of the Catholic Church have occasionally depicted Father Curran as irreverent, disrespectful, disloyal, and unprofessional. I believe that he is none of these. Such judgments of this good priest are sometimes written by those in the church who do not understand the probing and testing nature of the theological enterprise.[12]

Our spirits buoyed by Clark's letter, we entered the palace of the Holy Office. Häring led the way up the stairs and around corners to the proper room. Ratzinger came in and greeted all of us. Then Häring and I went with him to an inner conference room with Archbishop Alberto Bavone, the secretary, or number-two person, of the CDF, Father Thomas Herron, an American priest on the staff of the congregation, and Father Edouard

Hamel, a Canadian Jesuit who teaches at the Gregorian University and who was present for translation purposes.

Ratzinger began by stressing again that this was an informal meeting requested by me rather than an official part of the process. He spoke mostly in Italian, while I used English but also some Latin and Italian. Häring used all three languages about equally. Häring asked if he could begin by submitting a paper he had written titled "The Frequent and Long Lasting Dissent of the Inquisition/Holy Office/CDF." It was noteworthy that Häring had used the two older names of the CDF, to which he subsequently referred as the Holy Office. Ratzinger began to read Häring's paper, which was in English, but then gave it to Father Herron to read to the whole group. Häring's point was that on a good number of occasions the Holy Office had been wrong, and in a true sense had thus dissented from the teaching of the whole church community.

Even directly afterward, it was difficult to reconstruct the meeting because we moved rapidly from topic to topic; but I did write up a six-page memorandum and checked it with Häring. In the end, the meeting was unsatisfactory because there was no real exchange. Ratzinger claimed that one could not dissent publicly (which meant in writing) on the issues under consideration. Häring and I pointed out that many other Catholic theologians held the same positions I did. I mentioned five German theologians who had published dissenting positions with which Ratzinger was certainly familiar. Ratzinger responded that my comments were not pertinent because we were talking only about me. When I persisted, he said that if I wanted to accuse other theologians, the CDF would look into them. I responded that I was not accusing anybody but only stating facts. This was one of two testy exchanges between us.

Ratzinger admitted to some degree that I had dissented only from non-infallible teachings. Such dissent, I said, is not a denial of Catholic faith and therefore does not disqualify one from being a Catholic theologian, contrary to what the CDF had said in their letters to me. Ratzinger explained that the CDF's point was that such dissent stripped one of the mandate to teach in the name of the church. He said that the CDF hoped to correct the phrasing of this point in future correspondence, which to some extent it did.

Another testy moment came in the discussion of canonical mission. Here Ratzinger asked Bavone to explain what was involved. Bavone repeated that if you disagree with church teaching, you cannot teach in the name of the church. If he were to disagree with Cardinal Ratzinger, for example, he would have to do the honorable thing and give up his office and become just a parish priest. I replied that this was a terrible slight to parish priests. Ratzinger intervened to say that I had misunderstood Bavone; I insisted that I had understood him perfectly well. Ratzinger then responded that he himself would prefer to be a parish priest than to hold his current office.

Near the end of the meeting, Häring brought up the compromise. Ratzinger appeared not to understand what Häring was talking about (which seemed to confirm that Hickey had never discussed the compromise with Ratzinger in any detail). I showed Ratzinger the document that I had worked out with Hickey and Bernardin about the compromise. He gave the document to Father Herron to read to the group. Häring then pushed the compromise as the ideal way to solve the problem.

The meeting was scheduled to last from 11:00 A.M. to 1:00 P.M. Ratzinger had mentioned at the outset that we had to discuss whether or not to issue a press release, although I thought we had already settled this point and had in fact already sent Ratzinger a noncommittal draft. I personally wanted very much to have a press release so that no one could ever accuse me of being the first one to go to the press about this affair. In the end, we accepted my short, noncommittal draft more or less as written.

At the end of the meeting, I told Ratzinger that I had respected the confidentiality of the process but would now respond publicly to the questions that were going to come my way. I suggested that we close the meeting with a prayer and he agreed to lead us in prayer.

I was drained and exhausted but glad the meeting was over. That evening we had an informal debriefing session with Joe Fuchs and Dick McBrien, who happened to be in Rome. I was my usual realistic self and still expected no positive change to result from the meeting, but at least I could not be accused of passing up the opportunity to argue for change.

On Sunday morning Cenkner, Higgins, Muriel Curran (who had delivered Clark's letter to Ratzinger), and two others who had been at the same meeting with Muriel Curran—my classmate and friend Angelo Caliguiri and a Rochester priest, Gerry Krieg—went over to Häring's church for the Eucharist. Häring was more optimistic than I that Ratzinger might be willing to accept the compromise. I have sometimes found Häring's theology too optimistic, but there is no doubt that Häring also has experienced much personal suffering and difficulty. He was a medic in the German army during World War II and wrote a very moving memoir of that experience called *Embattled Witness*.[13] And he had had his own difficulties with the CDF. In addition, Häring, who had spoken to more people in more languages about moral theology than anyone else in history, had by then lost his larynx to cancer. He learned to speak from the diaphragm, but at times he was very difficult to understand. Häring was not only a mentor to me as a teacher of theology but also a witness and example of the Christian life.

During the liturgy that Sunday morning, it was at times difficult for us to understand him, but none of us will ever forget how moving that liturgy was. The gospel reading was the story of the prodigal son, and Häring's homily insisted on the importance of the two virtues of forgiveness and hope for the true Christian. In light of the gospel in general and the parable in particular, we can never think in terms of dividing the world into two camps—the winners and the losers. Häring ended the homily by softly repeating his last sentence—"Christians are people who have hope."

My Response to the Vatican Condemnation

We arrived back in Washington late on Sunday evening, March 9. The *New York Times* ran a long story on Monday morning, but it contained no statements from me because I was traveling. With the help of FACT, I scheduled a press conference for Tuesday morning, March 11. We made every effort to make this a teaching moment.

At the press conference, I read a prepared statement that was distributed to the press. The auditorium was filled, and some people connected with the university were present. I gave the historical background of the case and strongly reaffirmed my commitment to the Catholic Church and the Catholic faith. I pointed out yet again that I neither denied nor disagreed with the core elements of the Catholic faith. I had dissented from noninfallible church teachings on a few moral issues, but these by definition were far removed from the core beliefs of the Catholic faith. I told the audience I was neither a rebel nor an angry young man, and that history teaches us that the Catholic Church has always experienced disagreements, and even quite severe tensions, with regard to its past teachings, and that some of those teachings had changed over time. The teaching office of the church was legitimate and important, but it had its limits and these limits must be acknowledged. I also addressed at some length the importance of academic freedom for Catholic higher education in general and CUA in particular.

The questions that followed allowed me to develop some of these points in greater detail. Frank Somerville of the *Baltimore Sun* asked to what extent Cardinal Ratzinger was the problem. I replied that it was hard enough being a moral theologian in the church without being a psychiatrist as well. When the laughter had subsided, I added that Ratzinger would probably say the same thing. I also got the standard question about why I do not wear a Roman collar. I responded that many priests on college and university campuses do not wear Roman collars. If I wore it, people would say, "How can you wear a Roman collar and disagree with the Pope?" I suggested that the reporter ask the same question of the reporter from *America* magazine who was sitting in the row ahead of him—Father Tom Reese.

In the course of one humorous exchange, I pointed out that in the midst of my problems, it was necessary to keep a sense of transcendence that would help me rise above the current troubles. There were two great signs of transcendence, I said—prayer and humor. One person later commented that the sense of humor I displayed at the press conference was the best proof that I was no angry revolutionary.

One reporter asked whether I was going to release publicly all the documentation between the CDF and myself. I replied that I wanted to, because that would be in keeping with the idea of making this experience a teaching moment, but I was not sure I could because of the legal question as to who owned the letters. I then looked furtively around the room and asked if anybody wanted to help me leak them. Afterward, Jerry Filteau, the Catholic News Service reporter and a former student, told me that the Catholic News Service considers Vatican documents public documents and would be willing to publish them. A short time later *Origins,* the documentary service of the Catholic News Service, published most of the correspondence. I think it was very helpful to have this correspondence available to everyone.

To make sure we had clearly communicated the message, FACT had put together a press packet for the event that contained my C.V. and a four-page memorandum describing my positions on all the issues in dispute. The danger was that people would come to the conclusion, for example, that I supported divorce rather than a life-long marriage commitment. So the memorandum took pains to show that my differences with Catholic papal teaching were quite nuanced. We also distributed the procedures of the CDF and some background material on them.

FACT tried to keep the teaching moment going at CUA. On Wednesday, March 12, the group held a public "Call to Action" at which they announced that they were seeking signatures to a short statement deploring any possible action against me by church authorities. Through very hard, sustained work, they ultimately obtained more than 20,000 signatures and sent them to the Vatican. They also wrote letters to Catholic bishops and other leaders in the church seeking their support. And they announced that a statement signed by some past presidents of the CTSA and the CTS was being sent by them for signature to all members of the two societies. Ultimately, more than 750 theologians signed the statement, which was largely the work of Dick McBrien and concluded, "We can think of no Catholic theologian in this country who is more well liked and personally admired than Charles Curran. There would be much more than professional distress, therefore, if the contemplated action against him were carried out."[14] With support like that, I could not feel sorry for myself.

Finally, on Friday, March 14, the group held "A FACT Forum: A Teaching Moment," at which faculty and students talked about various aspects of the case.

Things were also happening in my home diocese of Rochester, New York. On March 12 Bishop Clark issued his public statement of strong support, cited above. Friends in Rochester formed a group called "Friends for Charles Curran," which sponsored three informational forums in the diocese and sent out the FACT statement for signatures around the diocese. In glancing through the signatures supporting the FACT statement before they were sent to the congregation, I came across a page from my mother's home parish—St. Ambrose in Rochester. She had died in July of 1985 at the ripe old age of eighty-five. One of her friends had forged my mother's signature and given her address as "heaven."

At CUA, Bill Cenkner explained in a letter to the faculty of the School of Religious Studies that he had accompanied me to Rome to show support for one who was recognized at CUA and beyond for his theological acumen, pastoral concern, and ecclesial loyalty. In my own department of theology, a resolution strongly supporting the letter of Bishop Clark and calling for the Vatican to accept the compromise passed by a vote of thirteen to four, with three abstentions. The larger School of Religious Studies modified the resolution somewhat but still strongly urged the Vatican to accept the compromise. This resolution passed by a vote of twenty-five to three, with one abstention.

Meanwhile, Ratzinger asked for my definitive written response. On April 1 I sent a statement that briefly summarized many of my earlier points, proposed the compromise once again, but concluded that "in conscience at the present time I cannot and do not change the theological positions I have taken." The reaction was predictable. The Catholic press reported that Cardinal Bernardin "supported a compromise that would allow Father Curran to retain his tenured professorship on the theology faculty in exchange for an agreement not to teach a course in sexual ethics." He had "spoken informally" with Ratzinger, but it would be inappropriate to discuss publicly that conversation.[15] I had a few letters from other bishops, but I knew of no other public support for me from bishops.

The Catholic theological community strongly backed me. The presidents of the CTSA and the CTS, in their addresses at their respective conventions, emphasized the urgency of the situation and strongly supported my position. I gave a plenary session on the theological aspects of my case to the CTS and received a standing ovation when I came onto the stage. I began by saying I would have preferred to have a standing ovation *after* the address! The CTSA had an informational panel on the case, and a resolution strongly urging that the Vatican take no action against me passed by a vote of 171-14.[16] In the spring, many Catholic campuses held forums on the case at the urging of the presidents of the CTS and the CTSA. Some faculties signed statements of support for me. And the moderate and progressive unofficial Catholic publications generally urged the Vatican not to take action against me.

On the other hand, my colleague William E. May sent out a statement asking for my removal from CUA that was signed by thirty-three Catholic scholars, almost all of whom were members of the Fellowship of Catholic Scholars, a group founded in the 1970s with the express purpose of supporting the magisterium of the church.[17] And the April 17, 1986, issue of the *Wanderer* supplied a postcard addressed to Ratzinger so that its readers could urge the CDF to discipline me. The *Wanderer* also urged that action be taken against me as a priest and that the Vatican punish anyone who dissented or allowed people under their authority to dissent.

I have no way of judging the sentiment of most lay Catholics. I personally received about 1,000 cards and letters, 15 percent of which were negative. Some national groups, such as the National Federation of Priests' Councils and the National Conference of Diocesan Directors of Religious Education, passed resolutions supporting me. I also received copies of letters of support from other groups on a regional or local level.

One expression of solidarity was most touching. Hans Küng gave a talk in New York in late March, and he flew down to Washington the next morning to see me. He came as a pastor, he said, since it appeared that I was going to be the only other person in the world besides himself whom the Vatican had declared was not a Catholic theologian. Küng told me that the hardest thing for him was the people who did not support him. At a time like this, he said, you find out who your friends are. That afternoon I put him on a plane for Frankfurt, from which he would arrive in Tübingen just in time for his 2:00 P.M. seminar, after having taken an all-night flight from Washington.

As expected, there was ecumenical support. Protestants were careful not to be seen as interfering too much in the internal life of the Catholic Church, but statements of support from my colleagues in the Society of Christian Ethics, as well as from various Protestant theological schools such as General Theological Seminary in New York and Wesley Theological Seminary in Washington, testified to my academic integrity and scholarship as well as my commitment to the Catholic tradition.

One historical note deserves mention. My friend Jim Coriden had written a letter to Cardinal Godfried Danneels of Belgium asking him, in his capacity as a voting member of the CDF, to oppose any action against me. Danneels responded on July 11, 1986, that the CDF as yet had sent him no "document concerning Father Charles Curran. . . . There is a plenary session of the congregation in December. I will be attentive if the question of Father Curran's canonical mission is raised." This told me that apparently my case was never brought to the full membership of the CDF.

The end came comparatively quickly. I met Hickey in his office on Monday, August 18. He handed me a letter from Ratzinger, dated July 25, 1986, informing me that "one who dissents from the Magisterium as you do is not suitable nor eligible to teach Catholic theology." The decision had been approved by the pope on July 10. In accordance with Ratzinger's instructions, his letter to me and Hickey's own press release were already in the hands of the media; they had not paid me the courtesy of notifying me in advance. That night, national television carried the news of the Vatican's decision, and it was in the newspapers the next morning. On Tuesday Hickey held a press conference together with Father William Byron, the president of CUA. A reporter asked Hickey about the 1968 statement of the U.S. bishops recognizing that the expression of theological dissent is acceptable under certain conditions. Hickey responded that the earlier bishops' statement was no longer acceptable in light of the declaration and action of the Holy See in my case.

I held a press conference on Wednesday at which I tried to prolong the teaching moment. I insisted again, against the insinuations in Ratzinger's letters, that I was dealing with noninfallible issues and not with issues of faith. I then raised three questions that were not addressed in Ratzinger's letter. Can faithful Catholics dissent from noninfallible teaching and still be good Catholics? What does the Vatican's decision say about the proper role of theologians, including the 750 American Catholic theologians who supported me? Does the action by the Vatican mean that it does not accept the principles of academic freedom in the American Catholic academy? On Friday I continued my defense as the ABC Nightly News "Person of the Week," and I did the same thing on Sunday morning on *Meet the Press*.

A long, difficult, and unsatisfactory seven-year investigation by the Vatican thus came to an end with the judgment that I was neither "suitable nor eligible to teach Catholic theology." This was similar to the condemnation of Hans Küng. In many other cases, before and since, the CDF has taken action against theologians, but it has never taken the step of declaring someone unsuitable or ineligible to teach Catholic theology.[18] Nevertheless, most people recognize that I am still a teacher of Catholic theology even though I have no institutional Catholic support. Ironically, in fact, the Vatican action against me has actually given me a much larger platform.

My Condemnation in Broader Perspective

The CDF's action against me was a very public sign of the move of John Paul II's papacy in a more conservative direction. The Vatican's condemnation dealt directly with the role of theologians and the need to control them. Ratzinger himself, even before the CDF's final decision, gave an interview to the Italian journal *30 Giorni* that was also published in English in the May 11, 1986, issue of the *National Catholic Register*. "When one affirms that noninfallible doctrines, even though they make up part of the teaching of the Church, can be legitimately contested, one ends up by destroying the practices of the Christian life and reducing the faith to a collection of doctrines." The opposition between the city of God (the church) and the human city (the world) comes through in Ratzinger's insistence that "The widespread dissent of many moral theologians . . . is the expression of a 'bourgeois Christianity.' . . . Christianity becomes a burden that must be lightened to the greatest possible extent. . . . This type of Christianity . . . enjoys considerable influence at the level of the mass media."[19]

In his book *The Critical Calling*, Richard McCormick pointed out some of the grave implications of these comments—namely, that they disallow dissent in principle, paralyze doctrinal development, blacken the personal integrity of theologians involved, and compromise justice in ecclesial processes. McCormick went on to explain "why 'the Curran affair' is far more important than its central subject. It is a reminder that when criticism is squelched and power enlists theology for its purposes, the entire church suffers because theology has been politicized, i.e., corrupted." McCormick then spelled out the self-inflicted wounds that resulted from such a coercive atmosphere, and their costs—the credibility of the papal magisterium, the weakening of the episcopal magisterium, marginalization of theologians, demoralization of priests, and disregard of the reflection and experience of baptized Catholic laypersons.[20]

The action against me fits into a broader picture of attempts by the Vatican to control what theologians write and say. Catholic colleges and universities in the United States since the early 1970s have generally accepted the principles of institutional autonomy and academic freedom. Only academic peers—not outside authorities of either church or state—can make judgments about the competence of a scholar to teach in the academy. Church authority cannot interfere in the hiring, promotion, or firing of faculty. The 1967 strike at CUA and the reaction to *Humanae vitae* had made me a symbol of academic freedom for Catholic theology. And this the Vatican could not countenance.

The action against me also had an effect on the church in the United States and was part of a bigger picture here as well. Kenneth A. Briggs, a Methodist and former religion editor of the *New York Times*, published *Holy Siege: The Year That Shook Catholic America*, referring to 1986–87. The book, which offers a snapshot of each month and interviews ten Catholics a number of times over the course of the year, focuses on "two celebrated cases [where] Catholic Americans found their loyalty to Rome set against their commitment to American constitutional values. . . . The test cases were (1) the deposing of the Rev. Charles E. Curran as a Catholic theologian for allegedly taking too many liberties with official church teachings, and (2) the usurping of the powers of Archbishop Raymond G. Hunthausen of Seattle on grounds that he had failed to keep proper church order."[21] These actions touched upon the American penchant for pragmatism and due process; and the theological issue pitted a classical Vatican view of the church as eternal and immutable against a more historical and evolutionary view of the church held by many Catholic Americans.

Journalists, even good journalists like Ken Briggs, live in the present. In comparison with the clergy sex abuse scandals of the early 2000s, no one today would ever refer to 1986–87 and the cases of Curran and Hunthausen as "the year that shook Catholic America." But there are some common threads here. The Curran and Hunthausen cases raised questions about how decisions are made in the church; the same problem, now magnified many times over, lay behind the clergy sex abuse scandals. Yes, my case did have some effect on American Catholicism, but it was only a small part of a much bigger whole.

These four perspectives—the move to a more conservative and restorationist Catholicism under Pope John Paul II, the role of theologians, the debate about academic freedom, and the clash between Vatican and American values—help put my case in a broader context. These perspectives also help to answer a question that has been frequently proposed to me—why did the Vatican choose to single me out for discipline rather than some other moral theologian?

The answer is, first of all, my visibility. I was teaching at the national Catholic university, often still referred to as the bishops' university. Ever since the strike and the organized response to *Humanae vitae,* I had been the most visible and public dissenter in moral theology. I also became a symbol for the importance of academic freedom for Catholic higher education. The very conservative Catholics in the United States had put a spotlight on me.

Second, the subject matter of sexuality has always been an area of great (in my estimation far too great) concern for the Catholic Church. People, Catholic or not, know in general the teaching of the Catholic Church on sexual issues, whereas the Catholic teaching on social issues, which in recent years has been very progressive and deeply admirable, has correctly been called our best-kept secret. Also, when sexuality and authority are joined, a neuralgic situation arises. Church authority is very conscious of its deep involvement in sexual issues and has become very defensive about its positions. Ironically, this defensive posture on the part of the pope and the bishops has caused the Catholic Church to lose much credibility in the area of sexuality.

Third, the U.S. church is one of the largest and most influential in the world, and the Vatican wanted to rein in the liberal tendencies on display in this country; thus it made sense to target an American. A word of caution is in order here, however. Too often Americans think they are the only or the most influential people in the world or in the church. But there have been tensions between the Vatican and many other countries. At about the same time it was seeking to discipline me, the Vatican took a lesser condemnatory action against Leonardo Boff, the liberation theologian from Brazil. In my judgment, there were more radical liberation theologians, such as Juan Luis Segundo of Uruguay, but the Vatican wanted to make an example of someone from the Brazilian church because it was also very large and influential.

Fourth, the Vatican decision in my case could be carried out somewhat easily precisely because I was at CUA, which still had the heavy involvement of the U.S. bishops. Individual diocesan bishops, and even the U.S. bishops as a whole, do not have that same level of influence and control over other Catholic universities. In short, I met several criteria that would satisfy Vatican objectives. I was, in effect, the perfect target.

A formal portrait with older brother and sister, John (Jack) and Kathryn (Kay).

With younger brother Ernest, left.

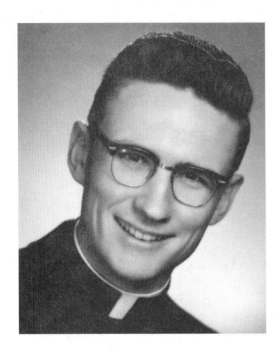

I was ordained a priest in Rome on July 13, 1958.

The retirement luncheon for my father in July 1965. *(Front, left to right)* my father, John, and mother, Gertrude, and *(back, left to right)* me, my sister, Kay, and brother, Ernest.

As president of the Catholic Theology Society of America *(center)* with Cardinal Terence Cooke *(left)* giving Fr. Richard McCormick *(right)* the John Courtney Murray Award in 1969.

With Father Walter J. Schmitz, Dean of the School of Theology at Catholic University, without whose support the 1967 strike would not have happened.

After the Eucharistic liturgy presided over by Fr. Bernard Häring at the Church of St. Alphonsus in Rome the day after my meeting with Cardinal Ratzinger in March of 1986. *(Left to right)* Msgr. George Higgins, Fr. William Cenkner, Fr. Angelo Caliguri, Fr. Bernard Häring, Fr. Charles Curran, Sr. Muriel Curran, and Msgr. Gerard Krieg.

Walking up to the Superior Court of the District of Columbia with my lawyers, John Hunt *(back)*, Juanita Crowley *(left)*, and Paul Saunders *(right)* for my lawsuit against Catholic University in December 1988.

At a press conference at Catholic University after the Vatican condemnation in 1986.

With friend Sr. Theresa Kane, who had confronted Pope John Paul II about the ordination of women.

I have been the Elizabeth Scurlock University Professor of Human Values at Southern Methodist University since 1991.

CHAPTER 6

More Trials

I HAVE HAD NO COMMUNICATION from the Vatican since Ratzinger's letter of July 25, 1986, informing me that I was neither suitable nor eligible to teach Catholic theology. What effect would this declaration have on me? That question would be answered by CUA and, ultimately, by the courts.[1]

CUA's Response

In his letter to me of August 18, 1986, and in the conversation that followed, Hickey told me that on the basis of the Vatican decision, approved by the pope, he, as chancellor of CUA, was initiating the withdrawal of the canonical mission that allowed me to teach theology there. According to the statutes, I had a right to request due process proceedings, but Hickey unilaterally imposed a September 1 deadline for me to accept those procedures. If I did not, then he would withdraw the canonical mission.

I responded that I had never received a canonical mission and that he had no right unilaterally to give me a deadline of two weeks. I was on sabbatical leave for the calendar year 1986 and under no obligation to participate in university business. Also, after the new statutes were adopted, I had written an official letter to the university dated August 12, 1982, saying that I was not obliged by the new statutes or the canonical mission since the university could not unilaterally add something to my contract as a tenured ordinary professor. I asked Hickey what effect the removal of the canonical mission would have on my tenure, but Hickey could not answer that question.

Immediately, Bill Cenkner, as dean, and the committee on academic freedom and procedures of the school encouraged me to ask for the due process hearing as allowed by the statutes, provided this would not interfere with my physical or mental health. In Cenkner's view the process was an important opportunity to emphasize again the role of the theologian/ scholar in the church. I also saw it as a chance to continue my long-standing struggle for academic freedom at CUA.

It is important to grasp the complex nature of CUA. In nonlegal language, before 1970 CUA was both a pontifical (or ecclesiastical) university chartered by the Vatican and able to give certain Vatican degrees, and a civil university chartered in the District of Columbia with U.S.-accredited degrees. In 1970 CUA, like most other Catholic institutions, cut its institutional ties to the church and control passed entirely to its independent board of trustees. At CUA, however, the forty-person board was made up of equal numbers of laypeople and clerics, and of the twenty clerics at least sixteen were bishops. Thus the bishops, for all practical purposes, still controlled the board.

The university had three pontifical or ecclesiastical faculties (the translation of the Latin word for "faculty" refers to what the American academy calls departments or schools). The three ecclesiastical faculties able to confer Vatican degrees (baccalaureate, licentiate, and doctorate) were the departments of theology and canon law and the School of Philosophy. But the matter was even more complex. The department of theology, in which I taught, also granted American-accredited degrees. In fact, 70 percent of our students were *not* in the Vatican degree programs. The department of theology was one of five departments in the School of Religious Studies, but three of the departments in that school—religion and religious education, biblical studies, and church history—were not ecclesiastical faculties.

When I came to the department of theology in 1965, I was never given a canonical mission because the older statutes calling for a canonical mission were not observed. The apostolic constitution *Sapientia Christiana* of 1979 called for each ecclesiastical faculty or university to develop its own statutes in light of the constitution and to have these statutes approved by the Vatican. The chancellor of CUA is also, by definition, the archbishop of Washington. The civil by-laws describe his role as the liaison with the Vatican and with the Bishops' Conference. In addition, the civil statutes confer on him special powers and responsibilities for the ecclesiastical faculties as spelled out in the statutes of those faculties, especially with regard to ensuring the orthodoxy of teaching.

Sapientia Christiana called for all full-time Catholic faculty members in ecclesiastical faculties to have a canonical mission from the chancellor. Before tenure could be granted, a *nihil obstat* (literally, a declaration that nothing stands in the way) had to be given by ecclesiastical authorities.

In light of the American principles of institutional autonomy and academic freedom, the majority of the faculty of theology resisted the canonical mission, as it seemed to give an outside authority the right to hire and fire. But Chancellor Hickey was adamant. The final statutes were a compromise that attempted to gloss over the basic disagreement by recognizing both the need for a canonical mission from the chancellor and the protections of academic freedom and due process for the faculty member. If the chancellor initiated the removal of a canonical mission, the faculty member had a right to a hearing by a committee of faculty peers that would determine whether the chancellor had "the most serious reasons" for withdrawing the mission. Under this uneasy compromise, both sides could say their principles were upheld, but what would happen in a crunch?

Even before I received the final word from the Vatican in August 1986, I was in contact with John Hunt and Jim Coriden about what to do if and when Hickey tried to take away the canonical mission, which I claimed not to have. I contacted them immediately after my August 18 meeting with Hickey, and on August 19 I wrote Hickey requesting the due process proceedings without waiving any of my academic or legal rights. Thus began a procedure that involved the due process hearing at CUA, further negotiations with Hickey and the university, and ultimately a lawsuit in the Superior Court of the District of Columbia. This whole process was to take two and a half years, ending in late February 1989. It was another long and draining experience, but fortunately I had the help and support of many people to whom I owe a great debt of thanks.

Above all, I can never repay John Hunt and the law firm of Cravath, Swaine, and Moore for serving as my legal counsel throughout the process. I could never have managed without them. John Hunt told me early on that he was not primarily a litigator, but he secured the services of his colleague Paul Saunders, who ultimately played the lead role in both the academic and legal cases. Ronald Chen and other associates also joined the team. Once we went to court, Juanita Crowley and some other lawyers from the Washington firm of Wilmer, Cutler, and Pickering also became part of our team. I could never have paid for such expert legal advice, which in the end amounted to $1.5 million. But these people were more than my lawyers; they became my friends. An editor in a Catholic publishing house once remarked that I was the only author who ever dedicated a book to a law firm! But that was the very least I could do.

I also had another offer of legal help. In 1985, after receiving the September letter threatening trouble if I did not change my positions, I had dinner with Dick McCormick and talked the whole matter over with him. Joseph Califano and his wife came into the restaurant and Dick motioned them over to our table. I barely knew Califano, but he and Dick were good friends. They exchanged pleasantries and were about to go on their way, but Dick asked them to stay and hear what I had just told him. Together we gave the Califanos a quick summary of the CDF's investigation, which was probably going to result in some disciplinary action against me.

Joe Califano kindly offered to represent me in any legal action. I thanked him and we went on chatting, but he reiterated his offer and added that he would represent me pro bono because obviously I would not be able to pay him. I thanked him profusely.

"Why don't you want to accept my offer?"

"I already have lawyers."

"Are they any good? Who are they?"

"Cravath, Swaine, and Moore."

"Well, they are very good, but, if you need any help, please do not hesitate to ask." Readers inclined to feel sorry for me can save their sympathy for someone more deserving. Here I had turned down an offer of free representation from one of the most famous lawyers in the United States!

I had hoped that the due process procedure at CUA would take place in the fall of 1986, but this hope was disappointed. Dean Cenkner suggested that I come off sabbatical and teach one course while going through the process. I agreed, but the university authorities, obviously under orders from Hickey, said no. I was scheduled to teach three courses in the spring of 1987 and these courses were listed in the preliminary schedule published in October. The vice president said my name should be removed from the list of spring courses. David Power, then the chair of theology, told the administration that its action was improper and that he was going to list my courses. The administration insisted. I protested in writing in early November. In the meantime, on November 21 the academic senate appointed a seven-member committee to hear my case. According to the statutes, both sides had a right to exercise challenges to the committee membership, but we had to do so within a month. Thus, the due process procedure would not begin until the spring semester.

Meanwhile, I was finishing the book *Faithful Dissent,* which told my story and included all the documentation between the Vatican and me. I had earlier accepted the invitation of the School of Religion at the University of Southern California to give a number of lectures there in October. They were ultimately able to schedule a public debate between Archbishop Roger Mahony and me on dissent in the church. On October 16, 1,700 people packed a USC auditorium to hear the debate. The exchange, according to one observer, was "amicable in manner but pointed in substance."[2] Mahony allowed for the possibility of some dissent from church teaching, but not public dissent. I pointed out that past noninfallible church teachings had been wrong and that public dissent was necessary for the good of the church and its search for moral truth in areas that are not core to faith. The *Los Angeles Times* published our prepared remarks.[3]

Back at CUA, Hickey was playing hardball. On December 19, against the urgings of Power and Cenkner, he wrote me that he was exercising his right as chancellor to suspend me from teaching in the ecclesiastical faculty of theology in the spring semester on the basis of the Holy See's declaration against me. I responded on January 7 that Hickey had no right by statute to suspend me from teaching in the nonecclesiastical programs in theology in which, in fact, 70 percent of our students were enrolled. In addition, I said, if his basis for suspending me was the letter from Ratzinger, none of my scheduled courses dealt with issues raised in that letter. I added that the threat of suspension presumed a specific outcome in the upcoming hearings. Again I offered the compromise that I become a professor at large within the university, teaching in my area of competence to nonecclesiastical students but not teaching sexual ethics.

On January 9 Hickey officially suspended me from teaching in the ecclesiastical faculty, pending the outcome of the proceedings. I responded that I would teach my classes to nonecclesiastical-faculty students and inform the ecclesiastical-degree students that they could not get credit for the course. The press got wind of the dispute. I released a public statement on Monday, January 12, summarizing the recent exchange and justifying my position. On January 13, at 8:00 P.M., I received a hand-delivered letter from Hickey. "[L]et me emphasize," he wrote, "that I regard it as untenable for you to teach your proposed theology courses this Spring in view of the Holy See's judgment." The letter argued that although there were nonecclesiastical programs in the department of theology, there were no nonecclesiastical teachers. But Hickey's letter recognized the weakness of his own argument. He went on to say that unless I informed him by noon the following day that I would not teach, he would exercise his authority "under canon 812 to revoke, suspend, or deny the required mandate to teach theological disciplines."

The reader will recall that canon 812, requiring a canonical mandate, applies to all Catholic institutions of higher learning, but the canon had never been invoked in the United States. Most leaders of Catholic higher education agreed with me that the invocation of this canon threatened the institutional autonomy and academic freedom of Catholic higher education. Hickey covered all his bases in his language of revoking, suspending, or denying the mandate, depending on whether I had one or not.

On January 14 I replied to Hickey that I would not teach my classes that spring in light of his threat. In view of the far-reaching consequences of his invoking canon 812, I said, it would be irresponsible for him to invoke this canon over the issue of a temporary suspension. "I do not want to be the occasion for the invocation of this canon since we are not now dealing with the primary issue itself. But, if you threaten to use canon 812 to suspend me from teaching, it suggests that you are prepared to invoke canon 812 if the faculty committee decides against your position. The faculty committee and all others concerned have a right to know if you will invoke canon 812 and thus make a charade of the whole process if the outcome is not in your favor." Hickey never responded to that part of my letter.

I gave a second reason for backing down—my concern for students who would take the course. Were I to appeal to a civil court to preserve my right to teach these courses, the right of the students to earn credit in those courses would be in question until the court issued a ruling. "I will not do an injustice to my students while fighting for justice for myself," I wrote. Thus did I back down and agreed not to teach my schedule of classes in the spring 1987 semester. Hickey went even further. He would not allow me to continue directing doctoral dissertations, including those of three students who were in the final stages of completing their work.

Two related developments occurred. On January 15, Jordan Kurland of the AAUP wrote President Byron concerning the suspension. He noted that the AAUP norms and the canonical statutes themselves accept the "immediate harm" standard in permitting the chancellor to impose a suspension "in an emergency case," and that the regulations governing all members of the CUA faculty permit suspension prior to the outcome of a dismissal proceeding "only if immediate harm . . . is threatened." The AAUP was aware of no "pressing" danger, no threat of "immediate harm." On February 27, 1987, I filed suit against the university in the Superior Court of the District of Columbia alleging that, by suspending me from teaching students in the ecclesiastical, and especially in the nonecclesiastical, programs, it had breached my contract.

The Due Process Hearing at CUA

Meanwhile, the due process hearing about the canonical mission had not even begun. Judicial processes take a long time, and the individual is always at a disadvantage. Institutions can easily put up with delay, but the individual hangs in a state of suspended animation until the process is complete. I had agreed in late August 1986 to submit to a due process hearing. The final report of the committee came in October 1987—more than a year later.

The academic senate of the university had to follow the complicated procedures set forth in the statutes and convened the seven-person ad hoc committee only on January 13, 1987, appointing Professor Urban A. Lester of the law school its chair. On February 11 the chancellor formally made his accusation, citing as his only reason for revoking my canonical mission that the "decision of the Holy See is a final, definitive decision by the highest authorities of the Catholic Church," and that this "decision of the Holy See constitutes a most serious reason for the withdrawal of Father Curran's canonical mission to teach in the name of the Church."

The ad hoc committee, however, had to postpone its work for a time because its counsel, John P. Arness of the firm of Hogan and Hartson, was tied up with other work. Cravath, Swaine, and Moore represented me, with Paul Saunders and John Hunt leading the team. Williams and Connolly represented the university, but because of the illness of Edward Bennett Williams himself, Kevin Baine was the leading attorney. The ad hoc committee asked both sides first to present their understanding of the jurisdiction of the committee and then held a hearing on their jurisdiction on April 20.

The chancellor maintained that the definitive declaration of the Holy See that I was neither suitable nor eligible to teach Catholic theology was not simply "a most serious reason" for the withdrawal of the canonical mission as required by the statutes but was incontrovertible proof that the mission must be withdrawn. This decision of the Holy See was binding on the committee as a matter of canon law. Even if not a matter of canon law, the Holy See's decision must constitute a most serious reason to remove my canonical mission to teach in the name of the church. A person cannot teach in the name of the church when the highest authorities in the church have declared him or her ineligible and unsuitable. The chancellor's lawyers also pointed out that this hearing had nothing to do with terminating my employment or tenure. Thus the committee's sole responsibility was to determine whether the chancellor had a most serious reason to withdraw the canonical mission. But in reality, as subsequent events clearly showed, the chancellor was determined that I would never again teach theology at CUA.

My lawyers took an entirely different tack. As mentioned earlier, the canonical statutes themselves tried to bring together a dual commitment. They "intended to assure fidelity to the revealing Word of God as it is transmitted by tradition and interpreted and safeguarded by the magisterium of the church," and at the same time to "safeguard academic freedom." The chancellor emphasized the first commitment; we emphasized the second. My lawyers pointed out that the canonical statutes themselves incorporated the principles of academic freedom and academic due process. The committee itself was an academic committee obliged to make a judgment on academic grounds. Due process, academic freedom, and recognized academic procedures called for a judgment about the suitability and fitness to teach made in the first instance by peers and ultimately by the board of trustees on the basis of the record. The university had provided for academic freedom and due process when it approved and promulgated the canonical statutes, which were also approved by the Vatican. This approach was very much in keeping with the decision made by the Marlowe committee in 1969 with regard to the dissent from *Humanae vitae*. If a theologian was competent and fit to teach Catholic theology, the canonical mission should not be revoked. If the committee simply had to accept the Vatican declaration as binding, as the university argued, then it was not functioning in accord with accepted academic due process procedures.

On April 22 the ad hoc committee outlined its own understanding of its jurisdiction and rejected the narrow view proposed by the chancellor. We found out only later, however, that it did not fully accept our position either. The substantive hearings of the committee took place on May 4, 5, and 6. At that time the committee said it would not hear oral testimony from the witnesses we had called to testify about my competence. In the end, the committee was going to assume my competence and even high standing in the field, but it was also going to accept the position that the canonical mission is a qualification added on top of competency and therefore could be removed from a competent teacher.

In the hearings of early May, the chancellor called no witnesses but relied on the earlier written testimony of Father Francis Morrissey, a canon lawyer from St. Paul's University in Ottawa. The chancellor rested his case on the CDF's determination that I was neither suitable nor eligible to teach Catholic theology and that this constituted a most serious reason for removing the canonical mission. The ad hoc committee did accept written testimony about my competence and the integrity of my positions from five different witnesses. In addition, they received letters from 150 groups, faculties, scholarly societies, and individuals. The two largest theological societies involving Roman Catholics—the Catholic Theological Society of America and the College Theology Society—strongly urged that no action be taken against me.

The statement from the board of directors of the CTSA, which was overwhelmingly approved by the membership at its annual meeting in June 1987, read in part:

> As The Board of the Catholic Theological Society of America, we affirm these stances of our society's membership and testify in the strongest possible way to Charles Curran's professional competence as a Catholic theologian, to the responsibility and integrity with which he fulfills his role as a Catholic theologian, and to the moderate character of his positions even when those positions disagree with the present official teaching of the church. Removing him from his teaching post is incomprehensible on professional grounds, unjust in the singling out of this one scholar from many of his peers with similar opinions, and indefensible in light of traditional understanding of what a theologian rightfully does.

The officers and board of the CTS closed their testimony with the statement that "To affirm that Professor Curran cannot be considered a Roman Catholic Theologian is in effect to deny the legitimacy of the theological enterprise for Roman Catholics."

Cenkner, Power, and I testified orally, as did Sister Alice Gallin, the executive director of the Association of Catholic Colleges and Universities, and Robert K. Webb, now a professor of history at the University of Maryland, Baltimore County, who once again generously served as my academic counsel.

After the hearing, both sides submitted briefs to the committee. The committee finally issued its report on October 9, 1987. Meanwhile, I had accepted a one-year appointment for the 1987–88 academic year as Visiting Kaneb Professor of Catholic Studies at Cornell University. The sixty-one-page committee report summarized the proceedings, including the testimony received, set forth the factual background, discussed the issues, and then made its conclusions and recommendations. The committee made no finding about my competence but merely accepted it. "It is undisputed," the report stated, "that Professor Curran's academic colleagues hold him in high esteem. Professor Curran has made extensive and continuing contributions to the functioning of the university and to the development of the field of moral theology" (35).[4]

The committee was keenly aware that the canonical statutes contained a potential conflict between the jurisdiction of the church and the institutional autonomy of the university. It also understood the canonical mission as a credential for a faculty member otherwise academically qualified for appointment to an ecclesiastical faculty (53–54) and as a qualification conferred upon a faculty member by the church (58–59). Since the chancellor was not seeking to terminate my employment or to abrogate my tenure, the committee ruled that the testimony concerning my academic competence was not directly relevant (54). But the committee could not consider the declaration of the CDF dispositive in this case because such a disposition "at least potentially infringes on the institutional autonomy of the university, generally accepted principles of academic freedom, and Professor Curran's rights as a tenured member of the faculty" (43).

In light of these understandings, the committee recommended that

1. The canonical mission of Professor Curran may be withdrawn, provided his other rights are simultaneously affirmed, to wit: a. That he remain a tenured faculty member at the Catholic University of America, with all the rights and privileges to which that status entitles him; b. That he continue to function as a professor in the field

of his competence, namely, as a professor in the area of moral theology and/or ethics.

2. If it is deemed impractical for Professor Curran to continue to teach in the department of theology, the committee recommends that arrangements for a suitable alternative academic position be made before Professor Curran's canonical mission is withdrawn.

3. If the foregoing recommendations cannot be implemented, the committee would oppose the withdrawal of Professor Curran's canonical mission and recommend against such action. In such circumstances, withdrawal of the mission would be unjust to Professor Curran and would be harmful to the university and its mission. (60–61)

Although the committee's report acknowledged my competence and assured me a tenured position in the university in my area of competence, I was disappointed with it. The report basically concluded that academic freedom does not exist within the ecclesiastical faculty of theology. A faculty member could be removed from the ecclesiastical faculty without a judgment made by peers about his or her competency and fitness to teach. For more than two decades I had fought for academic freedom for Catholic theology in general and for the theology department at CUA in particular. According to the committee, the hard-won victories of the past were now history.

But the chancellor had much stronger disagreements with the report than I did. The committee insisted that I had a right to teach at CUA in my area of competence even if the canonical mission was withdrawn. According to the statutes, if the chancellor agreed with the report, he would send it to the board of trustees. If the chancellor objected to the report, he should indicate to the committee in writing the reasons for his disagreement and the committee should respond. Finally, on December 14, Chancellor Hickey wrote the committee, agreeing with its decision that the canonical mission could be withdrawn but objecting to the condition that I continue to function as a tenured professor in my area of competence— moral theology and/or ethics. He contended that the committee, in imposing this condition, had exceeded its mandate, which was only to determine whether the canonical mission could be withdrawn. He also argued that the rationale of the committee involved a fundamental inconsistency. The committee acknowledged that canonical principles must be given precedence in determining the withdrawal of the canonical mission, but, for reasons not connected with canon law, concluded that "Curran should be permitted to teach theology somewhere in the university."

The committee responded firmly on December 21, 1987, and stuck by its conclusions. "If removal of the canonical mission, independently of any dismissal proceedings, were to terminate Professor Curran's function as a teacher in the field of his competence, the removal would impinge upon his contractual rights and upon the proper autonomy of this university as understood in the context of the American academic tradition."

Final Action by the Trustees

The statutes required that the committee report be sent to the trustees, who would make the final decision, and that I have an opportunity to address the board. Paul Saunders, John Hunt, and I made our case to the board on January 24, 1988. There was practically no discussion after our presentations; it was obvious to us that this was a pro forma hearing and that the board was simply going through the motions. That afternoon the board met in executive session to discuss the matter. Again, the procedures said that if the trustees disagreed with the committee report, they had to send their objections to the committee. On January 27 Cardinal Bernardin, as chair, responded to the committee that the trustees had determined that the canonical mission should be withdrawn. They objected to the condition that I continue to function as a tenured professor in my area of competence. In making this recommendation, Bernardin wrote, the committee gave insufficient consideration to the CDF's declaration that I was neither suitable nor eligible to teach Catholic theology. In addition, the board concluded that the committee had gone beyond its scope in addressing these other issues. After the withdrawal of the canonical mission, the letter concluded, the board would instruct the president to explore alternative teaching arrangements with me.

As I saw it, the board of trustees was apparently saying that I could not teach Catholic theology at CUA, period. On February 3 I wrote from Cornell to friends and supporters, indicating that I thought the university would not institute a dismissal proceeding against me but would offer me a position outside my area of competence, and would attach conditions that would make it impossible for me to accept the offer. Indeed, this is exactly what ultimately happened.

On February 16, 1988, in accord with the statutes, the committee responded to the board's objections. Again the committee reaffirmed its recommendations. It attempted to do justice to the dual commitment of the canonical statutes—fidelity both to the magisterium of the church and to academic freedom. Thus the committee made its two conclusions interdependent. The committee firmly restated its conclusion that the CDF's declaration was "not controlling with regard to Professor Curran's ability to teach in any department outside an ecclesiastical faculty. In such departments, the university must be guided by the American norms of academic freedom and tenure, including principles of academic competence and peer judgment which the university has accepted and embodied in the faculty handbook." It also suggested that the university enter into negotiations with me about alternative teaching assignments before withdrawing the canonical mission at the next board meeting, which was scheduled for April 12.

In the meantime, much consultation and strategizing was taking place on both sides. In December, we later discovered, a meeting took place at the Vatican involving Archbishop Hickey, President Byron, their attorney, Kevin Baine, Cardinal Ratzinger of the CDF, and Cardinal Baum of the Congregation for Catholic Education. On Holy Saturday, April 2, 1988, Archbishop Hickey was involved in a conference telephone call with Cardinal Baum, Archbishop Pio Laghi, the Vatican pro-nuncio, and several cardinals and archbishops on the board. We also discovered that church authorities were pressuring Bishop Clark to call me back to the Diocese of Rochester, or at least to revoke my permission to teach at CUA. This, of course, would solve the problem of what the university was going to do with me. Apparently this pressure came from a number of people, among them the chancellor and the chair of the board of trustees, but Clark refused in spite of repeated attempts to force his hand. I have always been most grateful for his courage and integrity in this matter. Had he taken such an action against me, I would have been forced to make a most painful decision.

Someone close to the situation also told me that Cardinal Baum wanted the pope to *order* Bishop Clark to bring me back to Rochester. Cardinal Ratzinger allegedly disagreed, and in the end, the pope himself decided not to order Bishop Clark to do so. To my knowledge, there is no documentary evidence of this Vatican discussion.

Meanwhile, the legal front was heating up. In February 1987 I had filed suit against the university in the Superior Court of the District of Columbia for suspending me. Both sides had agreed not to press this case while the faculty committee hearing was taking place. After that process was concluded, the university moved for summary judgment and dismissal of my case on the grounds that its decision was based on canon law and was thus immune from judicial review by a civil court. On April 5, 1988, Judge Bruce D. Beaudin of the Superior Court of the District of Columbia ruled that the university's position was without merit and that I had a right to have my contract case heard by the civil court.

Also, on April 5, a week before the trustees' meeting, Kevin Baine called John Hunt and started negotiations about possible arrangements. Hunt, Saunders, and I had been discussing all along what we could accept in terms of a teaching assignment, which we referred to as *conditiones sine qua non.* I could not accept the Vatican letter as binding on me; I could accept no loyalty oath; and I would be teaching Catholic theology whether it was called that or not. I was willing to accept the title of professor of Christian social ethics in the department of sociology provided my courses were open to all nonecclesiastical-degree students interested in them and were cross-listed in all the announcements and catalogues of religion and religious education. And, of course, I was willing to refrain from teaching courses in sexual ethics.

After their meeting on April 12, the trustees issued a press release announcing that they had withdrawn my canonical mission, thus barring me from teaching in the department of theology, but that this action did not affect my tenure. The trustees appointed a three-person committee— the chancellor, the chair of the board, and the president—to enter into discussion with me about an alternative teaching assignment within an area of my professional competence.

In light of what we had made known to the chancellor's lawyers, this statement seemed to offer some hope, but this hope, too, was disappointed. From the very beginning, Hickey was determined that I would not teach moral theology at CUA no matter what the faculty committee or anyone else said. On April 13 Kevin Baine sent a proposed agreement. I had to sign a statement saying that the Vatican declaration bound me and that I would not teach Catholic theology at CUA. I also had to agree to drop my lawsuit. We responded that such an offer was completely unacceptable because it had ignored the conditions we had laid out. On April 29 Baine responded with another offer that again demanded that I accept the CDF's decision as binding upon me and that I would not teach Catholic theology at the university. My counsel told Baine that if we did not hear otherwise by May 10, we would consider their April 29 offer final. We had no response and so, on May 17, 1988, I publicly announced that CUA had unilaterally broken its contract with me by refusing to offer me a tenured position in my area of competence.

On June 2 the trustees passed a new resolution. "The board accepts the declaration of the Holy See as binding upon the university as a matter of canon law and religious conviction." "[A]ny assignment allowing Father Curran to exercise the function of professor of Catholic theology, despite the Holy See's declaration that he is ineligible to do so, would be inconsistent with the university's special relationship with the Holy See, incompatible with the university's freely chosen Catholic character, and contrary to the obligations imposed on the university as a matter of canon law."

President Byron defended the trustees' action in a *Washington Post* article in response to my earlier article. There was "an ecclesial limit" on theological exploration and communication at CUA, he wrote, and claimed that the autonomy of the university was not threatened by such a condition because the trustees and the institution had freely chosen to abide by it.[5] The trustees and the university administration thus rejected and acted against the recommendations of the ad hoc committee. Twenty years earlier, the entire university had gone on strike to protest the trustees' action in firing me; but this time the faculty reacted with hardly a whimper. What explains the difference?

Times had changed in many ways. The late 1960s were full of ferment both in the church and in the academy. Catholic intellectuals were seriously debating the role of Catholic higher education in the post–Vatican II church. By the 1980s that ferment had long since died out. In the broader world of the American academy in general, faculty were often more committed to their particular disciplines than to the institutions at which they taught. Also, there was no dramatic flash of lightning to ignite the dry wood. The process had dragged on for eighteen months. The entire faculty, in a sense, never really owned the committee report. For a while it also seemed that the trustees might actually accept the committee's report. And when they finally did not, the school year was already over and the faculty dispersed. In addition, let's face it, after more than twenty years, I had accumulated plenty of scars from various academic struggles and encounters: I was no longer the shining young knight on the white horse.

There was one more act in the academic phase of the drama. The AAUP notified President Byron in July 1988 that it was appointing an ad hoc investigating committee to make a report. Byron agreed to cooperate but asked that the AAUP wait until the legal case was finished, which the AAUP agreed to do. The committee visited CUA in April 1989 and issued its final report in the fall, concluding that CUA had violated academic norms in suspending me from teaching pending the outcome of the due process procedure, but that the procedure itself had been properly carried out. By preventing me from teaching Catholic theology in a nonecclesiastical department, the university had deprived me of my tenure without due process and without adequate cause. "The administration, and particularly the Board of Trustees, failed in the case of Professor Curran to exercise their responsibility to protect the university's autonomy and the academy freedom of the faculty."[6] The AAUP then censured CUA.

The Court Case

There were three distinct phases in this whole matter for me personally. The first involved the issue between the authorities of the Roman Catholic Church and me with regard to public dissent from noninfallible teaching.

The second phase, the academic process at CUA, now gave way to the third, the legal phase. My purpose in taking the university to court was the same I had pursued from the beginning—the defense of the principle of academic freedom at CUA and in Catholic higher education more generally. By their action, the trustees and the administration of CUA had admitted that academic freedom did not exist at CUA. My only remaining course of action was to pursue the matter in civil court.

Judge Beaudin had already decided in April, in the case of my suspension from teaching pending the due process hearing, that I had properly turned to the court for a determination. On June 10, 1988, my attorneys amended our complaint to allege that CUA had now constructively terminated my appointment in violation of my tenured contract as a professor of theology.

At this point I was worried about how long the legal case would drag on and afraid that the university would be able to outlast me through its sheer institutional weight. Fortunately, the legal case took much less time than I feared, and was decided in February 1989. In the summer of 1988 interrogatories were posed and depositions, including lengthy depositions from me, from Cardinals Hickey and Bernardin, and from President Byron, were taken. Meanwhile, five graduate students in the nonecclesiastical-degree programs of the department of theology filed suit against CUA for interfering with their rights and academic freedom through its actions against me and other actions. These students were added as "intervenor-plaintiffs" to my case. Once again, I was happy not to be alone and was grateful for the willingness of these students to subject themselves to the ordeal of a lawsuit.[7]

In preparing our case, my lawyers took pains to make two points with me. First of all, they pointed out that I, by definition, dealt with morality and the question of right and wrong. They were afraid that I might confuse legal realities with moral realities, and they wanted to make sure that I understood the difference between the legal and the moral order and that I took a realistic view of the case. Second, they pointed out that the request for specific performance, namely, asking the court to order CUA to reinstate me as professor of theology, would be very difficult to obtain in a case of breach of contract. This was especially true in employment contracts and even more so in employment contracts in higher education. Ordinarily the courts awarded monetary damages, if anything. I had made it clear throughout this entire arduous process that my primary concern was not about money but principle. I had fought for academic freedom at CUA for more than twenty years, and I wanted the court to acknowledge the importance of that freedom, not so much for my benefit but, in spite of itself, for the good of the university. Paul Saunders used to kid me that we would ask for one dollar and one public lecture if we won!

On November 2, 1988, the university attorneys filed a motion for summary judgment similar to the one they had filed with regard to my suspension from teaching. They reiterated that the university's decision was based on religious conviction and canon law and that therefore, in light of the First Amendment separation of church and state, the civil court had no jurisdiction over the case. My attorneys filed a long opposition brief. We claimed that the case involved a broken contract and that the university's actions were not immune from judicial scrutiny merely because of its claimed rights to the free exercise of religion. CUA was not a religion or a church but a civilly chartered institution of academic learning in the District of Columbia.

The nonjury trial was scheduled in the court of Judge Frederick Weisberg from December 14 through December 23, 1988. At the beginning of the trial, the attorneys for CUA again asked for summary judgment and the court again denied it. In his opening statement, Judge Weisberg set the parameters for the case: it was a dispute about the nature of the tenure contract entered into by the parties.

By now the basic position of the two sides was clear. I held that CUA had accepted academic freedom and that this was a part of my contract. According to the principles of academic freedom, I could be removed from my teaching position only on the basis of a judgment of incompetence made in the first instance by my faculty peers. Such a process had not been followed in my case. Consequently I had been wrongly terminated from my right to teach theology at CUA.

The position of the university was also basically clear. CUA had a special relationship to the Holy See. Consequently, in light of a definitive judgment by the Holy See that I was neither suitable nor eligible to teach

Catholic theology, the university was bound to conclude that I could not teach theology there. There were, in short, ecclesial limits on academic freedom at Catholic University.

The court now had to decide what was contained in my contractual relationship with the university. Part of the problem at any university, and especially at CUA, is that there is no single contract in the form of a document spelling out the rights and obligations involved. The contract consists in the promises made in the faculty handbook and the annual appointment letter given to a professor, but in our judgment it also had to be understood as including the university's "course of dealing" with me.

Paul Saunders and a team from Cravath came down to Washington in advance of the trial and occupied an office in Virginia in order to prepare for the case. The Cravath team was also helped by lawyers from Wilmer, Cutler, and Pickering, especially Juanita Crowley. Once again, Kevin Baine was the principal lawyer from the team of Williams and Connolly defending the university.

This was certainly a landmark legal case for the Superior Court of the District of Columbia. As one wag put it, if not for prostitution and drugs, the court would almost have to go out of business. Now, two of the most prestigious law firms in America were squaring off over an issue not of money but of principle on both sides. John Tracy Ellis, generally known in those days as the dean of Catholic historians, said it was the first time that two cardinals ever testified in court in a lawsuit. Both sides committed themselves to carry out the proceedings precisely as a matter of principle and not to engage in any polemics or mudslinging. Spectators in the court, of whom there were many, were often amazed that during breaks people from the opposing sides would converse amiably. The skill and humor with which Judge Weisberg presided certainly made it easier for everyone.

I am not a lawyer and I will not attempt to describe in detail what transpired in these long, anxious days. The trial records are available to anyone who wants to study them in greater detail. I would, however, be remiss if I did not express my gratitude to those who testified on my behalf. These included four academics from CUA—James G. Brennan,

Frederick R. McManus, David Power, and Nivard Scheel, the acting rector of CUA in 1968–69, as well as Jim Coriden and Dick McBrien. As expected, I was on the stand longer than anyone else. My lawyers called President Byron, but of course his position was to support the university. The university lawyers called Cardinals Hickey and Bernardin, two former presidents of the university, Clarence C. Walton and Edmund D. Pellegrino, Carl Peter from CUA, and two academics from outside the university—James Burtchaell of the University of Notre Dame and Benedict Ashley of the Aquinas Institute in St. Louis. The trial ended three days before Christmas, and lawyers for both sides submitted their final briefs by January 25.

Judge Weisberg issued his ruling on February 28, 1989. The bottom line was very clear—I had lost the case. He ruled that my contract did not include a right to academic freedom, and he avoided all arguments based on the First Amendment, since the sole issue was the nature of the contract, the documents describing and expanding upon the contract, and the expectation of reasonable people at the time. One of the issues was whether or not I had a canonical mission from the chancellor. I and others from CUA claimed that no such canonical mission was ever given to us. The judge ultimately ruled that there was no requirement for me to have a canonical mission before 1981, but that the canonical statutes that went into effect then could be applied retroactively to me, even over the objection I had made that I had not accepted that as part of my contract. Since I had to have a canonical mission to teach on the ecclesiastical faculty, the court concluded, CUA had not broken my contract when it took away the canonical mission to teach on an ecclesiastical faculty. Did the university have an obligation to allow me to teach students in the non-ecclesiastical-degree programs in the department of theology? No, because I had not proved that there were or should be two different teaching bodies in the department of theology.

That left the final and most important question: Was the university obligated to allow me to teach theology in other schools or departments? The judge ruled there was no such legal obligation because my tenure was to the department of theology and not to any other department or to the university as a whole. But, more important, the court said that any reasonable faculty member entering into a contract with CUA should have known that, in the case of a definitive declaration from the Holy See that a professor was not eligible to teach Catholic theology, the university would enforce such a declaration. In addition, the judge ruled that even if he had decided in my favor, he never would have granted specific performance.

Judge Weisberg understood my theoretical position very clearly. I had claimed that academic freedom is a good both for CUA and for the Roman Catholic Church. But this was not a question that the court was competent to decide. The question presented was whether my contract gave me the right to teach Catholic theology at CUA in the face of a definitive judgment by the Holy See that I was ineligible to do so. "The court holds today that it does not."

The judge recognized that the crux of the problem was CUA's wanting to have it both ways—as a full-fledged American university and as a university that continued to place transcendent value on its unique and special relationship with the Holy See. "Perhaps it can fairly be said," the judge declared, "that the university wanted it both ways; but on most issues it can also be said that the university could have it both ways. On some issues—and this case certainly represents one of them—the conflict between the university's commitment to academic freedom and its unwavering fealty to the Holy See is direct and unavoidable. On such issues, the university may choose for itself on which side of the conflict it wants to come down and nothing in its contract with Professor Curran or any other faculty member promises that it will always come down on the side of academic freedom."

Paul Saunders read me the decision over the telephone. Over the two and a half years that this case, in all its various phases, had dragged on, I had made no decisions before consulting at length with my lawyers and others. I had discussed with many people the possibility of an appeal in light of a negative decision and had decided that in that event I would probably not appeal. Within three minutes of hearing Judge Weisberg's decision, I concluded definitively that I would not appeal. Paul Saunders and John Hunt concurred with this decision. Then I composed a short five-paragraph statement that was released to the press a few hours later, which read in part:

I have lost, but the university, its faculty, and students may have lost more than I. The court's opinion confirms what the university itself has asserted in this case: full academic freedom, as understood in American higher education, does not now exist at CUA. That conclusion strikes at the heart of the university's character as an American university.

I learned of the meaning and importance of academic freedom from my colleagues at CUA in the 1960s, and I will always remain grateful for the support of fellow faculty members and students who have stood for the same principle.

I have fought for academic freedom at CUA for more than twenty years. I have lost. As far as I am concerned, this was the last battle. I will not appeal the court's decision, and I will leave it to others to judge its significance. I will move on.

CHAPTER 7

Life after Condemnation

W HAT DOES A CATHOLIC THEOLOGIAN condemned by the Vatican and legally terminated from a tenured professorship do? From the beginning, I assumed that on the basis of my teaching and publications I could get some kind of teaching position in moral theology or, as it is often called in Protestant circles, Christian ethics. What had happened to me obviously closed some doors, but it could open others. In the end I found a very stimulating position as Elizabeth Scurlock University Professor of Human Values at Southern Methodist University in Dallas. But the path from CUA to SMU was hardly without its twists and turns. The Vatican and CUA actions affected me in many ways. Although my relationship to the Catholic Church changed, the Vatican action did not touch my status as a Catholic or as a priest. At the time, there was some talk of trying to oust me from the priesthood, but the Vatican stopped short of that, just as it had in the case of Hans Küng.

The Vatican's action cut me off from any official participation in the life of the church as a theologian. I was no longer invited to do any work for the hierarchical church in any capacity whatsoever. No official Catholic group would ever again invite me to address it. In one diocese I did give a few talks at a local parish and to a group of religious. Afterward, the bishop of that diocese received a letter from the CDF saying that perhaps he was not aware that I had given these talks, but that he needed to be more vigilant and to prevent anything like that from happening again. From the viewpoint of the institutional church, I am a nonperson.

People often ask me if I have had any official communication with the Vatican since 1986. The answer is no. In a certain sense, the Vatican in my case dropped the nuclear bomb. To the powers that be in Rome, I am no longer a Catholic theologian; I do not exist, yet I do. A few years ago I was involved in a discussion at the CTSA about the mandate that is now required of all those teaching Catholic theology in Catholic higher education. I said that I was the only objective person in the room because the mandate did not apply to me. From my perspective, however, there are some advantages in their having dropped the nuclear bomb rather than taking some lesser action. In other cases the Vatican has taken a less dramatic approach to disciplining a "troublemaker" but then has continued to harass that person. For my own part, I no longer have to worry about the Vatican; I do not have to spend the rest of my life looking over my shoulder. It is all over and done with.

I have already written of the support of my bishop, Matthew Clark. After the final decision by the Vatican, he issued a statement recognizing the final authority of the Holy Father and urging everyone to accept it. He went on to say that I was a priest in good standing and would always be welcome to exercise priestly ministry in the Diocese of Rochester.[1] He also told me that he would approve whatever teaching post I thought would work best for me.

A few attempts were made to find a position for me at a Catholic institution. These initiatives started at the faculty level but never went much further. It soon became clear that no Catholic institution was going to hire me, since it put them in opposition to the hierarchical church in general and the local bishop in particular. One president of a major Catholic university was quoted to me as saying that it was tough enough fighting his own battles. Even if he, or any other Catholic university head, wanted to hire me, the opposition of conservative Catholic donors would have been a powerful disincentive. Without doubt, I was both a controversial figure and a symbol. To some I am a hero, to others, an aging enfant terrible. The extreme right wing in Roman Catholicism in the United States had always strongly opposed me and was now gloating over its victory.

The hardest part about leaving CUA was losing the broader support system—on an academic, a spiritual, and simply on a human level. I lived and worked with people who recognized that faith and reason were not mutually exclusive. Of course we had our differences, but there was a spirit of collegiality and we took pleasure in working together. Here was a lively Catholic academic community interested in theology and the life of the church, a stimulating environment for faculty and students alike. Many of us gathered daily to celebrate the Eucharist. Our liturgical celebrations were lively, and we tried to incorporate women as much as we could. The support that I received from so many in this community of faculty, students, and friends was especially evident in 1986–87. So many people gave unstintingly of their time and energy to work on my behalf. It was not easy to leave all that behind.

Cornell and USC

My first peregrination started in the 1987–88 school year, even before the ad hoc faculty committee had made its final report. In the spring of 1986, Vice Provost Barry Adams of Cornell University had invited me to come to Cornell for a year as the first holder of the Kaneb Chair in Catholic Studies, a three-year revolving chair endowed by Al Kaneb, a Catholic trustee of Cornell. Cornell is the only school in the Ivy League that does not have a department of religion. Some even claim that the original founder of Cornell decreed that religion not be taught there. The president of Cornell at the time, Frank H. T. Rhodes, told me later that this was a myth, and I think that Kaneb and others hoped that this chair might augur a growing role for religious studies at Cornell.

After the CDF's final decision in August 1986, Adams contacted me again and renewed his offer. In January 1987, when it was clear that Hickey would not allow me to teach at CUA pending the due process procedure, I accepted the post at Cornell. Adams had set up a meeting for us with Al Kaneb in Rochester even before I was able to commit myself, and Kaneb was obviously leery. "Charlie," he said, "I don't want you coming to Cornell just to throw hand grenades at the pope." I told him I resented that comment. I had always been respectful in my disagreements with church authority, had never attacked people or their motives, and would continue in that vein. Also, I would never use my classroom to carry on my personal battles. In the end, Al and I became friends, though geographic distance has prevented us from keeping in close touch in recent years. I taught two courses in the fall semester of the 1987–88 academic year—the renewal of Roman Catholicism at Vatican II and fundamental moral theology; in the spring semester I taught Catholic social ethics and gave a series of four public lectures on Catholic moral theology. This was the first time I had taught undergraduate students, and I enjoyed it.

Before going to Cornell, I made a visit there to check out a number of things, especially the library, which of course was quite good. Despite the lack of a religion department, Cornell's library holdings in theology, even Catholic theology, were better than one might expect. I decided that I would spend my time at Cornell researching a monograph on Catholic higher education, theology, and academic freedom. The education literature was readily available there. Such a project tied together the disparate threads of my life at that time, and added some harmony to my various pursuits.

Cornell and Ithaca, New York, are geographically in the Diocese of Rochester, so I was close to many old friends. I was housed in the English department and enjoyed conversations with colleagues there; I lived in a house with the Catholic campus chaplains, and that too was very supportive. In addition to a spacious office, Cornell gave me a marvelous carrel that was really a small office on one of the library's top floors, with a large window looking out over Cayuga Lake. It was a great place to do research.

While still in Washington in the spring of 1987, when I was not able to teach, I went for a physical for the first time in thirty years. It turned out that I needed surgery for a hernia, and unfortunately I developed a blood clot in my leg after the operation. I don't think that the strain of recent events had in any way caused these problems, but I decided that I should get some exercise. I seldom if ever played golf in Washington, though I enjoyed the game and often played while on vacation. Once in Ithaca, I decided to play golf once a week on the Cornell golf course, which had been designed by the famous golf architect Robert Trent Jones as his master's thesis there in the early 1930s. Early in my stay, I ran into the president and the provost on the course. We exchanged pleasantries, and the provost suggested we get together to play golf sometime. I nodded and smiled, assuming that this was nothing more than the usual politeness. I was surprised when he called me a week later to suggest a game, and we ended up playing together five or six times over the course of the year. He was a biochemist and a nonbeliever, but he really liked playing golf with me. I think part of my appeal may have been that I was only there for a year, and thus would never be bugging him about something or other, as usually happened when he played with other faculty!

In the midst of a very busy year at Cornell, and with the ongoing academic and legal battles at CUA, I had not thought much about what I would do the following year. In February, William W. May from the University of Southern California called to see if I would be interested in coming there for a year as the Visiting Brooks Professor in Religion. I had pleasant memories of my week at USC in the fall of 1986, knew the faculty well, and was attracted by USC's doctoral program in Christian social ethics, so I accepted this kind invitation.

In August 1988 I set out on the long and lonely drive from upstate New York to Los Angeles. There was some serious talk of trying to fund a chair in Catholic ethics, but in the end it came to nothing. I had been approached by USC in the late 1960s about accepting a chair there in Catholic theology, but that had never materialized either, primarily because of restrictions imposed by the Archdiocese of Los Angeles.

Each semester at USC I taught a large general education requirement course on Christianity and American public life with the help of one or two teaching assistants. I did not enjoy the large class as much as I had my smaller classes. In addition, however, I had some upper-level undergraduate courses and a graduate seminar with doctoral students every semester. The topics of these seminars included Catholic social ethics, contemporary Catholic moral theology, and the reform of Catholicism at Vatican II. Since so many of my colleagues were in the area of Christian social ethics, there were good conversations and discussions—especially with Bill May, Jack Crossley, Henry Clark, and Sheila Briggs. USC was a very good place for me to be.

I lived with the Vincentian Fathers in their house on Adams Boulevard near the university and was one of the few people in Los Angeles who walked to work every day. I enjoyed my time with the Vincentians and made some good friends there. I had some relatives (my deceased brother Jack's family) and friends in the area, especially Marie Egan, a former doctoral student, and Alexis Navarro. Both taught in the M.A. program in theology at Mt. St. Mary's College. Some Irish-born priests also invited me to join their weekly golf game. Some of them, too, were trying to raise money for me to stay on permanently at USC.

While at USC I worked on editing a Festschrift for my friend Dick McCormick, titled *Moral Theology: Challenges for the Future; Essays in Honor of Richard A. McCormick,* and finished my monograph *Catholic Higher Education, Theology, and Academic Freedom,* both published in 1990. I stayed on for a second year in a visiting chair at USC, but I had to make plans for the future. I knew that the trial would take place during the 1988–89 academic year, and I felt I could not take a tenured position earlier because this would give CUA a reason to claim that I had unilaterally broken my tenure contract there. I had had enough of moving from place to place and was ready to settle down for the long term. I always felt that I could find another position, but in reality it was not that simple. There are not many openings at the senior level at any given time. With my background, I was a candidate for an endowed chair, but the availability of such chairs depended on many contingencies.

Even before the 1988–89 academic year began, Richard Penaskovic, the chair of religion at Auburn University in Alabama, approached me about an eminent scholar chair in religion that Auburn was going to advertise and then fill in the 1990–91 academic year. I was also in negotiations with two other universities about endowed chairs. There were two preliminary matters I had to clear up before I could enter serious negotiations with Auburn. For one thing, Auburn was on the AAUP list of censured institutions. I had a long conversation with Jordan Kurland, who made two basic points. He argued that I should not let Auburn's censure stand in the way of taking a position if I thought it was the best place for me. Moreover, Auburn was now attempting to get off the list of censured institutions.

The second problem was church related. Auburn is a small town with one Catholic church incorporating the campus ministry and run by the Vincentian Fathers. If the priests there were going to oppose my presence, it would not be a good place for me. I called a friend on the provincial council of the Eastern Vincentian Fathers to sound him out on this matter. He told me the Vincentians were quite open, and he was sure they would welcome my coming to Auburn. I then called the pastor, Father Mike Kennedy, and he was very friendly and welcoming. We agreed to meet when I came to campus for my official visit.

I had agreed with Dean Mary Richards of the College of Liberal Arts and the search committee to come to Auburn on March 14–15. I went through the usual routine of meeting with the faculty of religion, the search committee, Dean Richards, and Academic Vice President Ron Henry, and I gave a public lecture. All went very well, including my informal meeting with the priests of the parish. I learned that I was the last of three candidates to come to campus. The next day the search committee met and unanimously agreed to offer me the position. Dean Richards agreed and went through the normal channels to get the permission of the academic vice president and the president to offer me the position. She called me on April 2 with the offer and sent the official letter. Richards urged me to come to campus one more time, to finish up some negotiations, meet some other people, and look at housing, and she wanted this done as quickly as possible. I was scheduled to give a lecture at the University of the South in Sewanee, Tennessee, on April 5, and agreed to come from there to Auburn on April 6–8.

My biggest remaining question about Auburn concerned the library. The Auburn library was better than I expected (on my first visit, they proudly pointed out they already owned all my books), but I would need a better library if I were to carry on my theological research. My friend and former colleague at CUA Tom Flynn was now the chair of the philosophy department at Emory University in Atlanta and had a home right off campus. Tom offered me a key to his house and a bedroom whenever I needed to come over and use the very good library of the Candler School of Theology. Emory was only a two-hour drive from Auburn, and I thought this was feasible.

At Auburn I would be teaching only undergraduates, but I had found that kind of teaching energizing and enjoyable. Although Auburn had a very small department of religion, I would always be able to teach courses in my area of Christian ethics. We also worked out an arrangement whereby I would teach two trimesters a year and have the third trimester off for research and writing. Thus I would be teaching six months a year and doing research and writing the other six months. According to the offer, I would have a half-time assistant, a large, fully outfitted office, and a $10,000 research expense account to be used as I saw fit. I already knew Rich Penaskovic and immediately hit it off with Jim Dawsey, a New Testament scholar and the other full-time faculty member in the department. In addition, the people on the search committee and others I met seemed to be fine academic colleagues. I also met with Harry Philpott, the former president of Auburn, in whose honor the Goodwin/Philpott Eminent Scholar Chair in Religion was named. J. W. Goodwin was a businessperson who donated the money, but he also wanted Philpott's name on the chair.

The official letter offering me the position contained the usual formality: "Upon the recommendation of the tenured faculty in the Department of Religion, the University Promotion and Tenure Committee, and President Martin, you will receive a tenured professorship in the Department of Religion." Since we all knew that I was the unanimous choice of the search committee and the dean, and had been approved by the academic vice president and the president, we all assumed that my appointment was a done deal. The Auburn situation was not perfect, but nothing ever is. I judged it a good opportunity.

Before returning to Los Angeles on April 8, I promised Mary Richards a definite answer by Monday, April 16. I checked with the other two institutions I had been dealing with and learned that one was probably going to go in a different direction. At the other, I was still one of three finalists, but they had yet to make a final decision. A friend, however, told me that he thought the position would probably go to a candidate in the humanities rather than one in religion since it was a university-wide position. I then officially withdrew from consideration. Meanwhile, on April 11, both Philpott, the former president, and Henry, the current academic vice president, called to urge me to come to Auburn. I was happy with the decision to go to Auburn and called Dean Richards on April 16 to accept the offer—only to learn that my plan to finally settle down was not going to pan out.

Dean Richards informed me that President Martin now had doubts about giving me tenure. In the following weeks I stayed in frequent contact with Richards and even more with Henry, trying to find out what was behind the president's problem. I discovered several things. Martin had informed the trustees at a meeting on April 7 that the university was in final negotiations with me. A Catholic trustee cautioned that I was controversial and that Auburn should be very careful. On April 16 Martin told Henry that he had decided not to give me tenure. I asked Henry what the reasons were, but the president had not offered any. I suggested to the academic vice president names of three other university presidents who would vouch for me, and I also urged him to have Philpott, the former president, call Martin. I was very willing to talk to Martin myself, but Henry counseled against it. On April 20 Penaskovic and the two most senior faculty members on the search committee met with Henry. Henry told them that the president had decided not to give me tenure and would not be budged.

Dean Richards called me on April 25 to say that Henry now wanted to start the normal tenure process, with the department, the school, the dean, and the university committee finally sending their report to the president. I asked Richards if this meant that the president had changed his mind. She responded that she had not pushed on this but assumed that Henry would not send us on a kamikaze mission. The university tenure committee, chaired by Henry, met on April 30 and apparently voted in favor of my tenure.

On May 2 I talked to Henry and was quite surprised to learn that the president had not changed his mind. My friend Dennis O'Brien, president of the University of Rochester, called Martin and talked with him for more than fifteen minutes, but Martin was noncommittal. Henry told me that the president was going to meet with the university tenure committee on May 11.

I then proposed a compromise to Henry. I wanted to be at Auburn for a while and thus have a secure post from which to look for a permanent tenured position. It would be to the president's advantage if he did not have to go against all the faculty committees in denying me tenure. Thus I proposed that I be given a six-year nontenured position at Auburn. Henry liked the compromise and agreed to propose it to the president—but he called back a day later to say that the president would not accept the terms. On May 11 Martin met with the university tenure committee and told them he was not going to grant me tenure. Martin said he had more information than the committee did but that he was not going to share it with them. I went back and forth with Henry and Richards, finally receiving from them on May 25 an official offer for a temporary, nontenured, one-year appointment as visiting eminent scholar in religion at Auburn.

At that stage of the game, I had no choice but to accept. I figured I would go to Auburn and then make an all-out push for a tenured position elsewhere for the following academic year. I had no intention of making this a public matter. From a practical standpoint, there was little or nothing I could do. I would be a new faculty member with a one-year appointment and no connections of any kind on campus. Also, publicity about the situation would only add to the perception of some that I was a controversial figure that any university president would want to avoid.

My good friend Bill Donnelly, a Rochester priest, volunteered to drive with me from Los Angeles to Alabama and help set up my apartment. His company certainly made the trip much easier. And so I came to Auburn at the end of the summer, hoping that in the course of the year I could find a suitable position elsewhere.

My Year at Auburn

I found out only later that there was already rather strong opposition among the Auburn faculty to what President Martin had done, especially among senior faculty on the original search committee, the university tenure committee, and the university senate. Early in September a reporter from the *Atlanta Constitution* called me about the case, and I learned from my friend Penaskovic that someone on campus had leaked the story to the paper. On September 11 the *Atlanta Constitution* broke the story on the front page. Other papers in the area—Columbus, Georgia, Auburn-

Opelika, Montgomery, and Birmingham, Alabama—then picked up the story.[2] I was rather reluctant about all this publicity, thinking it would only make things more difficult for me.

As the situation unfolded at Auburn, I was really not a prime actor in any sense but rather the object of the story. The faculty had experienced many problems with the trustees and the president in the preceding years. In the course of the first trimester, on the advice of senior faculty, I wrote a few letters to the administration about procedural issues in my case. I also had two meetings with President Martin, but he refused to give his reasons for not granting me tenure. The primary actor was the university senate under the presidency of Professor Gary Mullen. My colleagues Penaskovic and Dawsey were also very active. The press was a major player and reported the developments in great detail in various area newspapers.

There was much sparring on campus and in the press, but I will relate only one significant incident. President Martin was quoted in the press as saying, "If you knew what I knew, you would have done the same thing."[3] How could one defend oneself against such a charge? This statement distressed me quite a bit (later the university senate censured the president for it), but what could I do? Fortunately, a reporter posed this question to Jordan Kurland in Washington. Kurland is a marvelous combination of realist and idealist in fighting for the principles of academic freedom. He told the reporter that I had been a very public figure in the Catholic Church and at CUA for twenty-five years. If there were any skeletons in my closet, they would certainly have been discovered by now.[4]

In October the university senate appointed an ad hoc committee chaired by Professor Michael Urban to investigate and report to the senate answers to three questions. The first concerned whether or not President Martin had followed the proper procedures in his action. The committee found that he had not followed procedures in two important areas. First, he had made "a final decision" to deny me tenure before even meeting with the requisite committee. Second, he never provided in writing the reasons for his decision, as the procedures call for. To the second question, whether trustees unduly influenced the decision, the committee found that some opposition to me had been expressed at a trustees' meeting on April 7. The third question was whether Martin's reasons for denying me tenure were acceptable in accordance with Auburn's guidelines and procedures. Martin admitted to the committee that he had never contacted my references, including three university presidents. Martin claimed that he alone had made the decision, but still he would not divulge his reasons.[5]

The committee report was very favorable to me and began with the statement that "Charles Curran is perhaps the most distinguished scholar ever to have served on the faculty of Auburn University." The realist in me knew that rhetoric tends to be overblown on such occasions, but the statement certainly gave some solace to a person who was desperately searching for a job!

The university senate had a tumultuous meeting on November 20. President Martin accepted an invitation to address the meeting but again refused to divulge his reasons for denying me tenure. He said again, in response to a question, "If you knew what I knew, you would have done the same thing." One faculty member referred to this remark as character assassination. Finally the university senate passed a resolution requesting that the president declare his reasons for the denial of tenure to the promotion and tenure committee and then follow the normal process for tenure. If President Martin did not do this by December 7, there would be a special meeting of the general faculty to discuss further action.[6] The president did meet with the committee on December 7, but again refused to give his reasons.

Two other significant events occurred in December. In a front-page story on December 11, the *Montgomery Advertiser* said that J. W. Goodwin, who had contributed $8 million to Auburn, including the money for the eminent scholar in religion chair, was taking Auburn out of his will. He complained about a "power-hungry trustee" who had put pressure on Martin. The newspaper article went on to say that the man judged to be the most powerful person on the Auburn board of trustees was Robert E. Lowder, a Montgomery businessman.[7] On December 13 I announced publicly that I had accepted a tenured university professorship at SMU—but I am getting ahead of the story.

The Auburn university senate met on January 8 to discuss a proposal to censure President Martin. Censure concerns a set of particular actions in a specific case but does not constitute a vote of no confidence as such. After much debate, the resolution was put off for a week. On January 15 the university senate, with its diverse membership of faculty, administrators, and staff, voted 48-39 to censure President Martin for four violations of academic principles and policies—deciding to refuse me tenure before receiving the required recommendations from the committee, allowing members of the board of trustees to influence his decision, approving the release of biased and mistaken information about me, and compromising the hiring of future eminent scholars and future faculty by saying that the university policies did not apply to them before they were officially hired.

In the course of the controversy, much speculation centered on who had pressured Martin to deny me tenure. Early on, there was speculation on campus and in the newspapers that the pressure came from the Catholic Church in Alabama and especially Archbishop Oscar Lipscomb of Mobile.[8] My own conclusion is that Archbishop Lipscomb was not the cause of but the occasion for Martin's action. Without intervention by Lipscomb, the controversy probably would never have taken place. How so?

I had contacted Father Mike Kennedy, the pastor of the Catholic church in Auburn, about my coming. He told me that on March 28 he had mentioned this to Archbishop Lipscomb and that Lipscomb had been stunned. After some conversation, however, Lipscomb concluded that I was a priest in good standing and that he knew me from the seminary in Rome, but said he was going to contact Cardinal Hickey and Bishop Clark about this. Lipscomb also talked about my controversial past to Bessie Mae Holloway, a university trustee from the congressional district of Mobile.

At the April 7 meeting of the trustees, Bessie Mae Holloway pointed out that I was a controversial figure. I do not know if any other trustees spoke, but they all heard her comment. It is unlikely that most of the trustees knew much about my controversial background in the Catholic Church. Vice President Henry told me that the president, even after this meeting, still planned to give me tenure. According to Henry, the president changed his mind between April 11 and April 16. Whatever Ms. Holloway said at the April 7 meeting, it was not enough to change Martin's mind—and in any case she, an African American Catholic in a small coterie of good old Alabama boys, did not have enough clout to change his mind. Neither the church nor Archbishop Lipscomb nor Ms. Holloway had enough influence to deny me tenure. But without Lipscomb's and then Holloway's involvement, the other trustees probably would not have raised any objections.

A person with much more influence on the board picked up on the fact that I was controversial and held somewhat liberal positions on issues such as homosexuality. Two different stories circulated on campus. One was related to the governor, Guy Hunt, a Primitive Baptist minister. His representative, Reginald Ray, was at the April 7 trustees' meeting and later, without identifying himself, wrote a letter to the *Montgomery Advertiser* supporting Martin's decision.[9] There was speculation that Ray had informed the governor of some of my moral positions and that the governor had pressured Martin.

Others theorized what I consider a more plausible scenario. J. W. Goodwin had been a business partner of Bobby Lowder's father, but they had had a falling out. Some people speculated that Lowder had used the information about my controversial background to get back at Goodwin, his father's enemy, who had endowed the eminent scholar chair. As I noted above, Goodwin had publicly mentioned a "power-hungry" trustee. But, to this day, I do not know for sure who pressured Martin.

In my judgment, the trouble at Auburn was a structural problem with the board of trustees. The trustees were too few, were political appointees, and were appointed for twelve-year terms. My faculty colleagues generally agreed with this analysis of the problem; in fact, they were the ones who really made me aware of it. Unfortunately, it is very difficult to reform a long-standing institution such as this one, and only a few changes have been made at Auburn. Even today Auburn suffers from undue trustee interference in the administration and life of the university.[10]

My case triggered three significant personnel changes. In April Vice President Henry and Dean Richards announced that they were leaving Auburn for positions at other universities, a step up for both of them. The general feeling among the faculty was that Henry had been caught in the middle of a difficult and untenable situation. In addition, at the end of April President Martin, at age fifty-eight, announced that he would retire at the end of the next academic year.

In the May–June issue of *Academe*, Committee A of the AAUP issued a report on my case at Auburn, which was still under AAUP censure. The report gave a detailed history of the case and concluded that the whole "sorry episode" revealed an unwholesome climate for academic freedom at Auburn University.[11] To its great credit, the faculty worked strenuously in the next few years to strengthen the academic freedom and due process provisions in the faculty handbook, so as to prevent the same kind of situation from arising in the future. The AAUP removed Auburn from its list of censured institutions in 1993.[12] The faculty and the new administration deserve great credit for learning from the problems of the past and trying to prevent them in the future.

I continue to have tremendous respect and appreciation for the faculty at Auburn. They took a courageous stand for me and, more important, for the principle of academic freedom that is so central to the enterprise of higher education. The situation at Auburn in 1990–91 was quite similar to that at CUA in 1967, though I was less well known to the Auburn faculty and had not even started teaching there when they began defending me. Auburn had a history of undue trustee interference and an administration that gave short shrift to academic principles and processes. Here again, my situation was the spark that ignited the fire. The faculty leaders at Auburn executed a strategy in defense of academic freedom, for which they, and indeed the faculty as a whole, deserve great credit and praise. They will always have my gratitude.

The spring semester of 1991 at Auburn sped by and was most pleasant. I received many invitations to speak on campus and was very glad to do so. I doubt whether a professor appointed for only one year ever got to know more people in an academic institution than I did. Before I left at the end of the school year, I invited more than thirty faculty and their guests to a dessert party to express my thanks.

SMU

Another great benefit of the Auburn experience was that it led to my coming to SMU. I had feared that the publicity about the controversy at Auburn would make it more difficult for me to find a suitable position, but I needn't have worried, for the nationwide publicity made everyone aware that I was looking for a job! A number of friends, including Rosemary Ruether at Garrett Theological Seminary and Stephen Lammers at Lafayette University, got busy trying to put together one-year appointments for me. Walter Bruggemann contacted me about a full-time position in Christian ethics at Columbia Seminary in Atlanta. But the best news came in a phone call from William F. May of SMU very early in October. Bill had been an acquaintance and colleague over the years, but we were soon to become very close friends. (Coincidentally, there have been three Bill Mays, all in Christian ethics or moral theology, who have had a great influence on my academic life. William E. May was a colleague at CUA who held positions very much different from my own in moral theology. William W. May had invited me to come to USC. Now, William F. May was talking to me about SMU.)

That October day, Bill May mentioned a one-year position in SMU's vacant Scurlock University Chair of Human Values. There were two such university chairs at SMU (his being the other) with the role of trying to bring the study of ethics into every part of the institution. I told Bill that I had had my fill of one-year visiting professorships and now really wanted to settle down into a full-time position that would be the last move of my academic life. Bill agreed to present this possibility to the search committee, and shortly thereafter I received a letter from the associate provost, Leroy Howe, inviting me to apply for a full-time position and asking me to send a detailed curriculum vitae. (Leroy is now my golf partner. We usually get the earliest tee time on Wednesday morning and play eighteen holes in two hours and forty-five minutes. We may not be very good, but we don't waste any time.) Leroy then sent me some catalogues, the faculty handbook, and other information about SMU. By October 18 we were trying to work out dates for my visit to campus.

SMU appealed to me in many ways. The Scurlock Chair was not in any department or school, but I was well acquainted with Joe Allen and Fred Carney, who taught moral theology in the Perkins School of Theology (interestingly, Protestant institutions usually call the discipline Christian ethics, but Perkins calls it moral theology). Including Bill May, I would thus have three strong colleagues in my own discipline. I also knew that Schubert Ogden, one of the top systematic theologians in the country, was at SMU. Schubert was on the AAUP investigating committee at CUA, and he was very familiar with my work and had been a strong supporter. I had heard about SMU's renowned Bridwell Library, and I later found it to be quite good even in Catholic theology. SMU also had a small Ph.D. program in religion, so I would be able keep a finger in Ph.D. work without being overwhelmed by dissertations.

I raised two concerns in my discussions with Leroy Howe. The chair was in "human values," but I was a Christian ethicist in the Catholic tradition. I told Howe that I would teach from the viewpoint of Christian ethics but would continue my research primarily from within the Catholic tradition. Howe assured me that this was exactly what people wanted me to do. Although the name of the chair was generic, it was most appropriate that it have a Christian dimension to it. My other concern was more personal. Having taught and lectured all over the country, I probably had twenty to twenty-five good acquaintances in every major city in the United States—except Dallas and Houston. Texas was simply never on my map. But certainly that would not be an insurmountable problem.

We finally agreed that I would visit the campus November 29–December 1, with the usual agenda of meetings with the search committee, prominent faculty, and the provost, and would attend lunches and dinners and give a public talk. I arrived at SMU expecting that I would be one of three or so candidates visiting the campus, but this was not the case. I learned later that SMU had been looking to fill this position for some time and that they frequently agreed in advance to interview just one candidate, since at the senior level candidates tend to be very well known. Soon after I arrived on campus, I realized that they were wooing me, not interrogating me, and that the job was mine if I did not have horns!

I met with Jack and Laura Lee Blanton, the donors of the chair, named in honor of Laura Lee Blanton's mother. The Blantons are marvelous people and philanthropic patrons of higher education and the arts. Jack had been chair of the board of trustees at the University of Texas in Austin. Early on in our conversation, they pointed out that, as donors, they had nothing whatsoever to say about who held the chair, but that as they happened to be on campus that day, the provost thought it might be good for them to meet me. They would be very happy to have me hold the chair, they said, but again they emphasized they had no say in the matter. Unfortunately, Laura Lee died of cancer in 1999. One could not ask for better patrons. They never intruded on me, and their only requests concerned how they could help me. Would that all academic benefactors were of the same stripe.

On the final afternoon of my visit, I met for an hour with Provost Ruth Morgan. After chatting for half an hour, we began to discuss the contract. She told me she could not offer me a tenured contract before checking with the faculty and other administrators I had met but that, from what she had heard, this would be a formality and I should have the official letter within a very few days. Lest I hear echoes of the experience with Auburn, she smiled when using the phrase "tenured contract." When I replied that she could not offer me tenure before receiving the approval of the president and trustees, she smiled more broadly and replied that SMU didn't have the same problems that Auburn did. A few days later she sent me the official letter offering me tenure, which contained no mention of the president or the trustees. We agreed that I would have a large furnished office (the two university chairs probably have the best faculty offices in the university), a half-time administrative assistant, and a $10,000 budget for research and travel to spend as I wished.

The future was looking very bright as I returned from SMU to Auburn, but there was still one small cloud. I discovered that Charles Grahmann, the Catholic bishop of Dallas, was trying to block my appointment. I called a friendly bishop in Texas to ask his advice about the Catholic scene in Dallas and to inform him of Grahmann's opposition. My friend told me that such opposition was not surprising as Grahmann was a very good friend of Ratzinger's German-language assistant, Josef Clemens, and also knew Ratzinger quite well. My friend pointed out, however, that Dallas was a large city and had a large and diverse Catholic population. I would find many Catholics there who were sympathetic to my approach. When I later asked Provost Morgan about Grahmann's opposition, she told me that he had apparently contacted the Methodist bishop and asked for his intervention with the authorities at SMU. She did not know what the Methodist bishop finally told Grahmann, but she herself had told the Methodist bishop that it was none of his business.

On December 10 I accepted the Elizabeth Scurlock University Professorship at SMU, and the following summer I moved for what I hoped would be the last time. My friend Bill Donnelly helped me to furnish and arrange my townhouse, about ten minutes by car from SMU. For the first time in my life, at age fifty-seven, I was a homeowner—thanks to the mortgage company.

My experience at SMU has fulfilled and exceeded my expectations. In the mid-1980s SMU adopted a new curriculum that called for undergraduates to take a capstone course involving an ethical reflection on their major. Two trustees showed their commitment to ethics by funding two chairs in ethics in the expectation that the chair holders would teach a capstone course and another course somewhere else in the university each semester. In keeping with SMU's goal to make the study of ethics part of the whole university, the two chairs were made university professorships responsible directly to the provost rather than to any one school or department. Bill May was the Cary M. Maguire University Professor of Ethics and I was now the Elizabeth Scurlock University Professor of Human Values. Professional ethicists were not to teach all the capstone courses, but the courses had to focus on ethical questions. In keeping with SMU's history and Methodist sponsorship, the holders of these chairs have approached the subject from a Christian perspective to date, although the chairs are deliberately described in open-ended terms.

I have taught one of the capstone or an equivalent course each semester I've been at SMU, and my second course in another department. I have taught in the department of religion and to the seminarians in the Perkins School of Theology. One year, Bill May and I, in successive semesters, directed a faculty seminar. Mine was on the role of religion in American public life and was a marvelous experience for all involved; it also allowed me to get to know ten colleagues from other parts of the university. I've also given directed as well as independent study seminars for doctoral students in Christian ethics. The two capstone courses (now called cultural formation courses) I have taught most often are Christianity and American public life and bioethics from a Christian perspective. In the past twenty years I have purposely moved away from research and writing in bioethics; but bioethics is a popular subject, especially for pre-med majors, so I do continue to teach it.

I teach these courses from the perspective of Christian ethics in general, which of course includes Roman Catholic ethics. In the mid-1990s the chair of the religion department asked me to teach a course on Roman Catholicism to undergraduates. I agreed, on the condition that someone else teach an undergraduate course on Methodism or the spirituality of John Wesley. Undergraduates had no such courses available to them. A Methodist bishop on campus heard about this, and as far as he is concerned, I walk on water.

Doctoral students and some Perkins seminarians have a vague knowledge of my background, but few Perkins students, and virtually no undergraduates, have a clue—or any interest. One day near the end of a semester, I ran into an undergraduate who apparently had read something about me. His comment was classic: "Professor Curran, I didn't know that you were a f—— Catholic priest."

A university professorship can be isolating, for one belongs to no department or school. I was lucky to avoid this danger, thanks especially to Bill May, who had been at SMU since the establishment of the two chairs in 1985 and had many connections throughout the university. By following in his footsteps, I learned a lot. Bill was a great friend and colleague. We spent a lot of time in each other's offices and on the phone, had lunch regularly once a week, and played golf together.

One great advantage in holding a university professorship is that I never again have to go to a departmental or school-specific faculty meeting! Henry Kissinger is alleged to have said that of all the kinds of politics, the worst is academic. This is because the stakes are so low! I do, however, serve on many university-wide committees that often deal with interesting and important issues, and in the process I have gotten to know many colleagues throughout the university. SMU is small enough that one can form collegial relationships and even friendships with a number of people in different disciplines and schools.

Through the Maguire Center, started by Bill May, all the ethicists on campus often come together. I also chair an ethics colloquy that brings these same people together twice a semester to discuss our work and that of others in the field. When Bill May retired a few years ago, I chaired the search committee that ultimately brought in Robin Lovin as his successor. Robin was in the process of finishing up his last year as dean of SMU's Perkins School of Theology. I had gotten to know him fairly well over the years, and we've since become close friends.

Life Outside SMU

SMU has also given me the opportunity to continue publishing in the area of Catholic moral theology, thanks to generous sabbaticals, competent and helpful administrative assistants (among them Carol Swartz, who efficiently prepared this manuscript for publication), and the marvelous holdings of the Bridwell Library. Because I am no longer invited to official Catholic functions, I have more time for my own research and writing, and have been able to publish more monographs than I was able to do while at CUA, where there were so many demands on my time. My writing is now the primary vehicle for working for change in the Catholic Church.

In 1993 I published *The Church and Morality: An Ecumenical and Catholic Approach,* a slim volume based on the Heim/Fry Lectures sponsored by the Evangelical Lutheran Church in America for their seminaries. I chose this subject because I wanted to explore further the relationship between ecclesiology and moral theology. In that the understanding of the church influences how one approaches morality, the book addresses primarily a church audience rather than an academic one as such. Catholicity (with a small "c") is shared by most mainstream Protestant churches as well as the Catholic Church. The catholicity of the church consists in three things—an inclusive community open to all and appealing to all; different levels of church, including the local and universal; and a recognition that church members belong to many other communities and institutions.

With regard to morality, catholicity means that the moral aspect of the Christian life touches all realities in our world and is open to both human and uniquely Christian sources of moral wisdom and knowledge. The challenge for any church catholic is to live out its catholicity and to maintain the tension between unity and diversity. On the more general aspects of morality, such as general principles (respect for life) or virtues (hope, justice), the whole church universal can and should find agreement. But on complex and specific concrete issues, there will be legitimate diversity precisely because no one can claim certainty on these issues.

My *Origins of Moral Theology in the United States* (1997) develops the history of the discipline at the end of the nineteenth century and the beginning of the twentieth. My goal here was to complement my earlier historical study of American Catholic social ethics. I have always had an interest in history, and I believe it is important for any discipline to understand its historical roots and development. My historical investigation turned up the fact that there was greater pluralism at the turn of the century than has generally been recognized. I studied three moral theologians in particular. Aloysius Sabetti, a professor at the Jesuit theologate at Woodstock, used a manualist approach; Thomas Bouquillon, a Belgium priest teaching at CUA, followed a neoscholastic approach and severely criticized the manuals; John Baptist Hogan, a Sulpician priest, never wrote a systematic moral theology, but he opposed neoscholasticism and called for a more inductive and historically conscious approach.

My Père Marquette lecture, published by Marquette University Press in 1999, developed a historical overview of the development of Catholic moral theology in the United States in the twentieth century. *The Historical Development of Fundamental Moral Theology in the United States: Readings in Moral Theology No. 11*, co-edited by Dick McCormick and me in 1999, brings together selections from the primary figures in fundamental moral theology in the United States in the twentieth century.

Theological Studies, the Jesuit journal generally recognized as the best Catholic theological publication in the United States, asked me to do an article in 1997 on the Catholic identity of the three major types of Catholic institutions—Catholic charities, Catholic hospitals, and Catholic colleges and universities, an invitation I readily accepted. The Vatican had taken away my identity as a Catholic theologian, but it could not prevent others from seeing me as an expert on what constitutes Catholic identity for Catholic institutional life in the United States. To understand the problem and also point toward a solution, I again built on the distinction between catholic with a small "c" and Catholic as in the Catholic Church. The institutions in question, I argued, must be catholic with a small "c." Thus Catholic hospitals must be good hospitals, but they must also integrate what is uniquely Catholic into their institutional identity. It would be a mistake, for example, to see the Catholic identity of colleges and universities as referring only to specifically Catholic subjects and not as embracing everything that takes place within the university.

For years, friends (to say nothing of enemies) have pointed out that I had never written a systematic moral theology putting the whole thing together. Chapter 4 of this memoir has attempted to describe how I developed the various aspects of my systematic fundamental moral theology, which I finally put all together in *The Catholic Moral Tradition Today: A Synthesis* (1999).

As I've said, I had specifically moved away from questions of sexual and medical ethics in the 1970s and put much more focus on social ethics. The hierarchical Catholic teaching dealing with social ethics has been called "Catholic social teaching" and is considered to have begun with Pope Leo XIII's 1891 encyclical *Rerum novarum* and to have continued down to the present with the three social encyclicals of John Paul II. Over the years I have written articles about many of these documents. I wrote *Catholic Social Teaching, 1891–Present: A Historical, Theological, and Ethical Analysis* (2002) to study the entire corpus of Catholic social teaching in a more systematic way. It deals first with the three different types of methodology involved—theological, ethical, and ecclesial—and then analyzes, criticizes, and shows the historical development of the teaching with regard to social and political ethics.

The long papacy of John Paul II, 1978–2005, significantly influenced all aspects of Roman Catholicism, including moral theology. My writings frequently dealt with John Paul's many moral teachings. A few years ago

I decided to write an analysis and criticism of the whole corpus of his moral theology, and in 2005 Georgetown University Press published this under the title *The Moral Theology of Pope John Paul II.*

In sexual and medical issues, John Paul II's methodology, despite his emphasis on personalism, continued to use the neoscholastic natural law approach. Such an approach, as I have tried to point out, has a number of problems—physicalism, a claim to too great a certitude, and a failure to recognize historical development and historical consciousness. I am much more supportive of this pope's social teaching precisely because it usually avoids these methodological shortcomings. Despite some occasional problems, John Paul II's social teaching, which is based on the dignity and social nature of the person, has made a very positive contribution to Catholic social ethics.

With regard to my official life in the Catholic Church, as a theologian I am still a nonperson. On rare occasions some national Catholic group will ask me to speak, but these are not clerical groups, and they are definitely the exception to the rule. Catholic colleges and universities, however, do occasionally invite me to lecture, and I invariably accept. After the Vatican's action against me, colleagues asked what they could do to help. I asked them, first, not to patronize me but to continue to disagree and challenge me when they thought I was wrong. Second, I asked them to invite me to speak at Catholic colleges and universities as often as they could.

The freedom of Catholic campuses enables them to issue such invitations, usually without too much opposition. Of course, many still do not, or feel they cannot, invite me, and even when they do, problems occasionally arise. Once I was invited to give a prestigious lectureship at a Catholic university. A few weeks later the chair of the theology department called to say that the committee had no right to issue the invitation and had not gone through the proper channels; therefore, I was disinvited. When I protested, the president of the university decreed that the entire theology faculty should vote on my coming and that the university would abide by that vote. The vote was heavily in my favor, and I was warmly welcomed for my lecture, which was also quite well received.

On another occasion, I accepted an invitation to give a lecture at a Catholic university on a weekend night, but problems arose. The solution? Before the weekend night lecture began, a university official announced that this was part of the curriculum for course X. All the students from that class apparently had to attend this weekend evening lecture. But, to their credit, they did not disinvite me.

On the local level of the Dallas Catholic Church, the bishop made the policy that I am not to speak at any official or parish event. But, here again, this gives me more time to do my own theological work, and I am not put in a situation of turning down a great number of requests. In the long run, this policy is beneficial to me. I am, however, frequently invited to speak to "liberal" groups in the church such as Call to Action, the Association for Rights of Catholics in the Church, and Future Church.

More than ten years ago some liberal Catholics in Dallas, sparked by a group that I meet with for liturgy and book discussions, founded a group called the Open Window that is affiliated with the national group Call to Action. The group meets once a month for liturgy and discussion and has a speaker once a year. When the treasury is low and we cannot afford outside speakers, I fill in. The first time I spoke before this group, the Open Window tried to take out an advertisement in the diocesan newspaper, as they had done with previous speakers, but they were refused. A few years ago, however, a reporter from the diocesan paper wrote a very favorable profile of me. I bet the reporter that it would never be published. I lost the bet, but when the profile appeared, the bishop of Dallas was reprimanded by the apostolic nuncio in Washington.

I have been invited twice, however, to address the judicatory leaders of the Texas Council of Churches, the leaders of all the Christian churches in Texas. The yearly meeting, from my experience, probably attracts between twenty and forty people, but the Catholic bishops take it seriously and are far and away the largest group there. Mark Herbner, then the Lutheran bishop of Dallas and an acquaintance of mine, first invited me. I explained to Mark that this would not go over well with the Catholic bishops, but Mark told me he had already consulted with two Catholic bishops on the committee and that they enthusiastically supported having me speak. The second invitation was issued by the Catholic bishop, who was head of the organization, himself.

I have also found a good home with part of the Catholic community in Dallas. I meet with two groups once a month for eucharistic liturgy and discussion, and I generally participate in the daily eucharistic liturgy in the parish where I live. On Sundays I sometimes preside at the liturgies for the adult community at SMU Catholic Campus Ministry and in some parishes. My work life, however, is centered around the university and not around the local church. I do not see myself and am not seen as doing pastoral ministry in the local diocese. I do get together occasionally with a few local priests, but I have little direct contact with the institutional Catholic Church in Dallas. My vocation is primarily in the academic world, with its service also to the church, but I do appreciate being a part of the Catholic people of God.

I have very much enjoyed my life at SMU and in Dallas. At CUA my personal, academic, and spiritual life centered around the university itself. At SMU I have found different ways and different communities to nurture the various dimensions of my life, and I have declined offers of academic posts elsewhere. I never dreamed that I would call Dallas home, but thanks to SMU and my many friends here, that is just what Dallas has become to me.

CHAPTER 8

My Moral Theology

A T A THEOLOGY INSTITUTE many years ago, I was talking about faith as the fundamental option we make that orients our entire life and all the choices we make. My Protestant theological partner asked me why I was a Catholic. At first I was quite flustered by the question. I knew my friend well enough to know that he was not trying to give me a hard time, but the question perplexed me. Then the light dawned. He was keeping my feet on earth with a call to realism. I was a Catholic because my parents were Catholics and raised me as Catholic. Yes, this was very true. Most of us do not make this fundamental choice out of the blue. But, as I grew, I did make that faith commitment on my own. Later, when I studied Catholic theology, I came to appreciate the Catholic theological tradition deeply. This general tradition continues to make great sense to me, and I feel very much at home in it.

Positive Aspects of the Catholic Theological Tradition

The Catholic theological approach is characterized by two related and overlapping concepts—catholicity with a small "c" and mediation. Other faith traditions also recognize these two important characteristics of theology, but I would argue that they are most central to Catholicism and are what make the Catholic tradition distinctive.

Catholicity and Mediation

Catholicism with a small "c" involves universality and the all-embracing belief that faith touches every aspect of human reality. By definition, the Catholic approach is universal. The Catholic tradition, consequently, emphasizes a both-and approach rather than an either-or approach precisely because of its emphasis on catholicity with a small "c."

Mediation refers to the understanding that the divine is mediated in and through the human. There are other names for this understanding—the incarnational or the sacramental approach or the analogical imagination. The incarnational approach recognizes that the divine enters into the human in Jesus and that our faith must continue to be incarnated and inculturated in the reality in which we live. The sacramental approach emphasizes all of creation as a sign of the divine reality itself: human reality contains the shadow of God. The analogical imagination stresses that our understanding of God is based on analogies of what we find here in creation and the human.[1]

Mediation characterizes many dimensions of Catholic self-understanding. The divine is mediated in and through the human and creation. No one has ever seen God. What is God like? All we can do is take the best human images and project them onto God. Thus God is both mother and father. There is always the danger that we may attribute what we consider the best of the human to God, when in reality this may not be so. I still cringe at many of the biblical writings that refer to God as a warrior. Still, we have to rely on images from creation and the human for our understanding of God. Nature and the human show forth the image of God. A pre–Vatican II Catholic apologetic went so far as to claim that human reason by itself can prove the existence of God. The famous five ways of Aquinas began with the human, such as cause and effect, or the mover and the moved, and went back to the first cause, or unmoved mover. But I do not think one can really prove the existence of God without faith. Thus at times the Catholic tradition has claimed too much on the basis of the principle of mediation, and yet the significance of mediation characterizes the Catholic self-understanding. Think, for example, about how the Catholic tradition has used both art and music to give us a better understanding of the divine.

The sacramental emphasis in Roman Catholicism well illustrates the principle of mediation. The primary sacrament is the Eucharist—the covenant meal. What is the primary way in which human beings get together to celebrate, to show their love, to share their stories, and to support one another? The answer is the celebratory meal. Even in this era of fast food, we still have some celebratory meals, for example, family celebrations, especially on special occasions like Thanksgiving and Christmas. Likewise, we celebrate important events like marriages and funerals with a meal. The sacramental system thus takes the basic way that human beings come together to celebrate their love and community in a meal and uses that as the means by which the divine comes into contact with the human. In the whole of the sacramental system, bread and wine, water and oil, are used as signs of the reality of God's becoming present to us in community. The whole Catholic emphasis on liturgy and ritual reminds us that the divine comes to us in and through the human.

Catholic ecclesiology illustrates the divine working through the human. The church is a visible human community with human members and human officeholders. The church is not simply an invisible community in which the individual is privately and immediately related to God. Mediation means that our relationship to God exists in and through the community of the church, which is composed of human beings, with all their strengths and weaknesses. Such an understanding of the church takes the human very seriously, but it also has its problems, to which I shall return.

The Catholic concept of natural law also illustrates the principle of mediation. I referred earlier to the distinction between the theological and the philosophical aspects of the natural law question. The philosophical aspect deals with what one means by human reason and human nature. I have seen human reason and experience as quite critical of the approach found in the older Catholic moral theology and in hierarchical teaching, especially in the areas of human sexuality and medical ethics. The theological aspect of the question addresses the sources of moral wisdom and knowledge. Do moral theology and the Christian church find moral wisdom and knowledge only in Jesus Christ and in scripture, or also in human reason and experience? Do we go immediately to God and ask her how we should act? No. Natural law is based on mediation. God created human beings and all that is in the world. We can look at what God has made according to her wisdom and knowledge and use our own God-given reason and wisdom to determine how God wants it to be used.

Beginning with Thomas Aquinas, Catholic tradition has defined natural law as human reason directing us to our end in accord with our nature. This same tradition also describes the natural law as the participation of the eternal law in the rational creature. The eternal law is the plan of God's wisdom and reason, according to which God created all that is. Our human reason participates in the reason of God and can thus examine what God has made and determine how it should be used. Thus the Catholic approach is open to all human sources of wisdom and knowledge but sees these not as merely human but as ways of discerning what God the creator wants for us. God's reason and wisdom come to us not directly and immediately but indirectly and mediately through the human sources of moral wisdom and knowledge.

The Both-And Approach

The Catholic emphasis on mediation and catholicity with a small "c," and its emphasis on inclusiveness, provide the ground for a "both-and" approach. Karl Barth, the great reformed theologian of the mid-twentieth century, once said his greatest problem with Catholicism was its "and." (I have often said that my greatest problem with Catholicism is not its "and" but its "butt"!) I think the "and" is the glory of the Catholic tradition, but whatever one thinks of the "and," one must acknowledge that it is distinctive of the Catholic theological approach.[2] Dangers have arisen and abuses occurred from the Catholic emphasis on "and," but the fundamental reality of the "and" is in a way the sine qua non of Catholicism, and it is a very beautiful concept in the abstract and, very often, in the concrete and particular. The Catholic tradition emphasizes scripture and tradition, grace and works, faith and reason, Jesus and the church, and Mary and the saints. Reformation theology by contrast emphasized scripture alone, grace alone, and justification by faith alone. (Jaroslav Pelikan, the great historian of Christian doctrine, has pointed out, however, that scripture alone never really meant scripture alone in the Lutheran tradition, and this is probably true of other denominations as well.)[3]

The fundamental reality of the coupling of scripture and tradition means that we cannot simply take scripture verbatim and apply it to our own circumstances today. The Christian community in our day must understand, appropriate, live, and bear witness to scripture in light of ever-evolving historical and cultural circumstances. The Catholic understanding of the church sees the Holy Spirit as guiding the whole church, and not just the officeholders in the church, to carry on this work of bearing witness to scripture in new and changing circumstances. Properly understood, tradition is an ongoing reality that never stops. Scripture is handed over to the Christian community to be understood ever anew in light of the ongoing realities.

Without question, the Catholic understanding of scripture and tradition has sometimes been abused. Vatican II itself corrected an older understanding that saw scripture and tradition as two totally different sources of revelation. A better understanding of their relationship sees that to a certain extent tradition itself mediates the scriptural witness to the present time. Catholics have often made the common error of thinking that tradition stopped fifty years before any one of us was born. But tradition by its very nature is an ongoing process that must always be nurtured and developed. Through the gift of the Holy Spirit, the Christian community is constantly striving to understand the implications of the scriptural witness for our world.[4]

The best of the Catholic tradition has held on to both grace and works, but not without some tension. It is important to recognize both God's gift and our response. Even though God's gift is the primary reality, we cannot do away with the matter of human works. Just as sometimes more importance has been given to tradition than to scripture, so in the course of time the Catholic Church often put more emphasis on works than on grace. The Catholic approach has always been tempted by the heresy of Pelagianism or semi-Pelagianism—the heresy that we can save ourselves by our own works. In Reformation polemics, Protestants overemphasized grace and Catholics overemphasized works. But recently, in a more ecumenical approach to the question, Lutherans and Catholics have been able to come to basic agreement on the concept of justification, which is the primary theological issue involved in the grace-works relationship.[5]

The coupling of faith and reason gives rise to the various sources of moral wisdom and knowledge for theology. The Catholic tradition has accepted the medieval adage that faith and reason can never contradict each other. Reason has thus played a most significant role in Catholic theology, understood as faith seeking understanding and understanding seeking faith. But human reason is limited and affected by sin.

The insistence on the goodness of the human and the goodness of human reason means that Catholic theology must always be in dialogue with all aspects of the human. An ancient axiom, frequently repeated among Catholic theologians, insists that nothing human can be foreign to the Christian. Christian theology must be in continuous dialogue with all aspects of the human—philosophy, culture, science, and human experience in all its different forms, including the ineluctable reality of sin. This means, too, that the church at times can and should learn from dimensions of human reality that are not explicitly Christian or even theistic. Thomas Aquinas's use of Aristotle is a good example, and a reminder, of how Catholic theology must always be in dialogue with all aspects of the human. In keeping with the principle of mediation, the Catholic tradition has always seen a positive relationship between nature and grace. An older axiom insisted that grace does not destroy nature but builds on nature. Many contemporary Catholic theologians accept the positive relationship between nature and grace but reject the two-layered anthropology often found in older Catholic theology.[6] My stance sees creation and nature in relationship with four other Christian mysteries.

The recognition of both specifically Christian and all other human sources of moral wisdom and knowledge as necessary for theology allows and even authorizes the Catholic theologian to criticize the tradition itself by going outside that tradition. The Catholic tradition must always be in dialogue with all other possible sources of truth, as I argue in an early collection of essays titled *Catholic Moral Theology in Dialogue* (1972). James Gustafson, the most respected Protestant ethicist in the United States at the turn of the century, characterizes such an approach as ecumenical and refers to me as an ecumenical moral theologian par excellence.7 Ecumenical here means simply catholic with a small "c." Thus the Catholic theological tradition by definition is not narrow or exclusive but is at its best a truly living tradition.

The insistence on catholicity and mediation has important consequences for moral theology. One cannot go directly, immediately, or with perfect certitude from a scriptural quotation or a theological statement (e.g., God is love) to a particular moral conclusion (e.g., this promise is no longer morally binding). One must deal with all aspects of the human before one can come to a specific conclusion about a particular action to be performed or avoided. There is no shortcut around the hard work of understanding the human in all its complexity.

The temptation for many religious people is to move too quickly and with unwonted certainty from scripture or faith to a specific moral conclusion. Religious people have often been dismissed as do-gooders precisely because they have failed to recognize the complexity of the human and have not done the necessary work of thinking and judging before making a moral decision or pronouncement. Some time ago a Catholic group working for peace and justice asked me to evaluate a short statement it had written on multinational corporations. The first paragraph cited the Last Judgment passage in Matthew's Gospel—when I was hungry, naked, thirsty, etc. The second paragraph concluded, "Therefore, multinational corporations are immoral." I responded to the leaders of the group that if they were going to get into a debate with the president of General Motors—Thomas Aquinas Murphy—they had better know more than Matthew 25. They had better know something about economics and the whole complex reality of the human.

Catholic theology in general and moral theology in particular thus recognize both complexity and tension. Theology must embrace all the complex realities that make up the human moral order and strive to hold them in tension. I remember once at CUA walking down the hall to my classroom on the day of an exam. Two students walking in front of me did not realize that I was just behind them. I overheard one student say to the other that he had not studied very hard for the test. The other one responded that you did not have to study too hard for Charlie's tests, you just had to remember: tension and complexity!

Dangers of the Catholic Approach

The emphasis of Catholic theology on catholicity, mediation, and the both-and approach makes great sense to me, though the church has not always avoided the potential dangers inherent in this approach.

If we accept that the divine is mediated in and through the human, there is nevertheless the risk that the human becomes too closely identified with the divine. Too often Catholic teaching has attributed divine qualities to the church. Pre–Vatican II ecclesiology identified the church with the reign of God. Vatican II rightly insisted that the pilgrim church, by definition, can never be perfect and is always in need of reform. The church can never fully mediate or make present the risen Christ, and, as the people of God on pilgrimage, it will always fall short of what it is called to be. Much of the authoritarianism in the Catholic Church stems from this confusion of the divine with the human.

The same problem appears in moral theology. Natural law is understood as the participation of the eternal law in the rational creature. The eternal law is the ordering of reason or the plan of God for human beings in the world. God gives us our reason, which, by reflecting on what God has made, can determine how we should live and relate to all of creation. Divine, and likewise natural, law is seen as eternal, universal, and immutable. But even Thomas Aquinas recognized that there are different levels of natural law and that the secondary principles of natural law oblige generally but can and do admit of exceptions.[8] One cannot claim for all natural law the status and certitude of eternal law.

A proper appreciation of eschatology also helps to avoid the danger of too readily identifying the human with the divine. Eschatology reminds us that the fullness of the reign of God will come only at the end of time. Nothing in this world can ever be totally identified with the divine or the reign of God. In light of the eschaton, all human reality, including the church, will always fall short and be imperfect.

Another theological safeguard against over-identifying the human with the divine is the recognition of the role of sin in human life. The Catholic tradition, in its insistence on the goodness of the human, has sometimes failed to recognize the power of sin in the world. It is true that pre–Vatican

II catechetics often emphasized sin, but it was sin seen primarily as an act against the law of God. Perhaps in reaction to Protestant views of sin as inherently and ineluctably compromising human goodness, the Catholic tradition after the Council of Trent tended to minimize the reality of human sinfulness. I myself learned to appreciate the importance of sin by reading Protestant ethicists such as Reinhold Niebuhr and Paul Ramsey.

No observant person can deny that the temptation in the Roman Catholic Church has been to claim too much certitude with regard to its particular moral teachings. The temptation arises from the view of natural law as eternal, immutable, and unchangeable, and from the conviction that the Catholic Church alone possesses the truth of the Holy Spirit and alone is fit to teach that truth. But, especially in moral matters, the church must learn the truth before it can teach. The best proof of the somewhat tentative nature of the teaching on specific moral issues comes from the many concrete areas in which hierarchical church teaching has changed over time. I edited *Change in Official Catholic Moral Teaching: Readings in Moral Theology No. 13* (2003), precisely to make this point. The hierarchical magisterium has changed its teaching on usury, slavery, the ends of marriage, religious freedom, democracy, human rights, the right of the defendant not to incriminate himself, and capital punishment. I have appealed to catholicity and mediation, and to the pilgrim nature of the church, in my criticism of the hierarchical magisterium's claim to absolute certitude on specific moral teachings. Thus the Catholic theological tradition at its best can criticize official church teaching when it fails to recognize the implications of its own theological tradition.

An Intrinsic Morality

Connected with catholicity and mediation is the insistence in the Catholic moral tradition on an intrinsic morality. Thomas Aquinas raised the question, is something good because it is commanded or is it commanded because it is good? One might be tempted to dismiss this as the esoteric musing of a medieval theologian, but the question has important implications for moral theology, especially in a church with a strong teaching office. Aquinas and the best of the Catholic tradition opted for an intrinsic morality that insists that something is commanded because it is good. In this view, the authoritative teacher or legislator must always conform to the moral truth.[9]

The characteristic Catholic championing of natural law gives the impression that the Catholic approach is deontological, legalistic, and open to the position that the will of the teacher or the legislator determines right and wrong. Most of us think of law as depending on the will of the legislator, but this is not the Thomistic or traditional Catholic notion of law. Law, in all its different aspects—eternal, natural, ecclesiastical, and civil—is an ordering of reason.[10] Unjust human law by its very nature is no law and does not oblige in conscience. Thus Aquinas and the Catholic tradition have always acknowledged the possibility and need for what is today often called civil disobedience. Aquinas recognized that every human law is essentially imperfect precisely because the legislator cannot possibly envision all the possible circumstances of any given situation or event.[11] Most of us obey the civil law that requires that we stop at a red light. But we also acknowledge that if you are rushing your bleeding child to the emergency room, you can go through a red light if there is no traffic coming. For this reason, Aquinas insists on the virtue of *epikeia* as the crown of legal justice. The virtue of *epikeia* may break the letter of the law in order to keep the spirit of the law. Thus, to break a law that is unjust is itself a virtuous act.[12]

We see the insistence on an intrinsic morality in the distinctively Catholic issue of an official hierarchical church teaching role. Because morality is intrinsic, the hierarchical teaching office must first learn the truth before it can teach it. In the past few decades the Catholic Church has struggled with the tension between conscience and church teaching, but this is a wrongheaded opposition. There should be three terms, not two—moral truth, the hierarchical magisterium, and conscience. Both conscience and the hierarchical magisterium strive to come to moral truth, which is the sine qua non, the primary consideration that governs all else.

My approach to natural law illustrates what I mean by the broad Catholic theological methodology and tradition. I applaud the natural law tradition for its acceptance of human reason and an intrinsic morality. But I have also severely criticized the natural law approaches found in the manuals of moral theology and in the teaching of the hierarchical magisterium, by appealing to a different reading of human reason and anthropology. Natural law in the Catholic tradition has lacked historical consciousness, has occasionally identified the human with the physical structure of the act, has given more importance to human nature than to the human person, has claimed too much certitude and universality for its specific conclusions, and has failed to recognize both the social location of human reason and the effect of sin on human reason.

Thus the broad Catholic tradition, with its insistence on catholicity, mediation, both-and approaches, and dialogue, appeals to me both because it makes sense and because it provides a perspective from which to criticize more specific approaches within the tradition itself. Precisely because of this approach, the Catholic tradition is a living tradition and the work of Catholic theology involves ongoing revision.

I am personally convinced of the truth of this broad Catholic approach, but my insistence on working in the Catholic theological tradition also has a pragmatic dimension. If one disagrees with a particular church teaching, it is very helpful if one can appeal to the broader Catholic tradition. What kind of credibility would a dissenter have if she was forced to go outside the tradition to support her position? It is of the utmost importance that thoughtful, responsible, and legitimate dissent can draw on the Catholic tradition itself for support.

The Discipline of Moral Theology in the Church

My theology has involved a commitment to the discipline of Catholic moral theology as such. I have been interested in the discipline as a whole, its methodology, and its approach to particular issues. In retrospect, I am very conscious that my concern for the discipline as a whole has colored and shaped my approach to specific questions and issues.

History and Method

In my youth, I enrolled at the Alfonsiana in Rome because that institution offered more complete coverage of moral theology from different perspectives—the biblical, the patristic, the historical, the systematic, the philosophical, the pastoral—than other institutions did. My studies there both reflected and reinforced my concern for the discipline as a whole.

Obviously I have been very much interested in the history of moral theology and how the discipline has evolved over time. Both of my doctoral dissertations dealt with historical topics—invincible ignorance of natural law in Alphonsus and the prevention of conception after rape. No one has written more on the historical development of moral theology in the United States than I have. My 1982 volume *American Catholic Social Ethics* analyzed five approaches to Catholic social ethics in the twentieth century and developed my own approach in the last chapter. My *Origins of Moral Theology in the United States* (1997) described and evaluated the approaches of the three most influential moral theologians in the United States at the end of the nineteenth century and the beginning of the twentieth. My 1999 Père Marquette lecture, *Moral Theology at the End of the Century*, picked up where the earlier study left off, analyzing the historical development of Catholic moral theology in the United States in the twentieth century.

The methodology of moral theology and how it relates to particular issues has always been an important consideration for me as well. For example, in my most recent book, *The Moral Theology of Pope John Paul II*, I analyzed and criticized John Paul's theology for its methodology as well as its substance. My *Catholic Social Teaching, 1891–Present* also analyzed both methodological and substantive positions.

In 1970 I published what appears to have been the first article by a Catholic moral theologian on the new genetics and its possibilities and pitfalls for the human future, structured as a dialogue between moral theology and the new genetics. The first section developed three emphases that I argued must be present in any theological approach to the problems raised by human beings' power over their own future development—the need for a more historically conscious approach, greater understanding of the human person as existing in community with other persons, and a deeper consideration of the power human beings have over their lives and creation. The second section criticized, from the viewpoint of Catholic moral theology, three dangers in the scientific literature—utopian schemes that fail to appreciate human limitations and sinfulness, the identification of the scientific with the human, and the resulting scientific or technological imperative.[13]

My interest in the discipline of moral theology and its methodology led me to study the different methodologies employed in hierarchical Catholic sexual teaching and in hierarchical Catholic social teaching at the end of the twentieth century—two bodies of teaching between which there is clearly great tension. Conservative Catholics often agree with papal sexual teaching but have difficulty with the social teaching. Many liberal Catholics have the opposite reaction. All, however, must recognize that Catholic social teaching changed quite a bit over the course of the twentieth century, whereas there has been little or no change in official Catholic sexual teaching.

I have argued elsewhere that the changes in Catholic social teaching have involved a change in methodology as well as in content, and that this stands in contrast to hierarchical sexual teaching, where the methodology has not changed. Three shifts occurred in the methodology of official Catholic social teaching as the twentieth century unfolded—first, the shift to historical consciousness; second, the shift to the person, with an emphasis on freedom, equality, and participation of the person; and third, a shift to a relationality-responsibility ethical model. Sexual teaching, by contrast, still employs a classicist rather than a historically conscious method, emphasizes nature and natural faculties rather than the person, and follows a deontological or legal-moral model rather than a relationality-responsibility model.[14]

The Limits of My Approach

My insistence on working within the broad Catholic tradition, with an emphasis on the discipline of moral theology, gave me a firm base for what I saw as my contribution to the ongoing revision of moral theology. I have also, however, tried to be self-critical and to recognize the limits of such an approach. The primary limit is that my work has been too thin—that it has not gone into enough depth. My fundamental reference point, whether I was addressing methodology or substance, has been moral theology and how a given question or issue was related to it.

When I started teaching moral theology in the early 1960s, it was still possible to take a broad approach, one that encompassed its methodology and all its various substantive issues. The manuals of moral theology in use before Vatican II were usually two- or three-volume works by one author and dealt with the whole of moral theology.

Things have changed dramatically since then, as ever more minute specialization has become the norm, not only in theology but in virtually every academic discipline. I realized early in the 1970s that one could no longer claim to deal with all of moral theology, and I made a conscious decision to move away from medical and sexual ethics and specialize in social ethics. I was forced back into the area of sexual ethics when the Vatican investigated and then condemned my teaching in this area, but even then I did not have to do much reading in contemporary sexual ethics but simply dealt with the older positions I had developed. No Catholic moral theologian setting out today would ever attempt to deal with the whole of moral theology, for its great complexity requires specialization in a particular area.

Regardless of the mandate to specialize, I continued to consider every question from the perspective of the discipline of moral theology. My early book, *Catholic Moral Theology in Dialogue,* is a good example. The first three chapters deal with the dialogue of moral theology with humanism, with the scriptures, and with science. Since my primary perspective was moral theology, I looked at the other things only to the extent that they related to it. Likewise in my later writings, whether the subject matter was natural law, feminism, or postmodernism, I addressed it from the perspective of moral theology.

Postmodernism has played a very significant role in contemporary academic debates in general, including theological debates. The postmodernists have dispensed with the very idea of a universal human nature and rejected the Enlightenment idea of the neutral, objective, value-free knower. Extreme postmodernists see all meaning and morality as socially constructed, and are prone to a thoroughgoing relativism in all judgments, moral and otherwise. My primary argument has been with an older, absolutist Catholic approach that put too much emphasis on universality and immutability, but in my view the extreme postmodernist position, which denies the very possibility of a social ethic, is equally unacceptable. I have expressed my agreement with Catholic feminist ethicists who have employed some of the tools and rhetoric of postmodernism but still maintain some universal principles. These Catholic feminist ethicists (Barbara Andolsen, Lisa Cahill, Margaret Farley, Christine Gudorf, Patricia Jung, Anne Patrick, and others) recognize that ethics must be particular, historical, and concrete but still strive for universality and strongly support the equal personal dignity of all human beings, both female and male. In general, however, the excesses of postmodernism seem to me just as pernicious as the excesses of the kind of moral absolutism practiced all too often by the Catholic Church.

The Emphasis on Intrachurch Controversies

My primary concern being the life of the church and the discipline of moral theology, I have been heavily involved in the internal debates within Roman Catholicism. Early on, thanks to Häring, I was prepared to criticize the manuals of moral theology, with their minimalist and legalistic approach, in light of the renewal of moral theology and Vatican II. My 1966 article, for example, was the first theological article in this country to challenge the teaching that had been accepted for more than three and a half centuries that all sins against sexuality involve grave matter.[15] The Latin phrase was *in re sexuali non datur parvitas materiae:* in sexual sins there is no parvity of matter. In other words, the matter is always grave; thus, presuming sufficient knowledge and volition, sexual sins are always mortal or grave sins, regardless of whether there was perfect sexual actuation, as in "impure" thoughts or touching. According to three theologians who taught at the Gregorian University when I was a student there—Sixtus Cartechini, Josef Fuchs, and Marcellino Zalba—this teaching brooked no dissent. Fuchs, who later changed his position, quoted others to this effect in his 1959 textbook and did not explicitly claim it as his own: "Today it is customary to say that this position is so certain that the opposite is temerarious and it is not permitted to act in that way."[16] Today this whole issue is merely a quaint historical footnote, but at the time it was very significant.

Understandably, given my perspective, I have dealt with the most contentious issues in the church. As important as some of these issues are, they are not the ones that many younger people in the church face today. In a sense, I had to continue to struggle against older approaches, but some of the internal church issues I have addressed will continue to be important for the church now and in the future.

When I turned my attention to social ethics, I was interested in particular issues of justice and peace, but always from the perspective of the Catholic tradition and Catholic social teaching, the name given to the collection of documents from the papal and hierarchical magisterium. My *Catholic Social Teaching, 1891–Present* (2002) proposed a systematic analysis and criticism of this teaching. David Hollenbach called this book "the single best analysis of the modern tradition of Catholic social teaching to be found in one place. . . . It will very likely remain for many years the best overview of the tradition of modern Catholic social thought through the early 21st century."[17]

Moral Theology for a Big Church

Another aspect of catholicity also affects the life of the church and its moral theology. The church strives to be universal in geography and open to all. The Catholic Church is a big church, embracing poor and rich, female and male, all colors, races, and tribes. Above all, the church embraces both saints and sinners and is not just a small group of elite believers. We members of the church are a sinful people who in our liturgies ask mercy and forgiveness from the loving God and from one another. The church itself is a sinful church despite the presence of the Holy Spirit uniting us through Christ Jesus to the God who is our parent. The big-church aspect of catholicity coheres with the catholic emphasis that faith touches all aspects of human existence. Catholics are not called to leave the world but to live in the world and strive to make the world a better place, while always remaining mindful of our limitations.

The self-understanding of the Catholic Church stands in contrast with what has been called the sect type. The sect is a small group of believers who withdraw from the world in order to live out the radical ethic of the gospel, often understood literally. In this view, the world is irredeemably sinful, and one cannot be faithful to the gospel while living in the world. The gospel, for example, tells us to take no oaths and to turn the other cheek, but anybody who lives in this world has to take oaths and cannot always turn the other cheek. The sect approach, which came into existence in Protestantism just after the Reformation, started the practice of adult or believers' baptism because infants and children are of course unable to make a radical commitment to live out the gospel. The sects have especially emphasized the centrality of nonviolence and opposition to war.[18]

Notice the sharp differences between the sect and what has been called the church type, best illustrated by the Roman Catholic Church.[19] The church lives in the world and tries to change the world for the better, but will sometimes have to make compromises. In this sinful world in which we live, one is not always able to turn the other cheek. The church embraces sinners as well as saints. Through baptism, children are born into the church, but the church does not take the strenuous commands of the gospel and the Sermon on the Mount literally. I see the catholicity of the church through the lens of the fivefold Christian mysteries. Our world shows forth the goodness of creation, incarnation, and resurrection, but sin and the lack of eschatological fullness will always challenge us as we attempt to live out our Christian lives.

The danger for the church type is that she will err on the side of conformity to the imperfect world. We are always tempted to use God and the gospel to support our own narrow and sinful perspectives. The Catholic Church is right in its insistence on living in the world, and it has learned much from the world, but we must always look with a critical eye on our own lives, our own church, our own culture, and our own country. Unfortunately, the church conformed to the mores of the people and the culture for eighteen centuries before condemning slavery, not one of the prouder episodes in our history.[20]

It is easy to criticize others, but what about oneself? I am aware that I have failed in my writing to deal with the issue of racism in our church and in our country. One can make all kinds of excuses for such a failure. I always went out of my way to encourage and help my African American and other minority students. I was busy with other issues. I meant well. But the truth is, I never addressed the subject myself.

Only recently have I become aware of the related and deeper problem of white privilege, which is systemic in our society. I enjoy many privileges because I am white, but these privileges come at the expense of African Americans who lack them. I was aware early on of the pervasive patriarchy in our society but was blithely unaware of my own white privilege, which remained invisible to me. In a 2005 paper to a session at the Catholic Theological Society of America, I recognized my need for growing and continual conversion on three levels—the personal, the intellectual, and the spiritual, in order to become more aware of all the levels of my white privilege.

Theological Controversy within the Church

Because I see the church as a community of moral discourse, the question arises, how does one carry on theological discussion and even disagreement in the church? It is not uncommon today for members of a particular denomination to get along better with members of other churches than they do with some members of their own church, with whom they are often in disagreement on specific issues.

The sharpest debates in Catholic moral theology today, and perhaps in the life of the whole church, center on dissent and the question of absolute moral norms. For better or worse, this has been seen as a debate between liberals and conservatives. On the conservative side, Germain Grisez has developed a new natural law theory that strongly supports the church's moral teachings and frowns on any form of dissent.[21] It is safe to say that most Catholic moral theologians writing today belong to the liberal or revisionist school, which disagrees with and dissents from some teachings of the hierarchical magisterium. Some years ago Richard McCormick and others developed a theory of proportionalism in their discussion of moral norms and moral acts from the liberal perspective.[22] A strong division exists within the church today on these issues. In 1977 conservative Catholic academics left the CTSA, which they felt had become too liberal, and founded the Fellowship of Catholic Scholars, whose members subscribe to a statement of purpose that accepts and supports the teachings of the hierarchical magisterium.[23] It is unfortunate that there is no one forum in which both groups can continue to debate the issues, but the opposition between them has hardened, as the so-called culture wars in the broader society have likewise driven liberals and conservatives further apart, perhaps, than ever before.

In the area of Catholic social ethics, there are three general camps. The first and largest group basically agrees with the social positions taken by the U.S. bishops, especially in their pastoral letters in the 1980s on peace and the economy. This group, to which I belong, is critical of, but not totally opposed to, the American capitalist system. Many theologians in this group have difficulty with the hierarchical magisterium's teaching in areas of sexuality and recognize the legitimate role of dissent within the church. A smaller, neoconservative position identified with Richard John Neuhaus, Michael Novak, and George Weigel strenuously defends the papal magisterium in all areas, but in social issues it claims that the U.S. bishops and many American Catholic theologians have been too critical of capitalism and the U.S. economic system.[24] A third and still smaller group, exemplified by the Catholic Worker Movement, takes a more radical position, calling on the church to be pacifist and to act as a countercultural force in the world.[25]

In light of these deep divisions, I have tried to carry on a respectful dialogue and have found four ways of doing this. First, I have tried to avoid all polemics, name calling, and attacking other people's motives in my writings. Most scholars in the Catholic debate have similarly tried to conduct themselves with respect for the views of others.

Second, in the Readings in Moral Theology series (now fourteen volumes), the late Dick McCormick and I tried from the very beginning to ensure that all sides were represented. I have been pleased to hear from people on all sides of the debate that they appreciate this attitude. A few friends have even suggested that I have bent over too far to make sure that all sides got a fair hearing.

Third, it is important for all of us to be both self-critical and critical of our allies as well as of our opponents. After my condemnation by the Vatican, I frequently urged my colleagues in moral theology not to "go easy" on me out of sympathy or pity. Theologians must always be honest in their pursuit of truth and express clearly their agreements and disagreements with one another. Only in this way can theology be true to itself and serve the needs of the church.

Finally, I have tried to encourage social interaction on the comparatively rare occasions when people on opposite sides of a question find themselves at a meeting together. I appreciated very much Germain Grisez's suggestion, a good number of years ago, that we both present papers at a CTSA meeting on a topic that happened to be one on which we were not deeply opposed to each other. We could all do more to carry on a respectful dialogue with other Catholic theologians with whom we disagree. Our differences do not go to the core issues of faith, where we share a basic unity that should always come through in our discussions. Respectful discussion within the basic context of the unity of the community of the disciples of Jesus is especially important to someone like me who insists on the need for a big church. A big church by definition should be a community of respectful moral discourse and discussion.

I have already mentioned my strong disagreements with Cardinal O'Boyle but also my appreciation for many things he did. Later in my controversy with the CDF in the 1980s, I strongly disagreed with O'Boyle's successor, Cardinal James A. Hickey, and I even took him to court, but I never thought Hickey was an evil person. Like all of us, he had some good qualities and some negative ones. The last time I saw Hickey, who died in 2004, was at the funeral of my good friend, George Higgins. George put in his will that I was to give a eulogy at whatever funeral service might take place in Washington, and Cardinal Theodore McCarrick carried out George's request by asking me to speak at the end of the liturgy. Cardinal Hickey came into the sanctuary of the church in a wheelchair just as the liturgy started. After my eulogy, the participants spontaneously broke into applause. I came down from the lectern and went over and embraced Cardinal Hickey, who was sitting a few feet away.

Some people described this embrace as a reconciliation, but I did not see it as a reconciliation. I still totally disagreed with what Hickey did in my case and thought he was terribly wrong, but we shared a friendship with George and a common faith and hope. That is what I was celebrating with that embrace. Basically good people can make very bad decisions that hurt people and the church very deeply. One must strongly point out such injustices without, however, accusing the perpetrator of being evil. In my early years of teaching, I often invoked what I called an old ethical axiom—a big heart does not excuse a stupid ass. In all my controversies, I have tried to respect the person while disagreeing with his thoughts and actions.

Before concluding this chapter, I should call attention to a critical study of my moral theology edited in 2002 by my friends and colleagues Jim Walter, Tim O'Connell, and Tom Shannon.[26] In this book, fourteen moral theologians critically analyzed my contributions to moral theology in light of both past realities and future needs.

I have tried to argue within the Catholic tradition for the ongoing revision of moral theology. Historical circumstances have greatly influenced what I have done and tried to do. I hope I am self-critical enough to see both the strengths and weaknesses of my own approach, but readers will have to decide this for themselves.

The Development of Theology in the Past Fifty Years

A FEW YEARS AGO Tom Roberts, the editor of the *National Catholic Reporter*, asked me if I thought there were today or would be in the future any theological giants comparable to the leading theologians of the Vatican II period. In his view there were not, and he saw this as one of the problems facing the church in our times. I disagreed with him, and he asked me to write an article for the *National Catholic Reporter* on the subject.[1]

Fascinating developments have taken place in Catholic theology, and in moral theology in particular, in the past fifty years. We are all conscious of the important role played by theologians at Vatican II. Today, even students of Vatican II have difficulty recalling the roles played by individual bishops, but many recall the significant role played by a number of theologians, although theologians had neither voice nor vote in the council hall itself. At its 2004 meeting, the Catholic Theological Society of America devoted a special plenary session to commemorate the hundredth birthdays of four leading theologians of the Vatican II era—Yves Congar, Bernard Lonergan, John Courtney Murray, and Karl Rahner. It was a joyful celebration, but here too the question arose: Where are today's theological giants?

In my judgment, no such giants dominate Catholic theology today, and this will probably be the case in the future. But this is good news. The four theologians celebrated by the CTSA in 2004 were all white male celibate clerics from Europe and North America. Today we have theologians from all over the world, including many countries in Africa, Asia, and South America—and there are more of them than ever before. Theology is no longer centered in the developed Western world. We recognize the need today for particular theologies to grow out of different cultures.

Today's theologians are also much more diverse than in past generations. Married, single, and gay people are all contributing to Catholic theology today. Women, single, married, and religious, play a significant theological role in many areas of the world. No one person or small, homogenous group can ever again speak for the worldwide Catholic theological community. This is a good thing.

I am of course deeply indebted to the four theologians celebrated in 2004, along with many others. My endnotes and references indicate my heavy dependence on these people, but my younger colleagues today cite these authors much less often, and this is as it should be.

Theology today is also much more complex than it was fifty years ago. Today's theologians must specialize in one particular area and thus, it stands to reason, no one or two theologians will ever again dominate the field. I firmly believe that Catholic theology is much better off than it was fifty years ago as a result of this diversity and increase in numbers. The Catholic lay public may not know these theologians well, but their contributions are very significant to the worldwide Catholic theological endeavor.

How, precisely, has theology developed in the past fifty years? I will trace this development in light of the three publics served by theology—the church, the academy, and society at large.

The Church

Three important events have greatly affected the Catholic Church in the past fifty years—Vatican II and its aftermath, *Humanae vitae,* and the long tenure of John Paul II as bishop of Rome. These events have crucially affected theology in general and moral theology in particular.

The Profound Impact of Vatican II

Two principles guided the renewal of the Second Vatican Council (1962–65)—*ressourcement* and *aggiornamento*. *Ressourcement* called for a return to the sources of scripture and tradition, whereas *aggiornamento* called for bringing the church up to date. The tension between these two principles of renewal has become more evident with the passing of time. Adherents of both principles rejected the neoscholastic theology of the old seminary manuals. As I noted in chapter 5, the *ressourcement* camp was made up heavily of patristic scholars who generally shared the Augustinian vision of the heavenly versus the earthly city and saw the world as seriously distorted by sin.

The *aggiornamento* approach relied on a theological Thomism that embraces the fundamental goodness of the human being and human culture without denying the limitations and sinfulness that affect all human reality. The Thomists at Vatican II included the four theologians mentioned above—Congar, Lonergan, Murray, and Rahner—as well as Chenu, Küng, Schillebeeckx, and others. This group, associated especially with the international journal *Concilium,* have been generally supportive of continuing developments since Vatican II. The *ressourcement* group, identified with the international journal *Communio,* has been more critical of contemporary developments in the church and theology.

While my convictions and orientation put me in the Thomist group, there is room in my theology for *ressourcement,* which is very important for moral theology. Vatican II's decree on priestly formation insisted that the scientific exposition of moral theology "should be more thoroughly nourished by Scriptural teaching" (par. 16). Thanks to Häring and the Alfonsiana, I was already convinced of the need for a strong scriptural basis for moral theology. I published an article in 1971 on the use of scripture in moral theology,[2] and in 1984 Dick McCormick and I edited *Readings in Moral Theology No. 4: The Use of Scripture in Moral Theology.* I insist that the Catholic tradition is a living tradition as exemplified in the title of my 1992 book of essays, *The Living Tradition of Catholic Moral Theology.*

The major issue concerns just how moral theology should use scripture. I contend that scripture plays a greater role in more general areas, such as the general dispositions, virtues, and attitudes of the moral life. Likewise, the whole Christian narrative based on scripture influences and shapes both the community of the church and individual Christians in their moral outlooks. The books of scripture are historically and culturally limited, and consequently the specific issues they deal with are not always the issues we deal with today. Thus, for example, we recognize today that we cannot follow what scripture says about the role of women in society or the question of slavery. Scripture has much to say about the basic response we make to the gift of God's saving love as exemplified in the teaching on discipleship or continuing conversion. Likewise, scripture tells us much about the dispositions, attitudes, and virtues that should characterize the Christian life, such as justice, mercy, forgiveness, care for the poor and the needy, as well as the important virtues of faith, hope, and love.

Aggiornamento has played a major role in moral theology since Vatican II. The insistence that the church move into the twentieth century was a call for a more historically conscious moral theology, with a greater role for induction than was found in the classicism of the manuals of moral theology, an approach that recognizes both continuity and discontinuity within the tradition. I personally have learned much from the work of John T. Noonan Jr. about how the Catholic moral tradition has developed and changed over time.[3] Most important, in my view, is how the Catholic Church has become an outspoken advocate of democracy, human rights, and political and civil freedoms, especially religious freedom. A historically conscious methodology gives due importance to the experience of Christian people, and the Catholic tradition has consistently recognized the *sensus fidelium* as a locus or place for wisdom and knowledge.

THE SCOPE OF MORAL THEOLOGY

The pre–Vatican II manuals considered almost exclusively the question of what was sinful and did not really address the question of what constituted the full Christian life in response to God's gracious gift. Vatican II's Constitution on the Church devoted the whole of chapter 5 to "The Call of the Whole Church to Holiness." All Christians are called to holiness and perfection, and moral theology must deal with this call and with the attitudes and dispositions that flow from it. Once again, thanks to Häring, I had recognized the need for such a focus even before Vatican II.

In addition to stressing the role of scripture in moral theology, Vatican II also emphasized the role of Christology, faith, and grace in the moral life. The Pastoral Constitution on the Church in the Modern World lamented, "This split between the faith which many profess and their daily lives deserves to be counted among the more serious errors of our age" (par. 43). The natural law basis for moral theology in the manuals failed to recognize the theological dimensions of the discipline—scripture, grace, faith, and Jesus Christ. I believe the Catholic tradition is correct in its insistence on the basic goodness of the human and human reason, but too often human nature and the natural law have been seen as the basis for life in this world, while the church's understanding of grace has involved the call to follow Jesus in religious life. The vows of religious life were called the evangelical counsels; thus the gospel became not an imperative for all but counsel for a few. The pre–Vatican II approach tended to see grace as a layer above nature. Vatican II emphasized that grace should be seen as transforming all of creation.

I agreed with the basic thrust of Vatican II, but the overly optimistic spirit of the 1960s pervaded Vatican II, and I criticized the Pastoral Constitution on the Church in the Modern World for being too optimistic.[4] The pastoral constitution tended to emphasize grace, faith, and Jesus Christ as directly affecting all of human life and reality in this world, but it failed to acknowledge the role of sin and the reality that the reign of God will never take place in this world.

Since Vatican II debate has continued over the relationship between the specific moral content of Christian ethics and the moral content required of all others in the world. In my view, the gospel does not call for Christians to do actions that are specifically different from the actions required of all other human beings working for a better world. My basis for this assertion was not only the common human nature that we all share but also my understanding of grace as bringing the human to its fullness and being present and effective outside the boundaries of the specifically Christian. Recall, for example, that many non-Christians have also recognized the importance of self-sacrifice, forgiveness, and willingness to walk the extra mile. My position did not claim that Christians and others will always agree on what people should do in their daily lives, but that, in principle, Christians and non-Christians can come to the same understanding of the basic conduct that we are called to live out in the world. The specific motivations behind these actions may differ, but the outcome can be the same. This conviction argues for dialogue not only with other Christians but with people from other faith traditions and with all people of good will.[5]

Vatican II departed from past practice in implicitly recognizing a pluralist approach to theology. In keeping with this recognition, Pope John Paul II insisted that Catholic theology does not endorse one particular philosophical or theological method, even while in practice he often accepted only the neoscholastic method.[6]

THE LOCAL CHURCH

Vatican II tried to overcome the one-sidedness of the First Vatican Council (1870), with its emphasis on the universal church, by recognizing the importance of the local church and the collegiality of all bishops, who, together with the bishop of Rome, have a solicitude for the universal church. The new importance given to historical consciousness and inculturation accentuated the emphasis on the local church.

In the years since Vatican II, particular theologies have continued to develop and mature. An early and excellent example is the theology of liberation as it developed in Central and South America. Today, in every part of the globe, theology is striving to be conscious of the need for its own local color and flavor. The church's dialogue with non-Christian religions in Asia is another example. No longer is one overarching Catholic theology, centered in Europe, proposed for the whole world, and the church is much richer as a result. This trend is bound to increase in the future.

To their great credit, the U.S. bishops recognized the importance of addressing the needs of the local church through their very significant pastoral letters on peace and the economy in the 1980s. I followed those developments very closely and wrote a good number of articles analyzing and criticizing the approach of the U.S. bishops.[7]

THE ECUMENICAL DIMENSION

Vatican II's decree on ecumenism brought the Roman Catholic Church into the ecumenical dialogue. On both the international and the national levels, the Catholic Church has established official dialogue groups with most other Christian churches, and the dialogue has expanded beyond ecumenism to all aspects of interreligious dialogue.

Before Vatican II, Catholic theology usually took an adversarial stance toward Protestant theology. The manuals of moral theology were virtually silent on the work of non-Catholic theologians. Thanks to Vatican II, Catholic theology has become much more ecumenical. In fact, all mainstream Christian theology today is ecumenical.

I took the ecumenical dimension of Catholic theology to heart especially after my experience at the 1963 Harvard colloquium. I had studied Protestant theological ethics in some depth when I began teaching at CUA in 1965, and my Protestant colleagues have taught me a great deal, much of which I have incorporated into my own theological perspective.

In the United States, the Society of Christian Ethics brought Protestants and Catholics together in a formal way. I was one of the first Catholics to join the SCE in 1965 and was elected its first Catholic president in 1971. I was frequently involved in projects and discussions with such Protestant ethicists as Paul Ramsey and James M. Gustafson, although they belonged to an older generation. I spent a sabbatical in the early 1970s working on my 1973 book, *Politics, Medicine, and Christian Ethics: A Dialogue with Paul Ramsey,* in which my criticism centered on what I saw as Ramsey's overemphasis on sin in the political order and his failure to see a greater possibility for justice in the role of the state. Since Ramsey frequently agreed with the specific conclusions of Catholic theology, he was well received by many Catholics, but his methodology was quite different from the Catholic approach. Ramsey basically employed a deontological ethical model based on the biblical concepts of covenant, faithfulness, and agape that differs quite a bit from the Catholic teleological approach, with its insistence on the intrinsic dynamism of the human person seeking happiness.

Ramsey was the first Protestant invited as an observer to the 1966 convention of the CTSA, through the work of its new secretary, my friend and colleague Warren Reich. Many of the old guard in the CTSA were not happy about the presence of this Protestant interloper, but they hospitably invited him to the officers' suite for a drink after the evening session. After an hour of conversation over drinks, their somewhat stiff politeness gave way to reverence, as the old guard realized that Ramsey was almost as conservative as they on many issues. He became, literally, the center of attention, as they sat around him in a circle soliciting his opinion on various issues. At one point, Ramsey, who was obviously enjoying himself, said with a flourish to the assembled gathering, "If only my fundamentalist preacher father could see me now—a pipe in one hand, a glass of scotch in the other, and a guest of the Catholic Theological Society of America!"

No Protestant ethicist is more familiar with the Catholic tradition than James M. Gustafson. Gustafson, who has directed the doctoral dissertations of more than twenty distinguished Catholic moral theologians at Yale, Chicago, and Emory, thanks "four close friends and professional colleagues" in his 1978 *Protestant and Roman Catholic Ethics: Prospects for Rapprochement*. I was honored to be among those four, together with Richard McCormick, Paul Ramsey, and David Tracy.[8] I learned a great deal from Jim Gustafson over the years, and we appeared on many platforms together and often shared a common agenda. We both recognize the complexity and the many dimensions of a sound moral theology, and I have always appreciated both his work and his friendship.[9] Gustafson has paid me many compliments, but his work has usually had much more depth than my own. I treasure two letters he sent me—one that I received after my dissent from *Humanae vitae* and the other that he wrote when he learned that I was under investigation by the Vatican.

I have always maintained my ecumenical orientation and involvement, but I have focused more on the Catholic tradition in recent years because of the various controversies in which I was involved. Gustafson himself astutely recognized that my work is "appropriately informed by the

Roman Catholic tradition and oriented toward the life of the Roman Catholic Church—its full membership, not only its hierarchy—but is inexplicable without his decades of ecumenical dialogue."[10]

During my years in Washington in the 1960s, I team-taught courses at Wesley Theological Seminary with Harold DeWolf and with J. Philip Wogaman. Phil Wogaman and I have enjoyed a professional and personal relationship ever since we met on a bus in 1966 on our way to a meeting of the SCE at Garrett Theological Seminary in Evanston, Illinois. In the midst of my struggles with the Vatican in the 1980s, Phil was the principal author of three statements of support that came from institutions and professional organizations. Sometime later, his wife, Carolyn, was called for jury duty in Washington in a case involving CUA. She was dismissed from jury selection because she said she was prejudiced against CUA in light of what they had done to me!

One of the reasons I came to Southern Methodist University was the people involved in Christian ethics there. I have already spoken of William F. May, who became my best friend at SMU and helped introduce me to its faculty. I also team-taught with Joseph Allen in the Perkins School of Theology and have shared much with him both professionally and personally. He once said that I was much more familiar with the Protestant tradition than he and many other Protestants were with the Catholic tradition. This may have been true, in that many Protestant theologians (with the important exceptions of Gustafson and Ramsey) received their training before Catholic theology became more ecumenical. But Robin Lovin, Bill May's successor at SMU, is deeply familiar with the Catholic tradition and has been a good colleague and friend.

Humanae vitae *and the Papacy of John Paul II*

Pope Paul VI's 1968 encyclical *Humanae vitae* and its reception in the church had a deep influence on the development of Catholic theology. The encyclical raised important issues for moral theology in terms of the method and conclusions of sexual ethics, and for ecclesiology in light of dissent and the proper functioning of the teaching office of the church.

But no pope in the modern era has had a greater influence on Catholic life and thought than John Paul II. John Paul was unquestionably a remarkable human being and Christian. He was a linguist, a dramatist, a poet, a philosopher, a theologian, a church administrator, and a very effective communicator with all people, especially the young. In my judgment, his role in world affairs and in the broad area of social ethics and teaching was very positive. We all recognize the part he played in the fall of the Iron Curtain and the overthrow of communist regimes in Russia and Eastern Europe. On his many travels throughout the world and in his prolific writings, he was an outspoken defender of democracy, human rights, the needs of the poor, and peaceful solutions to intractable social and political problems. It has often been said that John Paul was a great force for change, peace, and justice in the world but something quite different "at home" in the church, a judgment with which I concur. John Paul put heavy emphasis on central authority in the church and played down the role of national and local churches. He took several major strides backward, in my view, on issues of human sexuality and the rights of women within the church, and his appointment of bishops excluded anyone who had ever spoken out in favor of change on such issues as contraception, homosexual relationships, and the ordination of women.

The relationship between the hierarchical teaching office and the role of theologians in the church will always be fraught with tension, but the Wotyja papacy too often stood in the way of theological change. In addition, John Paul II had a very sacral view of priesthood and saw it as generically different from and superior to the baptismal role of the faithful. Educated women in the West were very upset with John Paul II, none more so than Catholic women religious. Non-Catholics would be astonished if they could hear the negative thoughts and feelings of religious women toward the pope and his teachings.

My book *The Moral Theology of Pope John Paul II* (2005) criticized John Paul's moral theology as expressed in his authoritative moral teachings. This pope made significant contributions to the discipline of moral theology with his personalism, his social teaching, and his use of scripture, but he failed to appreciate that moral theology is a living tradition. In his conviction that the magisterial church teaches "the truth," he neglected the different levels of truth and certainty, and he never understood that the hierarchical magisterium must learn moral truth before it can teach it. He never faced the fact that hierarchical teaching on some specific moral issues has changed in the course of history.

From a methodological perspective, John Paul II did not appreciate the need for historical consciousness but emphasized the universal and the unchanging. Even in his use of scripture on subjects of sexuality, he claimed to find God's plan for all time in Genesis. And, needless to say, the pope admitted of no dissent from noninfallible church teaching.

The Academy

The second "public" of theology is the academy, and here too there have been significant developments over the course of the past fifty years.

The Period before 1960

The home of Catholic theology in the United States (and in most of the world) before the era ushered in by the Second Vatican Council was the seminary. I joined the CTSA in 1961, while finishing my graduate studies in Rome, and attended my first convention in Pittsburgh in 1962. The members were all priests, except for two or three religious brothers, almost all of them seminary professors. Nearly all had received a pontifical or Vatican-accredited graduate degree in theology, and the vast majority had graduated from Roman universities. These institutions were called universities but they dealt primarily with the ecclesiastical sciences—philosophy, theology, and canon law. The pontifical doctoral degree was not a Ph.D. but an STD, or *Sacrae theologiae doctor*.

Scholarship was not the primary goal of the seminary; the purpose was to train future priests for the ministry. Today we would call seminaries professional schools. Seminary professors were often very dedicated and committed people, but scholarship was not their primary concern, and very few seminary professors published scholarly articles. In the early part of the twentieth century there were two theological journals in the United

States—the *American Ecclesiastical Review* (started in 1889) and *Homiletic and Pastoral Review* (started in 1900)—but these were really pastoral journals for priests in ministry.[11] In the late 1950s the *American Ecclesiastical Review*, which had been at CUA for some time and was then under the editorship of Joseph Clifford Fenton, became a bastion of Catholic conservatism. After Fenton left, during Vatican II, the journal became much more open. I published four articles in this journal in the early 1970s, but unfortunately it ceased publishing in 1975 for financial reasons. I also published three articles in the late 1960s in the *Homiletic and Pastoral Review*, but since then this journal has moved decidedly to the right. The *Linacre Quarterly*, the journal of the Catholic Medical Association, took a similar rightward turn in the 1970s.

Although the seminary was the primary place for doing theology before Vatican II, there were some moves toward a more scholarly approach to theology. In 1939 the Dominicans started the journal the *Thomist*, which dealt with both philosophy and theology; and in 1940 the Jesuits started *Theological Studies*, which has become the premier Catholic theological journal in the United States. The CTSA came into existence in 1946. Similar developments occurred in related areas; in 1939 the new Catholic Biblical Association started publishing the *Catholic Biblical Quarterly*, and the Canon Law Society of America was established the same year, and the canon law faculty of CUA started publishing the *Jurist* in 1940.

Another development in the 1940s contributed to the more scholarly aspect of theology in the United States. For all practical purposes, the only center for doctoral studies in theology in the United States before 1960 was the Catholic University of America. A significant exception was a doctoral program begun in 1943 at St. Mary's College in South Bend, Indiana, which in its existence conferred degrees on twenty-five women, most of them nuns.[12] CUA conferred its first S.T.D. in 1895, but between then and 1938 only about fifty doctorates were given in all areas of theology, including scripture. During this time, as noted above, the vast majority of seminary professors earned their doctoral degrees from the pontifical universities in Rome. But things changed dramatically after 1939 because of World War II. From 1940 to 1950 CUA conferred more than 100 doctorates in theology, which showed that it was becoming a center for scholarly work. In moral theology in particular, Francis Connell directed many significant dissertations of a casuistic nature, all of which were published.[13] At the same time, the Jesuits John C. Ford and Gerald Kelly, writing in *Theological Studies,* became leading moral theologians in the United States, thus contributing to a greater professionalization of the discipline.

But what about the many Catholic colleges in the period before the 1960s? In general, Catholic higher education in those days did not see itself in the mainstream of secular American higher education and in fact tended to see itself primarily in opposition. In his 1949 inaugural address as the thirty-fifth president of Georgetown University, Father Hunter Guthrie attacked secular higher education in the United States in no uncertain terms. His approach was anti-intellectual, his tone arrogant, and his rhetoric biting. "The lowliest child who has completed his penny catechism," said Guthrie, "knows more about the full meaning of this . . . universe than the assembled faculty of some of our universities." The secular university too often resorted "to a fatuous liberalism, which ranges all the way from polite skepticism to the shoddy 'science' of statistics." The Catholic university, on the contrary, emphasized the religious, moral, and intellectual virtues by which human beings can achieve their full moral stature within the limits of human nature.[14] Few would have put the matter so strongly, but Guthrie's speech suggests the extent to which mainstream Catholic higher education saw itself as set apart.

Every Catholic college required religion or theology courses for all students, but these courses were primarily catechetical and were seen as an extension of the pastoral arm of the church. They were not looked upon even by the teachers themselves as academic courses. Very often a teacher's status as a vowed religious or an ordained priest was the only qualification needed for teaching theology or religion in these institutions. However, some attempts to fashion a distinctive Catholic college theology began at CUA early in the twentieth century, and by midcentury the Dominicans and Jesuits were developing ways of teaching college theology.[15] Catholic higher education at this time emphasized neoscholastic philosophy, around which the Catholic college curriculum was centered.

In the 1950s the winds of change began to be felt in Catholic higher education. The growth of Catholic colleges after World War II meant that more laypeople—among them many who had received their doctorates at secular universities—were teaching in Catholic colleges. But such laity were still considered second-class citizens in Catholic higher education until the 1960s.[16] In 1955 John Tracy Ellis, the renowned church historian at CUA, wrote his famous article decrying the failure of American Catholics to contribute to the intellectual life of our country.[17] This article and the debate it occasioned began to have their effect. The 1950s also witnessed some debate about the nature of teaching theology in Catholic colleges. The first meeting of what was then called the Society of Catholic College Teachers of Sacred Doctrine was held in Washington in 1955. The purpose of this society (since 1967 known as the College Theology Society) was to improve the quality of undergraduate teaching in Catholic colleges, for it was universally recognized that such courses were not truly academic but doctrinal.[18]

Change after 1960

The understanding of theology as an academic discipline began to change dramatically in the 1960s and has continued to evolve since then. The changes brought about by Vatican II made theology a very appealing field of study for many Catholics. In addition, the changed understanding of the role of the church in the modern world gave rise to greater professionalization and a greater acceptance of the norms governing secular higher education in this country. The ethos of theology courses in Catholic colleges and universities moved from a pastoral and catechetical orientation to a truly academic one. This involved the need for professors of theology to have good academic degrees, and many Catholic universities responded very creatively to this need in the 1960s. Gerard Sloyan, in the department of religious education at CUA, and Bernard Cooke at Marquette were significant leaders in developing such doctoral programs.[19] Notre Dame and Fordham also developed top-notch theological doctoral programs. Today many Catholic universities offer doctoral programs in theology.

Since the 1960s the academic aspect of Catholic theology has continued to intensify. Professors of theology, like all university professors, are expected to publish as well as teach. The number of books and articles published in Catholic theology today far exceeds the number published fifty years ago. Both the number and the quality of professional Catholic theologians have thus increased dramatically in the last thirty years.

This situation contrasts starkly with what I experienced when I first started teaching theology in a Catholic seminary in 1961, where I had virtually no institutional support or encouragement for writing and publishing. But I remain grateful to some of my professors in Rome and to my colleagues at St. Bernard's Seminary in Rochester, who encouraged me to do research and helped me do it.

I have also tried in my own small way to encourage scholarly publication and research in theology. As an officer of the CTSA and the SCE in the late 1960s and early 1970s, I introduced discussion sessions in which we reflected critically on new books published by members of the society. When I introduced this change at the SCE, one of my more pessimistic and curmudgeonly colleagues commented that we would be lucky to have two or three books to discuss at each annual convention. At the 2005 convention, we discussed twenty-nine books, but we ran out of time and rooms to discuss all the books that had been published in the previous year. I regret that the CTSA dropped these seminars after a while, but perhaps they are no longer necessary.

THE DIVERSITY OF THEOLOGIANS

The movement of Catholic theology from the seminary to colleges and universities has been an extremely positive development, not least because it has encouraged diversity among theologians. The most startling change concerns the number and quality of women theologians working in the academy. When the Second Vatican Council concluded, there were no women at CTSA and only one African American priest, Joseph Nearon, who later started the Institute for Black Catholic Studies at Xavier University in New Orleans.

At the 1966 meeting of the CTSA in Providence, Rhode Island, I happened to be standing near the registration desk as we were preparing to go into the annual banquet, and I could not help overhearing a very animated conversation between the secretary of the society and a woman. The secretary was telling this woman that she could not attend the banquet and that if she persisted he would have to call the police and have her thrown out. I introduced myself to this woman and learned that she was Elizabeth Farians and a teacher of theology at Sacred Heart University in Bridge-port, Connecticut. She told me she had joined the CTSA in 1965 and had come just to attend the banquet. I telephoned Eamon Carroll, the president of the CTSA and a colleague of mine at CUA, and told him that he had to come down immediately to remedy this injustice; Eamon, to his credit, overruled the secretary. Elizabeth thus became the first woman to attend a meeting of the CTSA. This incident made me quite conscious of the difficult road that women faced in entering the field of Catholic theology, and I was grateful for the lesson. Ever since, I have tried to be very supportive of the role of women in Catholic theology.

At CTSA meetings my roommate Tom Dailey and I (Tom was my best friend in the theological community) would invite people up to the room for drinks in the evening. We made a special point of inviting new women members of the society. One of the largest groups of new women theologians in the CTSA came from St. Michael's College in Toronto. The first wave of woman Catholic theologians was primarily religious, but soon many single and married laypeople also joined their ranks.

African American Catholic theology has developed more slowly. I have already mentioned my own failure to deal with racism. Now there exists a small and, one hopes, growing number of people—more women than men—doing Catholic theology from an African American perspective. We all need to do more to encourage this development. The few African American Catholic theologians often carry intolerable burdens because they are asked by so many constituencies to do so many things.

Latino/a and Hispanic Catholic theologians are more numerous. The CTSA, especially under the leadership of Anne Patrick, has promoted the importance of these voices in American Catholic theology today. The Academy of Catholic Hispanic Theologians of the United States has been in existence for more than fifteen years. In 1993 this group started publishing a quarterly journal called the *Journal of Hispanic-Latino Theology*. The growing need for diverse competencies in the academy has also provided teaching opportunities for a growing number of Latino/a and Hispanic theologians in this country.

The American academy has thus played a very significant role in the quality, quantity, and diversity of Catholic theologians. Since the United States has well over 200 Catholic colleges and universities, the number of theologians in the United States is far greater than in any other country in the world. Although Asia, Africa, and South America have fewer academic institutions, the challenges facing Catholicism and Christianity on these continents, plus the need for local and inculturated theology, have increased the number of well-qualified Catholic theologians in these areas.

The Effects of Academic Professionalization

What are the practical consequences of increased academic influence on Catholic theology? First, the number of published theologians has increased exponentially. Second, newly minted Ph.D.s today are much better trained than we were in my day. When I read their work or hear them lecture, I am amazed at the breadth and depth of their knowledge. Scholarly publishing in theology in general and in moral theology in particular has increased a hundredfold. Many new scholarly journals have come into existence. More books are published in moral theology each year. When I return from professional meetings of such groups as the CTSA and SCE, I am humbled and even a bit depressed. There are so many important new articles and books in my own field that I cannot possibly keep up with them. It seems that every year I fall further and further behind.

As noted earlier, the growing breadth of the field means that theologians must specialize comparatively narrowly. Even in the area of bioethics, many moral theologians feel the need to specialize in a particular area, such as genetics. What a change from the 1960s! Most people would agree that Richard McCormick and I were the dominant figures in revisionist Catholic moral theology in this country from the mid-1960s through the 1970s. But since then there has been an explosion of interest and work in this area.

The earlier orientation of moral theology toward Rome has also changed. After Vatican II and *Humanae vitae,* moral theologians in Rome—especially Bernard Häring and Josef Fuchs—still played a significant role; both of these men were under Vatican surveillance and investigation, but they continued to provide leadership for Catholic moral theology throughout the world. Häring and Fuchs have had no real successors in Rome, primarily because the authoritative atmosphere of Rome has made it impossible for theologians to explicitly and publicly dissent from hierarchical church teaching. As a result, the development of Catholic moral theology has shifted from Rome to other parts of the globe.

When I was beginning in this work, there were few enough moral theologians in the world that most of us knew one another, even when this meant crossing language barriers. I have much less contact today with moral theologians in other countries, in part because the older generation has died (e.g., Louis Janssens in Leuven), but even more because today so much is written in English that I do not have time to read as much in foreign languages.

My younger colleagues, who were trained for the most part in the United States, and who also of course have ready access to a huge literature available in English, have even less contact with Catholic moral theologians abroad, and sometimes none at all. This is not surprising, yet I find it somewhat lamentable, as I would hate to see the discipline lose its universal character. James Keenan of Boston College has worked to bring about greater dialogue between Catholic moral theologians in the United States and others around the world.[20] No longer can our dialogue be Eurocentric. It will not be long before Europe and the United States will cease to be the center of world Catholicism. Catholic theologians need to be in dialogue beyond national and linguistic boundaries, and this kind of communication has been greatly facilitated by the internet.

Academic Freedom

Ever since the strike at CUA in 1967, I have been a strong defender of academic freedom for Catholic theology both in practice and in theory. In the late 1980s, after my third controversy at CUA involving academic freedom, I wrote a monograph on the subject—*Catholic Higher Education, Theology, and Academic Freedom*. Academic freedom means that no authority outside the academy can intervene in the hiring, promoting, and dismissal of faculty. A tenured professor, according to the norms of the AAUP, which are generally accepted in American higher education, can be dismissed only for cause, including incompetency, after a due process hearing by faculty peers, with a final decision by the governing board of the institution on the basis of the record of the hearing.

Until the 1960s Catholic colleges and universities strongly opposed academic freedom. In the late '60s, spurred on by Vatican II, the professionalization of higher education, and fears of losing government funding, Catholic higher education in general came to accept and support academic freedom. But the Vatican was always suspicious and did what it could to oppose academic freedom in American Catholic universities. In spite of practical developments "on the ground," no one had made the theoretical case for why the Catholic Church should accept academic freedom in its institutions of learning, and especially in the teaching of theology. I developed what I called a pragmatic argument for academic freedom, but this was actually a misnomer, for my argument was one of principle, based on the common good.

From my earliest writings, I have opposed the absolutizing of freedom or conscience as the only criterion in ethics. Why should academics have tenure and freedom to say what they think, when practically no other class of workers does? The secular answer is: Because this promotes the common good. Society benefits when professors enjoy academic freedom and when no force external to the academy can make decisions about what takes place within its walls, especially with regard to the hiring and firing of faculty. So, too, the common good of the church justifies academic freedom, even in the area of theology.

The Roman Catholic tradition is a living tradition and has consistently recognized the need for a theology that is both creative and faithful. Academic freedom guarantees to theology such a creative role, free from any direct church control. At the same time, I have always insisted that a Roman Catholic theologian must demonstrate competence, which means, among other things, that he or she respect the proper role of the hierarchical magisterium. Ultimate judgments about fitness to teach must be made first by peers and then by the trustees of the institution on the basis of the earlier record, and not by any external source. But is it not possible that academicians will make mistakes, and even mislead the people of the church? The answer is that their mistakes can be contained. The hierarchical magisterium itself always has the right to point out what it thinks are errors and ambiguities in the work of a theologian, but it cannot hire or fire anybody in the academy. Especially in the United States, the general public recognizes that academics often make mistakes in their search for the truth, but the public values their role highly enough to allow this to happen.

A free press in the Catholic Church is a good analogy for a free academy. Before Vatican II, the official national Catholic press in this country was controlled by the hierarchical church. Since Vatican II, the Catholic News Service has gradually become free from hierarchical control. Freedom of the press can create some problems in the short term, but in the long run it is for the good of the church. In the same way, a free academy is also ultimately for the good of the church. The Vatican today finds it difficult to accept complete academic freedom because the hierarchy is very fearful of what many theologians in the church are saying. The church's requirement that anyone teaching Catholic theology in a Catholic university must have a mandate from the church, and its power to remove that mandate from a qualified academic, violates academic freedom. Even where the mandate is not enforced, this church law is still on the books.[21]

Larry Witham, religion reporter for the *Washington Times,* wrote a book on my court case that provides a helpful summary of the trial but unfortunately oversimplifies the whole issue at stake as one of freedom versus authority.[22] This simplistic framing of the matter distorts our understanding of the issue in terms of both Catholic theology and academic freedom.

Society

The third public served by theology is the broader human society. By its very nature, the social dimension of theology is much more diffuse than the ecclesial and academic. As theology has become more historically conscious and culturally sensitive since Vatican II, its relationship to particular cultures and societies has become more important. Local and particular theologies are now developing in all parts of the world. Today people speak of African and Asian theologies, but in the future we will recognize that these general approaches must be broken down into even more particular theologies relating to particular cultures and societies within Africa and Asia.

Catholicism in America

It is beyond the scope of this book to describe how Catholic theology in general has been in dialogue with American culture and society. I can only reflect on how I have dealt with this relationship. The stance that I developed in 1970 provides the perspective from which moral theology and the Christian in general look at the world in terms of the fivefold Christian mysteries of creation, sin, incarnation, redemption, and resurrection destiny. This stance was derived not only from the gospel and from theological premises but also from my perception of what was happening and what should happen in society and culture. My 1982 book on American Catholic social ethics used as a frame of reference the question that had faced the Catholic Church in the United States from its very beginning: Could one be both Catholic and American? My answer to that question avoided the extremes of seeing Catholicism as in complete harmony with the American ethos or in complete opposition to it. The church has both learned from American culture and also been critical of it, and it is important that this tension be maintained.

The immigrant Catholic Church in the United States in the nineteenth and early twentieth centuries went out of its way to prove to other Americans that Catholics were just as American as they were. After World War II, when the United States and the Vatican were the leading opponents of communism in the world, the tendency to identify U.S. Catholicism with U.S. culture and society became even stronger.

The great temptation for any believer or any religious group is to use God for one's own purposes. Too often the United States, following its

Puritan founders, has seen the United States as God's chosen people and as having a God-given leadership role in the world. We see this tendency today as strongly as ever before. But American Catholics have often made the same mistake. We can never identify our own finite perspective totally with God's omnipotence. The gospel perspective always stands in judgment over every finite human perspective.

On the other hand, Catholicism has learned and can learn from American culture. Catholicism traditionally has failed to give enough importance to human freedom and the active participation of the citizen in government. Without glossing over the very real dangers inherent in the American notion of freedom, which stresses freedom from rather than freedom for, all can agree that the Catholic Church has come to appreciate the importance of individual freedoms, and that the United States has been one of its teachers in this respect. The Catholic Church was slow to embrace human rights and democracy because of its fear of rampant individualism and the sins that it breeds. The procedures of canon law still fail to protect adequately the rights of the accused, and this stands in stark contrast to the procedures of American law. The church universal should learn from the more open style of writing church documents that the U.S. bishops used in their pastoral letters on peace and the economy, a style in keeping with the larger American ideal of open processes.

This is not to say that the church has been in the wrong to mistrust unbridled individualism—far from it. Catholicism, based on its biblical foundation and also borrowing from Aristotle, has traditionally insisted on the solidarity of all human beings; indeed, the church is in its very essence a corporate body. And the church is right to criticize the abuses that flow from privileging individual rights and liberties at the expense of the common good.

In political matters, Catholic social teaching steers a middle course between the two extremes of minimal government intrusion into people's lives (the individualist ideal) and maximum government control over people's lives (collectivism). The church recognizes the need for intermediate institutions between the individual and government. In the economic arena, Catholic teaching calls for significant limits on the capitalist system to ensure that all human beings are guaranteed a minimally decent human existence. The church must teach and live the preferential option for the poor. One reason why I moved away from sexual and medical ethics into the study of social ethics in the 1970s was that I had realized that sexual ethics was often a middle-class agenda. Social ethics addresses issues that have a broader impact and that concern not only or primarily the middle class but also the working class and the poor.

Other Social Issues

While, as I have said, I regret that I never directly addressed the issue of racism or white privilege in this country, I am quite proud of my essay on the community organizing approach of Saul Alinsky, which had been adopted by many Catholic social activists.[23] Saul Alinsky, an agnostic Jew, had been organizing poor people in Chicago in the 1950s with strong support from the Catholic community and Father Jack Egan. In 1970 the U.S. bishops, following Alinsky's model, established the Campaign for Human Development in response to the urban riots of the 1960s. This project funded a good number of community organizations that helped poor people work for their own betterment.

Until this time, Catholic theology had ignored what was the most significant development in Catholic social practice in the United States. I was very impressed by the Alinsky approach and how it fit in with the Catholic theological tradition, but I also argued that we need to deal with substantive issues and institutional structures, not just with tactics and strategies, including the conflictual ones that Alinsky emphasized. Alinsky's approach to community organizing impressed upon me the important role that solidarity and its challenge to entrenched power must play in bringing about social change, even though these things can never be absolutized. Official Catholic social teaching has not adequately recognized the importance of power and conflict to social reform.

In 1979 I argued that the Catholic understanding of distributive justice calls for the right of all citizens to an adequate level of healthcare.[24] A later essay maintained that the Catholic tradition of justice calls for a progressive taxation system. Although the U.S. income tax is somewhat progressive, more and more tax revenue in recent years comes from regressive taxes such as the sales tax. A more communitarian, socially responsible approach recognizes that those who have more should pay more, and proportionally more, to support the common good.[25] In all my writings on social ethics, I have pointed out that the common good is the cornerstone of Catholic social teaching, and this is reflected in the church's teaching documents.[26]

I have often written on the development of the church's social teaching on human rights.[27] In the late nineteenth and early twentieth centuries, the church was wary of the language of individual rights, though papal teaching began to recognize some rights, such as the rights of workers, in the late nineteenth century. Only in 1963, however, did John XXIII pen the first thorough exposition of the concept of human rights in Catholic social thought, in his encyclical *Pacem in terris* (pars. 11–38). *Pacem in terris* recognizes duties as well as rights and insists on two kinds of rights—civil and political rights, including freedom of religion, speech, press, and association, and economic and social rights, including food, clothing, shelter, education, and healthcare. The United States, with its individualistic perspective, has been slow to legislate social and economic rights.

In the 1980s I wrote a number of essays analyzing the two pastoral letters of the U.S. Catholic bishops on peace and war and the economy.[28] The U.S. bishops deserve great credit for these two letters, which made a real contribution to public debate on these issues. My most significant contribution to this debate was to point out the continuity and discontinuity in the various drafts of the pastoral letter on peace and war. The drafting committee of this letter agreed early on that they would not call for total unilateral nuclear disarmament, advocating instead bilateral disarmament by the United States and the USSR. Pope John Paul II also took this position in his 1982 address to the United Nations.

Earlier drafts of the pastoral letter, especially the second draft, built on the congressional testimony of Cardinal John Krol in 1979 and maintained that deterrence through the threatened use of nuclear weapons aimed at population centers (as distinguished from nuclear weapons aimed at military targets) was an acceptable option. But in their 1976 pastoral letter, "To Live in Christ Jesus," the bishops claimed that not only was it wrong to attack population centers with nuclear weapons, it was also wrong to threaten such attacks as part of a deterrence policy. Their argument was based on the principle that one cannot threaten to do what is morally wrong to do. Krol's testimony thus was inconsistent with the 1976 pastoral letter.

How could the bishops still maintain the position of not demanding total unilateral nuclear disarmament if they accepted this principle that one cannot threaten to do what is morally wrong to do? The final approach was both elaborate and subtle. The bishops condemned the use of countercity or counterpopulation weapons. They also condemned the first use of counterforce nuclear weapons, but they did not absolutely condemn retaliatory second use of counterforce nuclear weapons if the other side had already used them. In the words of Bryan Hehir, the staff person working on the document, there was a centimeter of ambiguity about the use of retaliatory, second-strike counterforce nuclear weapons. The centimeter of ambiguity made it possible to hold onto some limited deterrence. Countercity or counterpopulation deterrence is wrong, but counterforce deterrence is not necessarily wrong because there might possibly be a legitimate use of counterforce weapons.

The reasoning was so complex and subtle that the body of bishops as a whole did not understand it. At the discussion of the final draft by all the bishops in 1983, a large majority passed an amendment proposed by Archbishop John Quinn that read, "Nevertheless there must be no misunderstanding of our opposition on moral grounds to any use of nuclear weapons." Accepting such an amendment logically meant that the document had to support total unilateral nuclear disarmament. Later in the meeting, at the strong urging of Cardinal Bernardin, the chair of the drafting committee, the bishops reversed themselves on this amendment. The centimeter of ambiguity about the use of retaliatory second-strike counterforce nuclear weapons was necessary to preserve the conditional acceptance of some deterrence based on such weapons.

The most significant aspect of the two pastoral letters was the process through which they were written. The bishops insisted on a broad consultation and a public discussion of their drafts. We in the Catholic Church would be much better off if our major church documents followed such a public drafting process. Unfortunately, Vatican documents are drafted in secret, usually by a small and unknown group of men.

Church and Politics

Ever since my book on Paul Ramsey in the early 1970s, I have addressed the involvement of churches in general, and the Roman Catholic Church in particular, in the political order, an issue closely related to the relationship between morality and law, discussed above. In *The Church and Morality* (1993), I presented my most concentrated discussion of this issue, proposing five general roles for the church in politics—to teach and to inspire the faithful to work for a more just society; to provide for those in need; to empower and enable others through such means as sponsoring community organizations; to advocate for the poor and the needy; and to serve as a model in its own constitution and actions for the broader society.

Should the church, as a whole or through its leaders, take stands on particular social issues such as a specific war, capital punishment, abortion law, or the best way to structure social security? At times the church and its leaders can and should take such stands, provided they study the question from every angle and recognize that there is room for disagreement within the church. Only then is it possible to maintain the tension between the role of leadership, the freedom of the believer, and the unity of the church.

Ordinarily, Christians and their leaders should not support a particular political candidate because there is bound to be disagreement among church members on the candidate's record and position on various issues. Likewise, the church should never identify itself and its gospel message too closely with one individual. In extreme cases (e.g., Hitler's Germany, apartheid in South Africa), the church and its leaders can properly come out against a particular candidate when that person holds a position that is abhorrent to Christian or Catholic beliefs.

How does the First Amendment's separation of church and state affect the involvement of the church and its leaders in working for a better and more just human society? When the public welfare is at stake, the church should be able to advocate on its behalf. Legislation and public policy should be based on what is in the interest of public order, and that includes social justice, public peace, and public morality. In a pluralistic society, churches have no right to advocate for things, such as prayer in public schools, that are not a matter of public order. Because the ultimate criterion is the substance proposed (a matter of public order), the motivation behind the position should not be the determining factor. Thus one could oppose capital punishment or euthanasia as a Buddhist, a Hindu, a Muslim, a Christian, an atheist, or a utilitarian. In a pluralistic society, religious people, if they are to succeed in their aims, must convince others, and therefore their arguments need to have broad appeal.

CHAPTER

10

My Relationship to the Catholic Church

A FTER THE VATICAN CONDEMNED ME in 1986, many people asked why I stayed in the Catholic Church. I was certainly hurt by the Vatican's action. My primary role in the church had always been as a moral theologian, and in many ways this was my vocation. But now I stood condemned as a Catholic theologian by the Congregation for the Doctrine of the Faith and the pope himself.

In recent years, this question has taken a slightly different form: "Why stay in the church when there seems to be no hope for the church?" We who rejoiced in the reforms of Vatican II have seen the promise and bright future of that time wither away.

As it enters the new millennium and moves on from the long papacy of John Paul II, the Roman Catholic Church is pervaded by an authoritarianism and centralization that seem to go against the Vatican II reforms. It is unlikely that Pope Benedict XVI will change this course, and the first months of his papacy suggest a continuation of the same. To be appointed a bishop in the church today, a candidate must never have uttered a word against any existing papal teaching. The centralization of church authority may be seen in a number of ways, including the Vatican's choosing to decide the smallest matters of liturgical language and custom for specific language groups and countries.

Many theologians throughout the world have been condemned in one way or another. No teaching field has felt this chilling effect more deeply than moral and pastoral theology. The list of the condemned is long and distinguished—Ambrogio Valsecchi, Stephan Pfürtner, Bernard Häring, Josef Fuchs, Anthony Kosnik, John McNeill, André Guindon, René Simon, Marciano Vidal, Sean Fagan, Charles Curran. And many more moral theologians have suffered at the hands of church authority or have been investigated privately. My good friend Tom Dailey was removed from two different seminaries.

Moral theology has been a neuralgic area precisely because moral theologians deal with the practical issues that people face in their daily lives. As we know, most of these contentious issues involve sexuality—contraception, sterilization, divorce, homosexuality, and the use of reproductive technologies.[1] On the whole, Catholic moral theologians have been dedicated members of the church, striving to be faithful both to the gospel teaching and to the needs of the times. When they have dissented from church authority, their dissent has involved specific moral issues, not the central core of Catholic faith and belief.

The tensions felt by Catholic moral and pastoral theologians are also felt by practically everyone engaged in full-time ministry in the church. People ministering in the field often feel torn between the official teaching of the church and the needs of the people to whom they minister. Many of them try to avoid or sidestep contentious issues as much as they can, but this is not always possible.

In my opinion, women in the Catholic Church face more obstacles and frustrations than any other group. The hierarchical church will not even consider the ordination of women. Even apart from ordination, women are barred from any true leadership roles in the church. Most of the female graduate students I taught at CUA have suffered at least one crisis of faith somewhere along the line. What they experience in the church is not at all what the church professes to stand for and believe. I can readily appreciate why some Catholic women have left the church, but I admire and support as much as I can those who have remained, working for change in spite of the obstacles they face.

The recent pedophilia scandals that have rocked the church have reminded us that we are a sinful church. The cries of the poor innocent victims can be heard all over the globe. The priests and ministers who took advantage of these innocent and vulnerable children in order to satisfy their own sexual desires are rightly condemned, but many people see the behavior of their bishops as even more unconscionable. These men put institutional survival and "the good name of the church" above the needs of the innocent victims. This issue has deeply upset not only Catholics but people of conscience the world over.

Yet there are many good things that the church is doing today, and we must take pains not to forget these things. Still, many of us who lived through the changes of Vatican II face the contemporary church with disappointment, anger, and frustration. Why should one stay in the church? Is there any hope for this church? Let me try to give my own answers to these questions.

Theological Aspects

As I have said, I feel very much at home working within the parameters of the Catholic theological tradition and would not feel comfortable in any other tradition. My problems are with particular church teachings, not with its core dogma or broad theological approach. I strongly disagree with those who charge that this is cafeteria Catholicism—in which one selects what one likes and disregards the rest. One cannot deny the core teachings of Roman Catholicism and still be called a Catholic. But those who uphold the core beliefs of a benevolent God, creation, redemption, sanctification, the Trinity, the sacramental system, the role of overseers or bishops in the church, and the role of the bishop of Rome can consider themselves good Catholics even when they disagree with a specific noninfallible church teaching. The Nicene Creed is one succinct expression of our faith that Catholics recite regularly, which professes that we are one in faith with other Christians down through the centuries and, in the present, with other believers throughout the world.

I have always framed my understanding of legitimate dissent in terms of noninfallible—i.e., fallible—church teachings. The CDF and the pope have tried in the past few decades to respond to dissenters like myself by extending infallibility to more church teachings. In addition, the hierarchical magisterium has been unwilling to admit the somewhat provisional nature of all noninfallible teaching. Such approaches illustrate once again the recent growing authoritarianism in the Catholic Church today.

The distinction between infallible and noninfallible teaching may not be the best way to approach the issue of dissent. This distinction was not the primary way of viewing the core-periphery debate until the twentieth century. It does tend to frame the issue legally and canonically rather than doctrinally. At the same time, however, it is both a useful and an accurate way to distinguish different levels of Catholic teaching.

In fairness, there has also been debate about which beliefs are part of the core of Catholicism and which are not. Pope John Paul II, for example, claimed that women's exclusion from the ordained priesthood is a matter of divine law issued by Jesus himself and thus cannot be changed by any human being, not even the pope.[2] In my view (and that of many others), this is extending divine law too far. In fact, Jesus did not ordain any priests in the sense that we use the term today. Although there were no women among the group we call the apostles, the New Testament mentions significant women leaders in the early church. That the group we call the twelve apostles included no women is a simple matter of the prevailing social mores of the time. In the era of Jesus women did not play leadership roles in society in general and hence were not given leadership roles in the church. The issue is primarily sociological rather than a matter of divine law. If women today should be barred from ordained priesthood because there were no women among the twelve apostles, then so should non-Semites, because all the apostles were Jews.

The Pilgrim Church

My book *The Moral Theology of Pope John Paul II* (2005) claims that John Paul II took a triumphalistic view of the church, in which the church is the kingdom of God and the bride of Christ, holy and without spot. This was the view promulgated in the ecclesiology I studied in Rome in the 1950s. Vatican II overturned it, insisting that the church is a pilgrim church—not the reign of God itself but a sign of the reign of God in this world. Vatican II recognized the importance of the axiom often used in the churches of the Reformation—*Ecclesia semper reformanda*—the church is always in need of reform.

I first experienced the pilgrim reality of the church when I was a seminarian in Rome in the 1950s and saw the human element at work in the church all too clearly. As in any institutional bureaucracy, there was infighting, ambition, bickering, and rumors galore. It was not hard to see that some clerics came to Rome to seek promotion and further their own careers. I remember laughing almost uncontrollably at the beginning of the 1963 movie *The Cardinal,* based on the novel by Henry Morton Robinson. The opening credits rolled over a background in which an impeccably dressed Roman cleric in cassock, coat, and Roman hat climbed the various well-known stairs of the city. This seemed to me a marvelous illustration of the ambitious cleric trying to climb the ecclesiastical ladder.

I was quite taken with an early essay by Karl Rahner on the sinful church,[3] which helped me to see that the sinfulness of the church was of a piece with the sinfulness of all human beings. The Catholic tradition makes a well-known distinction between mortal sin and venial sin. Mortal sin breaks our relationship with God, but we are all, without exception, guilty of venial sin. We all fall short and never live out fully what we are called to be in our baptism. So too the church. The Holy Spirit animates the church, but the church always falls, and will always fall, short.

John Paul II did not accept the concept of the sinful church. To his credit, he apologized for more sins of members of the church throughout history than any pope ever had. But he could not say that the church itself sinned—only its members. But if the church is the people of God, including the hierarchy, then the church itself is sinful.[4] It is inherent in the nature of the pilgrim church that it will never fully respond to the presence of the Holy Spirit.

Historical Illustrations of Tensions and Disputes

Too many Christians see the early church as a utopia—a time when everything was perfect and there were no disputes or disagreements. Nothing could be further from the truth, as the New Testament clearly shows.

Given my disappointment with various aspects of the church today, I am especially consoled by the Gospel of Mark. The original ending of Mark, according to scripture scholars, occurs in Mark 16:8. The angel instructs the women, the heroines of other gospel accounts, to tell the disciples that Jesus will go to Galilee and be with them there. But the women fled the tomb, were very fearful, and said nothing. Thus ends the good news according to Mark! Recall that, throughout Mark, Jesus' disciples, the future leaders of the church, do not understand his mission, and they ultimately abandon him. But the early church was not willing to have Mark's Gospel end on such a sour note, so they added verses 9–20, in which the risen Jesus appears to the eleven and sends them to spread the good news to the whole world. After the ascension, the disciples preached and baptized everywhere, and their message was confirmed by divine signs.

Why did the original Gospel of Mark end on such a low note? Those who heard Mark's story knew full well that Jesus had risen and that the new community was alive and well. Mark wanted to emphasize that the growth of the early community did not depend on the work of the human ministers and leaders in the church. Despite the many shortcomings of the disciples, the new community, thanks to the Holy Spirit, was flourishing.[5]

The most divisive question facing the early church was whether or not Gentile converts had to obey the Jewish law. The Acts of the Apostles answers this question, but one can easily imagine the divisiveness it caused before it was resolved. Recall too how Paul criticized some Christians for getting drunk and not sharing their food with others at the agape meals. I take solace in the splitting up of the team ministry of Paul and Barnabas in Acts 15—a pericope that, unfortunately, we do not use in our liturgical lectionary. Paul and Barnabas differed over bringing John Mark with them on their new missionary journey because he had abandoned them earlier. So Paul took Silas and went one way, and Barnabas took John Mark and went the other way. Here we have the first story of the breakup of a team ministry because two saints could not get along with each other!

The frictions and factions in the Johannine community were so strong that John developed a new understanding of Christian love. For John, the object of love was not the neighbor in need or the enemy, as in the other Gospels, but rather the other members of the Christian community. John insists on love of the sisters and brothers precisely because of all the divisions that rent the community. The early church was as much a pilgrim and a sinful church as it is today. So it was, and so it will always be.

The triumphalistic view of the church is not restricted to John Paul II and pre–Vatican II theology. I am afraid that many so-called liberals and progressives in the church today have the same triumphalistic view. They expect the church to be perfect as they—or we—define perfection. Many of us are unwilling to live with the tensions, the divisions, and the struggles that will always accompany the sinful pilgrim church. But such tensions and struggles are not in themselves negative—they are a sign that the church is a living community striving to be ever more faithful to its covenant commitment. Without tensions, there would be no living church. We must all learn to live with the shortcomings, imperfections, and tensions of the church, as well as with our own.

We theologians, with our sense of history, are acutely conscious of the controversies and sharp disputes that have marked the church since its inception. The term *odium theologicum* (theological hatred) illustrates the strong and even venomous character of theological arguments in the church. Theological hatred is a special kind of hatred precisely because of the antagonisms it provokes.

Take, for example, the controversies at the University of Paris in the thirteenth century, which dwarf those of the twentieth century. The professors, who were secular clergy, and the mendicant orders were engaged in what felt at the time like a life-or-death struggle. The archbishops of Paris and Canterbury condemned the teachings of Thomas Aquinas himself immediately after his death, and the acrimonious *de auxillis* controversy between Jesuits and Dominicans lasted from the sixteenth to the twentieth century. The debates over probabilism in the seventeenth and eighteenth centuries were also deep and bitter, as I learned while working on my doctoral dissertation, on Alphonsus Liguori's "invincible" ignorance of natural law.[6]

Older theologians today are very familiar with the Vatican condemnations of scriptural scholars in the early twentieth century and of the *nouvelle theologie* of the 1950s. These positions, condemned only a few decades ago, are now generally accepted even by the Vatican. A number of theologians under suspicion and explicitly condemned by the Vatican before Vatican II—most notably Yves Congar and John Courtney Murray—were rehabilitated by that council.

The Church as the People of God

Vatican II reminded us that the church consists of the people of God and not just their leaders in the church hierarchy. From early times, Catholic theology attached great importance to the *sensus fidelium* (sense of the faithful) as an important source of knowledge of what the Spirit is saying to us.[7] Contemporary theology once again emphasizes the need for the whole church to receive the teaching of the hierarchical magisterium.[8] It is true that the hierarchical magisterium itself does not give as much importance to these theological positions today, but they are nonetheless deeply embedded in the Catholic tradition and should be used by all of us. One can say truthfully not only that many in the church but to some degree the church itself has already changed its teaching on a number of the sexual issues discussed earlier.

When I am asked how I can stay in the church when the church has condemned me as a theologian, I can answer that the church did not condemn me—the hierarchical magisterium did. Yes, I was hurt by the action of the hierarchical magisterium, but I have received much support and solace from the broader Catholic theological community and from many of the people of God, who continue to nourish and support me in many ways.

Ironically, I play a greater role in the Catholic Church today than I would have had the Vatican not condemned me. After the Vatican action against me, a cartoon appeared in a daily newspaper that depicted, in the first frame, the pope saying he was silencing me as a Catholic theologian. The second frame showed me speaking before two dozen microphones! When Josef Ratzinger was elected Pope Benedict XVI, in April 2005, almost all of the major newspapers, news magazines, and national television networks interviewed me. I cannot imagine that this would have happened had the Vatican's condemnation not made me such a prominent public figure within the church.

Spirituality for the Pilgrim Church

Many people urged me to accept the 1986 decision by the CDF and the pope quietly and not to fight it. They thought it would be better for the church and also enhance or deepen my own spirituality to leave it to the Holy Spirit to right the wrongs of the church. The great theological heroes of Vatican II, John Courtney Murray and Yves Congar, had acted in this way, these people said. I disagreed.

I have always been attracted to a theology and spirituality based on the Paschal Mystery—the dying and rising of Jesus. Through our baptism we are incorporated into this mystery—we die in order to rise. In this life we will always know frustration, opposition, and failure. We all are called to die in order to live.

I addressed this issue of spirituality in my book *The Crisis in Priestly Ministry* (1972), in which I used Yves Congar as a good example of the spirituality of the Paschal Mystery.[9] When his diaries were published a few years ago, we learned even more about the anguish he suffered when he was relieved of his teaching function by church authorities, who also made it difficult for him to publish any works on controversial issues or to engage publicly in the ecumenical movement.[10] He had earlier written of his anguish and suffering in light of the Paschal Mystery in *Chrétiens en dialogue* (1964), translated into English in 1966 as *Dialogue between Christians,* and in a short article he addressed to his brother priests in 1965.[11] In the article, Congar, who had suffered in silence for many years, tried to encourage priests and others who were suffering and not seeing the fruits of their actions. Fortunately, Congar lived to see Vatican II and to hear Pope Paul VI say that no theologian had influenced him more deeply than Yves Congar.

But I raised some questions about Congar's approach. "Perhaps reform would have been achieved more quickly if he would have resisted more actively or perhaps even left his ministry. Perhaps such a spirituality is too passive and too easily accepts the imperfections and sinfulness of the institution and people in it. There are times when one cannot passively suffer, but must speak out boldly and resist the wrong that is being done. Congar himself realizes there is no meaning in suffering just for the sake of suffering. Although one might raise questions about Congar's response, one can only admire the man and his spirituality."[12]

I also had theoretical problems with understanding the Paschal Mystery only in terms of paradox. Yes, at times we experience life in the midst of death, power in the midst of weakness, joy in the midst of sorrow. But the Catholic tradition, with its emphasis on mediation, rejects the total paradoxical view of the Christian life. We also experience God's goodness in human goodness, God's joy in human joy, God's power in human power, God's truth in human truth.[13] On both theoretical and practical grounds, therefore, I chose a different path. The Catholic Church is as much my church as it is the pope's. The pilgrim people of God will always experience the tensions and frustrations of the journey, but we must strive to respect one another in our struggle and disagreements.

We all need a spirituality for living in and participating in the church as the pilgrim people of God. I have always appreciated the spirituality found in the famous axiom *in necessariis, unitas; in dubiis, libertas; in omnibus, caritas*—in necessary things unity, in doubtful things freedom, in all things charity.[14] Julia Fleming, a graduate student of mine at the time of my confrontation with the CDF and now a tenured professor of moral theology at Creighton University, gave me a needlepoint of this saying that now hangs in my dining room. We must continue to work for change in light of what we think is best for the church but always in the awareness that we may be wrong, and we must always treat our opponents with charity.

I did not leave the church, because the church is not only the people of God; it is the way in which God determines to come to us with her saving love. The Catholic Church is not a voluntary society that one joins because one likes the other members or the music. Nor does one leave it, necessarily, if one becomes disenchanted (although it is true that many Catholics today do seem to view the church as just another voluntary society). The Catholic Church sees itself more as a family. You cannot cease to be a member of your family no matter how much you might want to. You can chose to have nothing to do with your family, but you cannot escape the fact that you belong to it. God made a covenant not with individuals but with a people. In many Christian churches, especially in the United

States, God makes a covenant not with a community but with individual persons—Do you accept Jesus Christ as your lord and savior? For many Americans, the relationship to God is direct, immediate, and invisible. But in the Catholic understanding, God comes to us and we go to God indirectly, mediately, and visibly through the community of the church.

When Protestants are asked about their church, they will invariably say, for example, "I am a member of the First Methodist Church." Catholics, especially older Catholics, will respond, "I belong to St. Augustine's parish." Catholics don't choose, they belong. We see the same tendency throughout church history. When Protestants have differed with their church, their tendency has been to go out and start another church. When Catholics disagree with the church, they have more often struggled to reform it.

With such an understanding of the church as the people of God, Catholics have a strong reason to work to reform the church despite all its problems: it is their church just as much as it is the church of the hierarchy. More accurately, it is *God's* church, which we are all trying to make more faithful to what it is called to be. The covenant people of God will always struggle to make the church a better sign of the reign of God in our midst.

Structural Change

In the years preceding Vatican II, the Roman Catholic Church had become more centralized, authoritarian, and defensive than it had ever been in its history. Vatican Council I, in 1870, dealt only with the papal office in the church, emphasizing the primacy of its jurisdiction. Other aspects of ecclesiology, such as the local church, the role of bishops, and the people of God, were simply not on the agenda. In the early and mid-twentieth century, the Vatican defensively condemned new developments in theology as modernism and refused to have any dialogue with modern thought. According to John Tracy Ellis, long recognized as the foremost American church historian in the twentieth century, the Vatican's fear and suspicion of modernism killed off what little creative church scholarship there was in the United States at the time.[15] In addition, new technologies, especially in transportation and communication, allowed the

Vatican to be in instant communication with people and institutions all over the world. Thus the Vatican was able to give rapid solutions to issues that were arising in the Catholic Church around the world.

Illustrations of this growing centralization and authoritarianism are abundant. In the field of moral theology, the papal magisterium, in the late nineteenth century, began to intervene frequently in deciding particular ethical questions. This was a significant change. The first strong intervention of the papal magisterium in Catholic moral issues occurred in the seventeenth and eighteenth centuries, when the Holy Office, the predecessor of the CDF, condemned the two extremes of laxism and tutiorism in the midst of the debate about whether or not it is legitimate to follow a truly probable opinion. The condemnation of these two extremes left plenty of room for theological debate. But that changed in the latter part of the nineteenth century. In 1899 Thomas Bouquillon, a professor of moral theology at CUA, chastised Catholic theologians for seeking answers from the Vatican congregations when there was no need to do so.[16] By the middle of the twentieth century, a dramatic change had taken place in Catholic theology. Now the papal magisterium became the primary arbiter of moral questions.[17] The direct appointment of bishops by the pope is a development of the past 150 years. American Catholics may be surprised to learn that the first Catholics in Maryland celebrated the liturgy in English. This was the New World, and it called for new approaches. But today the Vatican decides even the smallest of liturgical details for the whole world.

The Second Vatican Council changed our theological understanding of the church by insisting that the church is the people of God and not just the pope and bishops. Vatican II put more stress on the collegiality of all bishops, together with the pope, in their mutual solicitude for the whole church. The role of local bishops and churches also received much more attention. These significant changes called for a corresponding change of structure, but unfortunately, for all practical purposes, the pre–Vatican II structure, with its emphasis on centralization in Rome, remains in effect.

This is not the place for a full-scale description of the structural changes needed in the church today, but the practical basis for such reforms lies in the principle of subsidiarity, which is emphasized in Catholic social teaching. The individual human person, who is both sacred and social, is the basis of the entire social order. In ascending order come the family, the neighborhood, the nation, and a host of voluntary associations covering all aspects of human life. We are born into the first three kinds of society, but we freely join the voluntary associations. According to the principle of subsidiarity, the higher levels of association do all they can to help the individual and the lower levels accomplish all they can on their own. Higher levels should do only what cannot be done on the lower levels. The principle of subsidiarity thus avoids the opposite extremes of individualism and collectivism and tries to bring about the unity of the whole social order. Despite some controversy about applying the principle of subsidiarity to the church, it is totally compatible with contemporary Catholic ecclesiology.[18]

Under the principle of subsidiarity, the international synod of bishops should not be simply consultative and advisory to the pope but should make decisions for the whole church. The principle of subsidiarity calls for a much greater role for national and regional groups of bishops, who can and should make final decisions on the particular issues facing the church in their areas. Unfortunately, under the papacy of John Paul II, the role of national and regional bishops' conferences was greatly reduced. But bishops are not simply vicars of the pope; they are bishops in their own right. Bishops fulfill their rightful role only if, both individually and collectively, they can disagree publicly with the pope. In addition, if the church is the people of God, then laypeople need to play a much greater role in the life of the church.

The church itself has recognized that in the past it overemphasized unity and universality and gave short shrift to diversity and local differences. Only in the past fifty years, for example, has the eucharistic liturgy been prayed in the vernacular. Today we are much more aware of the diverse and the particular in our world. In addition, change today occurs much more rapidly than ever before. We do not have the leisure to wait 100 years for change, as we did in the case of religious freedom. If it is to address the needs of the present, the Catholic Church badly needs institutional structures that recognize the legitimate requirements of historical change and diversity today.

Greater recognition of particularity and diversity within the church does not mean denying its universality. These two ideals must be kept in tension. That the church is universal means that it can never be totally identified with any particular language, nation, or culture. In the midst of my struggles with the Vatican, many people proposed to me that we should start an American Catholic Church, but this was the last thing I wanted to do. A universal church by definition is bigger and broader than any particular nation or culture and can and must serve as a check on the pretensions of any one nation or culture, especially one that looks upon itself as a superpower.

Thanks to technological advances and economic change, the world today is smaller than ever before. We desperately need a global ethic that can bring greater justice to the four corners of the earth. The twentieth century has seen an unprecedented concentration of power and wealth, while the poor and the weak of the world have become poorer and weaker. Only if the worldwide community becomes more conscious of itself as such will we avoid the grave injustices that result from globalization in all areas except ethics.[19]

As a universal community by definition, the church has the advantage of basing our unity on the forgiving and merciful love of God, which has been poured into our hearts through the Holy Spirit. We in the church are challenged to model a global community that also strives to recognize the rightful place of diversity and particularity. If the church cannot achieve this goal, how can we ever expect the secular worldwide community to even approach it?

As essential as structural reform is for the Catholic Church, it will not solve all our problems. The Anglican Church has open and participatory structures, but this has not saved it from divisions over the issue of homosexuality. The Archbishop of Canterbury thinks the church should change its teaching on homosexuality, but he does not want to break up the church over this issue. How to work for change within a commitment to the worldwide unity of the community of the disciples of Jesus is a great challenge for all of us. Here we all need the three gifts of wisdom, courage, and patience.

The Meaning of Hope

To respond more completely to the question of whether there is hope for the Catholic Church today, we must understand what hope means. In Romans 4–8, Paul reminds us that merely seeing the goal ahead does not amount to hope. Hope is truly hope only when it prevails in the midst of darkness. It is a matter of "hoping against hope," as Abraham and Sarah did when they put their faith in the power of God to give them a child against all odds. This is what hope must mean to the pilgrim people of God.

The very fact that we raise the question—is there any hope for the church?—in difficult times reflects a poor understanding of the concept of hope. We are reminded of the true meaning of hope in the witness of our mothers and fathers of the Old Testament and their descendents in the Jewish faith today. They did not lose hope after the destruction by Sennacherib. They did not lose hope after the slaughter of 6 million Jews in the Holocaust. For those who believe the Spirit is present and working in the church, there will always be hope.

Just as the Catholic acceptance of mediation modified the paradoxical understanding of the Paschal Mystery, so too it modifies the paradoxical meaning of hope. Hope ultimately rests on the loving power of God; but the Catholic tradition, with its notion of mediation, recognizes that God is even now present and working in our world and in our church. At the same time, and this truth must never be forgotten, the church, despite the presence and power of the Spirit, will never be perfect, and will always be on its pilgrimage to the Promised Land. There are always signs of God's presence in the church today, if we would but see, even though the fullness of God's presence and power will never be realized perfectly in the church. We can and must use God's presence to work continuously for reform in the church.

Congar was fond of referring to Romans 5:4—patience breeds hope—and there is a very close connection between suffering and patience, and both are connected to hope. The French and English words for patience come from the Latin word meaning to suffer. Congar points out that one would expect Paul to say that hope helps us to be patient and to suffer.

But Paul puts it the other way around—patience and suffering *breed* hope. Paul has hit on a deeper reality. One who has not suffered does not know how to hope.[20]

I must confess that patience is not my strong suit, to say the least. I am reminded of my impatience every time I drive a car because I always have to find the quickest way to get there and frequently change lanes to do so. We who work for reform in the church need hope and patience. We must continue the struggle for change and reform in the church the same way we continue the struggle for growth and continuing conversion in our own Christian lives.

My Personality and My Relationship to the Church

There are common elements that all of us reformers in the church can and should share, but there are also personal characteristics that each of us brings to our life in the pilgrim people of God. This section will discuss my spirituality, my understanding of priestly ministry, and my recognition of the acceptance of complexity and tension in all aspects of my Christian pilgrimage.

Spirituality

Like Congar, I have tried to develop a spirituality based on the Paschal Mystery of dying in order to live, but I understand this in transformational rather than paradoxical terms. There are no purely rational solutions to the problems of evil, suffering, and death. Faith gives us answers to these mysteries, but it is above all in the person of Jesus, the Christ, that we experience existentially the meaning of these realities and the possibility of God's love overcoming evil, suffering, and death itself. Through baptism, we are incorporated into the rhythm of the Paschal Mystery of Jesus—the dying and the rising. I have tried to live out that spirituality in my own life.

I am very conscious that my relationship with God is not as strong as it could be. Likewise, I have to admit that my commitment to others and to the community could be much greater. In my writing and teaching, I have consistently pointed out the dangers of individualism in our society and the failure of so many people to be concerned about others and society as a whole. In theory, we Christians recognize that love of God and love of neighbor are inextricably joined. How can you love the God you do not see if you do not love your neighbor whom you do see? I worry that at times I become too self-centered with my own theological work. I have insisted in my writing on the need for "the uneasy conscience of the Christian." No one ever lives up fully to what we are called to be and to do. The uneasy conscience reminds us of two important realities—that we are redeemed by God's love and not by our own efforts, and that we are called to continual conversion precisely because we continually fall short.

A couple of years ago my friend Beth Johnson reminded me of something I had forgotten. Before leaving CUA for the last time and setting out for the University of Southern California, I went out to dinner with four close faculty colleagues who were part of the committee that had supported me during the Vatican's investigation. After dinner we came back to my room for conversation and a final drink together. Beth said that after the others left my room in the wee hours of the morning, they stood outside talking for almost an hour. They marveled that my primary concern about leaving CUA was that I was leaving a faith community that had nourished and supported me for many years. I had spoken that evening of my hope that I would find a similar community wherever I wound up in the future. Beth told me that the four of them had stood there for an hour complaining about the action taken against me by the Vatican, Cardinal Hickey, and CUA, and what a contrast this had been to my own concern about losing my faith community. Despite my own shortcomings, or perhaps because of them, the faith community is the most important part of my life.

Priestly Ministry in the Church

Another significant part of my personal identity is being a Catholic priest. Although my primary role has been that of theologian and teacher, I still consider myself, and am looked upon by others, as a Catholic priest. My concept of priesthood has changed dramatically since I was first ordained a priest in 1958. Then I understood the priestly calling in terms of the eighteenth- and nineteenth-century French spirituality of the time—that is, as the mediator between God and human beings. The priest brought God to the people and the people to God. Today I see that this was a very mistaken application of the Catholic concept of mediation. The priest is primarily a member of the community of the people of God who has a particular function to perform for that community—that of presiding at its liturgical celebrations.

Distinctive clerical dress and titles help to perpetuate the sacral notion of the priest, which I now see as an error, however widely it may still be held by practicing Catholics. I stopped wearing clerical garb in the early 1970s, except at peace marches and similar events, where I would sometimes wear the collar. I also discourage people from addressing me as Father Curran and have long encouraged colleagues, students, friends, and foes to call me, simply, Charlie.

Although the eucharistic liturgy is an important part of my life, I feel no need to preside at the liturgy. In my judgment, everyone who participates in the liturgy is a celebrant; the priest is not the only celebrant but rather the presider. As I mentioned earlier, during my first year in the seminary in the early 1960s, I strongly opposed the need for priests to celebrate a private Eucharist or to concelebrate if there already was a community celebration with a presider. At CUA I organized and promoted a daily eucharistic liturgy in Caldwell Hall, where some faculty and students came together to celebrate, but I presided no more than once a week.

I enjoy presiding at the Eucharist, and many people have told me that they appreciate the way I do so. For example, I always use inclusive language, even about God, and I spontaneously pray all the prayers of the liturgy, which is not exactly in accord with liturgical laws. When groups of Catholic theologians get together for meetings, I am often asked to preside at the liturgy. Two of my women friends, Beth Johnson and Margaret Farley, asked me to preside at the convention liturgy when they served as presidents of the CTSA. Even then, however, I insisted that they call me out of the community to preside and that they give the homily.

In the case of Margaret's presidency, a few members were quite upset by the way I presided. One complained that even on Pentecost Sunday I omitted the Nicene Creed. Ironically, the reality was quite different. The local liturgical arrangements committee told me in advance that they had decided not to have the creed recited, but I convinced them that it should be. No one told the choir, which immediately after Margaret's homily went into the bidding prayers. At recent meetings of the Society of Christian Ethics, a couple of us have invited the Catholic members to a Saturday night liturgy that we follow with drinks and conversation. I think it is important for Catholic theologians to encourage one another, not only in our theological work but also in our faith commitment and the connection between the two.

One of my concerns before ordination was celibacy. I have missed sexual intimacy with a spouse and having children, but I have developed a way of living that I think has been basically healthy both spiritually and emotionally. From the beginning, I knew, of course, that the lack of sexual intimacy and children of one's own would be costs of my decision, and some years ago I was hit by the absence of grandchildren when I saw my contemporaries being so energized by theirs. But I am also sure that, like many celibates, there have been compensations for my celibacy.

Nonetheless, I do not think the Catholic Church should require celibacy as a necessary condition of priesthood. Celibacy is nothing more than a human law, and it has not been enforced always and everywhere. Today, somewhat ironically, we have permitted married former Episcopalian priests to become Roman Catholic priests. (I have a feeling that if they, as a group, had been more liberal, the Vatican would never have allowed them to become Catholic priests!) In the United States, Western Europe, and South America, the shortage of priests in recent years has deprived a good number of Catholic communities of the weekly Eucharist and has forced the Catholic bishops of the United States to come up with various formats for noneucharistic Sunday liturgies in this country. But for Catholics the Eucharist has always been the font and center of our spiritual lives. How can the church deprive its people of the Eucharist because of a manmade law? Many good Catholic priests, including friends of mine, have left the ministry because of the requirement of celibacy. I know and admire many committed, celibate Catholic priests, but I also know priests who have not kept their vow of celibacy or who have been stunted by it.

Why, then, do the bishops and the pope still require celibacy of Catholic priests? In a significant way, the celibacy issue is at bottom very much an issue of authority. Authorities can have greater control of celibate priests than of noncelibate ones. Noncelibates would have more independence in the way they are trained (they could not live in a celibate seminary) and in their lifestyles. The authority issue also explains why Catholic bishops in the United States and in the Western world will not raise their voices to call for a married priesthood despite the needs of so many Catholics, and the needs of the aging celibate priests themselves. The bishops, individually or as a whole, are unwilling to disagree publicly with the pope on this subject because of the authority issue. But the collegiality of bishops in the Catholic Church will not be a reality until individual bishops or groups of bishops can say publicly, "Holy Father, we revere you as the bishop of Rome and admire you personally for many things, but on this particular issue we think you are wrong." On this and similar issues, there could also be different disciplinary regulations in different parts of the world, as appropriate. We often pray for vocations to priesthood. My prayer is a little different. I pray that the church might open its eyes to see the many priestly candidates—including women—who are now in our midst.

But what about the argument that celibacy frees a priest to be totally dedicated to God, and that it constitutes a higher form of the spiritual life? This argument does not jibe with our experience. We all know committed married people who have dedicated themselves thoroughly to the service of others. One of the significant developments in Catholic theology has been the growing number of married Catholic theologians in the church. I have many friends in this category and admire not only their theology but also their Christian commitment, as exemplified in their lives. Indeed, they put me to shame. Let me give two examples. Lisa Sowle Cahill of Boston College is a superb moral theologian who has written extensively and from whom I have learned much. But, in addition to her great contribution to theology, she and her husband adopted three foreign-born orphans, whom they have raised and educated in addition to their two biological children.

Christine Gudorf, now at Florida International, is a leading feminist moral theologian from whom I have learned a great deal as a theologian, but I have also learned from her what it means to be a committed Christian. She and her husband adopted two extremely disabled very young children and cared lovingly for them, with all the heartache that this entailed. The older one died in 2004 at age thirty-five. Chris disagrees with the hierarchical teaching on abortion, but I wish that prolife people and all of us in the Catholic Church showed as much commitment to human life as she has shown. I could give a long list of married lay theologians who have inspired me by their dedicated Christian commitment.

Experience, on both a macro and a micro level, has convinced me that celibacy is not a higher form of the spiritual life than marriage, nor is it necessary for priesthood. We all make the same baptismal commitment, but it can then be developed and expressed in different ways. Ironically, I have to recognize that not having a spouse or children made it much easier for me to publicly disagree with official church teaching and be willing to face the consequences of that. If I were to lose a job, I figured sooner or later I could find something else. I could move comparatively easily to three different universities in four years because I did not have to worry about a spouse or children. But this does not mean that celibacy is a higher form of spiritual life for Christians, or that married people cannot be dedicated ministers of the gospel.

One final point on priesthood in the Catholic Church. I believe that the people who suffer most in the Catholic Church today are women. Women in very real respects are second-class citizens in the church. Some people in the Vatican maintain that the women's issue is a first-world issue and is not relevant in the developing world. In my judgment, the equal role of women is a Christian and a human rights issue not limited to any one culture, and it will ultimately become an issue throughout the world. To make matters worse, the Vatican and the pope claim that divine law prevents the church from ordaining women priests, an argument that has been refuted by more gifted thinkers and writers than I. But I worry about what might happen in the future. The Catholic Church could finally accept married male priests but not women priests. This would be a disaster.

Realism and Complexity

My personality obviously has affected my approach to theology and my response to what is going on in the church. I am no more independent of subjectivity and social location than anyone else. Because of the public controversies I have been involved in, some people see me as a radical, a rebel, a revolutionary. But I am none of these things, nor am I an idealist or utopian. I am a realist who recognizes the complexity, tension, and ambiguities in every aspect of human existence.

This realism has affected my theology in my insistence on these complexities and tensions. My theological stance views life through the lens of five Christian mysteries, not just one or two. I have proposed a relationality-responsibility model for moral theology because the other two models—of deontology and teleology—are too narrow and simplistic, in my judgment. In my understanding of relationality, I insist on the multiple relationships one has with God, others, the world, and self. My primary argument for the possibility of dissent from noninfallible church teaching is based on the complexity of concrete issues about which one cannot claim to have moral certitude. Because of this complexity, the physical aspect of an act cannot determine its moral content.

My approach to life and to theology precludes the possibility of real radicalism. Indeed, I have worried in the past that my approach was not radical enough. The simple, black-and-white view of the radical has its appeal, but common sense and pragmatism seem to me a more honest and integrated approach to life.

The church today faces many problems, but it is probably better off than it has been at many other times in its history. For one thing, the leaders of the church, the pope and the bishops, are on the whole better Christian role models then they have been at times in the past. John Paul II's papacy had significant negative consequences for the church, but also some positive ones. And while I was disappointed in the election of Josef Ratzinger as Benedict XVI, I respect him as the pope, and I pray for him every day. The hierarchical leaders of the church today see themselves primarily as spiritual leaders and not as princes or warriors or politicians. We should never forget that leadership in the church today is not easy. The work of any church leader is to challenge the people of God while also acting as the center of unity for the Christian community. This is a much taller order than it was in the past because we are so much more conscious today of the diversity and differences that exist in the church at every level.

Many priests have told me how they admire the way I have worked for change in the church and dealt with tension and adversity. But I remind them that as pastors they play a much more difficult role than I. Within any local church community today, there are Democrats and Republicans, liberals and conservatives, rich and poor, male and female, introverts and extroverts, young and old, gays and straights. Parish priests have to deal every day with the tensions and problems that arise from all of this diversity, and they must try to both challenge and unify the people of God. If I give more than 5 percent of my time to addressing these tensions, that is a lot.

Supporters have often praised me for my courage in challenging authority in the church. But, at least in the popular sense of the word, courage alone is not enough. Terrorists can be courageous; thieves can be courageous; racists can be courageous. Here again complexity recognizes the danger of absolutizing courage. What is needed is the twofold gift of the Spirit—courage and wisdom. We have to know when to stand firm and when to compromise, when to oppose and when to tolerate. Courage without wisdom is not worth very much.

My personality also helps me to deal with the problems and struggles that are a part of life in the pilgrim church. There are days when I am tired and discouraged, but I am not by nature a brooder. I generally try to deal with problems head on and move on to the next challenge. I am blessed with a sense of humor, which is a big help. The two great sources of transcendence—prayer and laughter—prevent me from being imprisoned in the present. The virtue of hope reminds me that there is something better and deeper than present realities and difficulties. In the end, what more could anyone want?

Notes

Notes to Preface

1. For a complete bibliography of my writings from 1961 to 2002, see James J. Walter, Timothy E. O'Connell, and Thomas A. Shannon, eds., *A Call to Fidelity: On the Moral Theology of Charles E. Curran* (Washington, D.C.: Georgetown University Press, 2002), 273–98. This bibliography is based on Thomas W. O'Brien, "Bibliography of Charles E. Curran, 1961–90: Thirty Years of Catholic Moral Theology," *Horizons* 18 (1991): 263–78, and Thomas W. O'Brien, "Bibliography of Charles E. Curran, 1990–2000: Another Decade of Catholic Moral Theology," *Horizons* 28 (2001): 307–13. A bibliography of the books I have written and edited appears at the end of this volume. I have not listed all of my articles and essays there; the essays collected in many of my books first appeared in journals and other books, but in such cases, for the sake of convenience, I refer only to the collection in which the essay is found.

2. Charles E. Curran, "A Place for Dissent: My Argument with Joseph Ratzinger," *Commonweal* 132 (May 6, 2005): 18–20.

Notes to Chapter 1

1. Curt Gerling, *Smugtown U.S.A.* (Webster, N.Y.: Plaza, 1957), 97–98.

2. Charles E. Curran, *Christian Morality Today: The Renewal of Moral Theology* (Notre Dame: Fides Press, 1966), 13–26.

3. Louis Janssens, "Morale conjugale et progestogènes," *Ephemerides Theologicae Lovanienses* 39 (1963): 787–826.

4. Curran, *Christian Morality Today*, 67–76.

5. Ibid., 107–19, 93–105, 29–45, 121–38.

Notes to Chapter 2

1. For the history of CUA, see C. Joseph Nuesse, *The Catholic University of America: A Centennial History* (Washington, D.C.: Catholic University of America Press, 1990).

2. Charles E. Curran, *A New Look at Christian Morality* (Notre Dame: Fides Press, 1968), 201–21.

3. Ibid., 73–128; Charles E. Curran, *Contemporary Problems in Moral Theology* (Notre Dame: Fides Press, 1970), 97–158.

4. William B. Smith, "The Revision of Moral Theology in Richard A. McCormick," *Homiletical and Pastoral Review* 81, no. 6 (1981): 8–28.

5. For the story of my termination and its aftermath, see Robert B. Townsend, "Culture, Conflict, and Change: The '67 Strike at Catholic University," available at http://mason.gmu.edu/~rtownsen/67StrikeIntro.htm; Albert C. Pierce, *Beyond One Man: Catholic University, April 17–24, 1967* (Washington, D.C.: Anawim Yahweh, 1967). Much of my discussion here relies on these two sources.

6. Connell to Vagnozzi, December 1, 1966, Connell Papers, Holy Redeemer College, Washington, D.C.

7. Connell to O'Boyle, April 16, 1966, ibid.

8. Samuel J. Thomas, "A 'Final Disposition . . . One Way or Another': The Real End of the First Curran Affair," *Catholic Historical Review* 91 (October 2005): 714–42.

9. "Minutes of the Twenty-Second Annual Convention," *Proceedings of the Catholic Theological Society of America* 22 (1967): 347–49.

10. "Secretary's Report: The Twenty-Third Annual Convention," *Proceedings of the Catholic Theological Society of America* 23 (1968): 283–84.

Notes to Chapter 3

1. For a more detailed discussion of my involvement in the opposition to *Humanae vitae* and the subsequent inquiry at CUA, see Charles E. Curran,

Robert E. Hunt, et al., *Dissent In and For the Church: Theologians and Humanae Vitae* (New York: Sheed and Ward, 1969), and John F. Hunt et al., *The Responsibility of Dissent: The Church and Academic Freedom* (New York: Sheed and Ward, 1969).

2. Andrew M. Greeley, William C. McCready, and Kathleen McCourt, *Catholic Schools in a Declining Church* (Kansas City, Mo.: Sheed and Ward, 1976), 3–157.

3. National Catholic News Service (domestic), July 31, 1968.

4. *Washington Post*, August 2, 1968, A2; *New York Times*, August 2, 1968, A1.

5. National Catholic News Service (domestic), August 2, 1968.

6. Ibid., August 1, 1968.

7. National Catholic News Service (documentary service), August 22, 1968; *Washington Post*, August 22, 1968, B1.

8. Hunt et al., *Responsibility of Dissent*, 19–20.

9. Ibid., 23–29; "News Release by Carroll A. Hochwalt, chairman of the board of trustees," ibid., 206–7.

10. *Dissent In and For the Church* deals with the theological aspects of the case, while *The Responsibility of Dissent* deals with the issue of academic freedom.

11. Hunt et al., *Responsibility of Dissent*, 39.

12. Ibid., 42.

13. National Conference of Catholic Bishops, *Human Life in Our Day* (Washington, D.C.: United States Catholic Conference, 1968), 18.

14. Curran, Hunt, et al., *Dissent In and For the Church*, and Hunt et al., *Responsibility of Dissent*.

15. Curran, Hunt, et al., *Dissent In and For the Church*, 221.

16. For the trustees' actions with regard to the report, see Hunt et al., *Responsibility of Dissent*, 163–72.

17. National Catholic News Service (domestic), June 17, 1969.

18. *Tower*, November 21, 1969, 1.

19. Joseph Byron, "The Case of the Washington Nineteen: A Search for Justice," in *Judgment in the Church*, ed. William Bassett and Peter Huizing (New York: Seabury, 1971), 104–12.

20. Cardinal Ratzinger to Charles Curran, July 25, 1986, in Charles E. Curran, *Faithful Dissent* (Kansas City, Mo.: Sheed and Ward, 1986), 268.

21. Kevin Kelly, "Serving the Truth," in *Readings in Moral Theology No. 6: Dissent in the Church*, ed. Charles E. Curran and Richard A. McCormick (New

York: Paulist Press, 1988), 479–80; Linda Hogan, *Confronting the Truth: Conscience in the Catholic Tradition* (New York: Paulist Press, 2000), 176–79; Lisa Sowle Cahill, "Sexual Ethics," in *A Call to Fidelity: On the Moral Theology of Charles E. Curran,* ed. James J. Walter, Timothy E. O'Connell, and Thomas A. Shannon (Washington, D.C.: Georgetown University Press, 2002), 113–14.

22. George A. Kelly, *Keeping the Church Catholic with John Paul II* (New York: Doubleday, 1990), 46–47.

Notes to Chapter 4

1. Charles E. Curran, *Catholic Moral Theology in Dialogue* (Notre Dame: Fides Press, 1972), 184–219; Charles E. Curran, *Transition and Tradition in Moral Theology* (Notre Dame: University of Notre Dame Press, 1979), 59–80; Charles E. Curran, *Critical Concerns in Moral Theology* (Notre Dame: University of Notre Dame Press, 1984), 73–98.

2. Charles E. Curran, *New Perspectives in Moral Theology* (Notre Dame: Fides Press, 1974), 212–76.

3. Charles E. Curran, *Issues in Sexual and Medical Ethics* (Notre Dame: University of Notre Dame Press, 1978), 3–29.

4. Curran, *New Perspectives in Moral Theology,* 163–93.

5. For overviews and analyses of McCormick's proportionalism, see Bernard Hoose, *Proportionalism: The American Debate and Its European Roots* (Washington, D.C.: Georgetown University Press, 1987); Paulinus Ikechukwu Odozor, *McCormick and the Renewal of Moral Theology* (Notre Dame: University of Notre Dame Press, 1955); James J. Walter, "The Foundation and Formulation of Norms," in *Moral Theology: Challenges for the Future; Essays in Honor of Richard A. McCormick,* ed. Charles E. Curran (New York: Paulist Press, 1990), 125–54.

6. Curran, *New Perspectives in Moral Theology,* 164–71.

7. John Courtney Murray, *The Problem of Religious Freedom* (Westminster, Md.: Newman, 1965), 7–17.

8. Charles E. Curran, *Ongoing Revision: Studies in Moral Theology* (Notre Dame: Fides Press, 1975), 107–43.

9. Curran, *New Perspectives in Moral Theology,* 194–211.

10. Congregation for the Doctrine of the Faith, *Declaration on Certain Questions Concerning Sexual Ethics* (Washington, D.C.: United States Catholic Conference, 1976).

11. Curran, *Issues in Medical and Sexual Ethics,* 30–52.

12. Charles E. Curran, *Moral Theology: A Continuing Journey* (Notre Dame: University of Notre Dame Press, 1982), 35–61.

13. Curran, *New Perspectives in Moral Theology,* 47–86.

14. Curran, *Catholic Moral Theology in Dialogue,* 111–49.

15. Charles E. Curran, *A New Look at Christian Morality* (Notre Dame: Fides Press, 1968), 157–75.

16. Curran, *Catholic Moral Theology in Dialogue,* 184–219.

17. For my early development of this relationality-responsibility model, see Curran, *New Look at Christian Morality,* 223–49; Charles E. Curran, *Contemporary Problems in Moral Theology* (Notre Dame: Fides Press, 1970), 104–36; Curran, *Catholic Moral Theology in Dialogue,* 150–83. My most systematic treatment of the ethical model is found in *The Catholic Moral Tradition Today: A Synthesis* (Washington, D.C.: Georgetown University Press, 1999), 60–86.

18. H. Richard Niebuhr, *The Responsible Self: An Essay in Christian Moral Philosophy* (New York: Harper and Row, 1963).

19. Curran, *New Look at Christian Morality,* 25–71.

20. Charles E. Curran, *The Crisis in Priestly Ministry* (Notre Dame: Fides Press, 1972), 51–102.

21. Curran, *New Look at Christian Morality,* 203–08.

22. Curran, *Moral Theology: A Continuing Journey,* 69–74.

23. Charles E. Curran, *Directions in Fundamental Moral Theology* (Notre Dame: University of Notre Dame Press, 1985), 63–97.

24. Charles E. Curran, *Themes in Fundamental Moral Theology* (Notre Dame: University of Notre Dame Press, 1977), 191–231.

25. Curran, *Moral Theology: A Continuing Journey,* 35–61.

26. Ibid., 173–208; Curran, *Catholic Moral Theology in Dialogue,* 111–49.

27. Pope Paul VI, *Octogesima adveniens,* par. 22, in *Catholic Social Thought: The Documentary Heritage,* ed. David J. O'Brien and Thomas A. Shannon (Maryknoll, N.Y.: Orbis, 1992), 273.

28. Charles E. Curran, *Tensions in Moral Theology* (Notre Dame: University of Notre Dame Press, 1988), 87–109.

29. *National Catholic Reporter,* April 6, 1979, 1ff.

30. Edward LeRoy Long Jr., *Academic Bonding and Social Concern: The Society of Christian Ethics, 1959–1983* (N.p.: Religious Ethics, 1984).

31. "Secretary's Report," *Proceedings of the Catholic Theological Society of America* 27 (1972): 175–76.

32. Richard A. McCormick, *The Critical Calling: Reflections on Moral Dilemmas since Vatican II* (Washington, D.C.: Georgetown University Press, 1989), 6.

33. Frank Morriss, "CU's Fr. Curran," *Washington Catholic Standard,* October 31, 1974, 8.

34. Archbishop Robert J. Dwyer, "Catholic University: Who's in Charge?" *Twin Circle,* April 13, 1975, 2ff.

35. *Oregonian,* March 26, 1977, B7.

36. *New Freeman,* January 30, 1971, 1; for the story on the lecture and the reactions to it, see *New Freeman,* January 23, 1971.

37. Louisiana State University, *Daily Reveille,* February 20, 1979, 1.

38. *Davenport Catholic Messenger,* February 1, 1973; *National Catholic Reporter,* February 2, 1973, 3.

39. United States Catholic Conference, "Statement on Capital Punishment, November 1974," in *Quest for Justice: A Compendium of Statements of the United States Catholic Bishops on the Political and Social Order, 1966–1980,* ed. Brian Benestad and Francis J. Butler (Washington, D.C.: United States Catholic Conference, 1981), 221.

40. Bishop Joseph V. Sullivan, "An Open Letter to the Academic Community of Louisiana State University," *Catholic Commentator,* February 21, 1979, 1; for the earlier *Wanderer* columns, see Charles R. Pulver, "In Curran's Own Words . . ." *Wanderer,* December 8, 1977, December 28, 1977, January 12, 1978.

41. *Wanderer,* March 1, 1979, 1; "Open Letter of Catholics United for the Faith, New Mexico Chapter," August 22, 1979, in author's possession.

42. *National Catholic Reporter,* April 6, 1979, 1ff.

43. Father Matthew L. Lamb, "In My Opinion," *Milwaukee Journal,* June 13, 1979, A21.

Notes to Chapter 5

1. All the correspondence between the CDF and myself is found in Charles E. Curran, *Faithful Dissent* (Kansas City, Mo.: Sheed and Ward, 1986).

Rather than document all the correspondence in endnotes, I shall rely on the interested reader to use the date of the correspondence to find it in *Faithful Dissent*.

2. *Le Monde*, October 25, 1979, 17; *Tablet* (London), November 3, 1979, 1081; *Economist*, November 10, 1979, 66; *Times* (London), December 3, 1979.

3. National Conference of Catholic Bishops, *Human Life in Our Day* (Washington, D.C.: United States Catholic Conference, 1968), 18.

4. Pope John Paul II, *Apostolic Constitution Sapientia Christiana on Ecclesiastical Faculties and Universities* (Washington, D.C.: United States Catholic Conference, 1979).

5. *Washington Star*, December 20, 1979, A2.

6. The leaders of Catholic higher education in the United States tried unsuccessfully to prevent the acceptance of this canon. In April 1985 the Vatican Congregation for Catholic Education published the first draft of a document on higher education insisting that bishops are to see that Catholic doctrine is faithfully taught in these institutions and requiring a mandate from church authority for teachers of theology. For a further elaboration of these and other actions by the Vatican in opposition to academic freedom, see Charles E. Curran, *Catholic Higher Education, Theology, and Academic Freedom* (Notre Dame: University of Notre Dame Press, 1990), 130–36. The U.S. bishops later accepted the Vatican requirement that theologians have such a mandate, but tensions over this issue persist in the United States to this day. See James A. Coriden, "Moral Theology and Academic Freedom: The New Context," in *A Call to Fidelity: On the Moral Theology of Charles E. Curran*, ed. James J. Walter, Timothy E. O'Connell, and Thomas A. Shannon (Washington, D.C.: Georgetown University Press, 2002), 77–94.

7. The statements of the CDF can be found in Charles E. Curran and Richard A. McCormick, eds., *Readings in Moral Theology No. 8: Dialogue about Catholic Sexual Teaching* (New York: Paulist Press, 1993), 485–97; for an overview of what was happening in American Catholic sexual ethics at this time, see Leslie Griffin, "American Catholic Sexual Ethics, 1789–1989," ibid., 469–77.

8. National Catholic News Service, July 12, 1984, 3–4.

9. "Vittorio Messori a colloquio con Cardinale Josef Ratzinger," in *Jesus* (November 1984): 77; for the somewhat altered version that appeared later in book form, see Josef Cardinal Ratzinger, with Vittorio Messori, *The Ratzinger Report: An Exclusive Interview on the State of the Church* (San Francisco: Ignatius, 1985), 86–87.

10. For an analysis of Ratzinger contrary to mine, see John L. Allen Jr., *Cardinal Ratzinger: The Vatican's Enforcer of the Faith* (New York: Continuum, 2000).

11. Bernhard Häring, *Fede, Storia, Morale: Intervista di Gianni Licheri* (Rome: Borla, 1989). Häring himself translated this original Italian interview-based volume into a smaller German book; for an English translation of the German, see Bernard Häring, *My Witness for the Church,* trans. Leonard Swidler (New York: Paulist Press, 1992).

12. "Statement of Bishop Matthew Clark," March 12, 1986, in Curran, *Faithful Dissent,* 279–80.

13. Bernard Häring, *Embattled Witness: Memories of a Time of War* (New York: Seabury, 1976).

14. "Statement Signed by Some Past Presidents of the Catholic Theological Society of America and the College Theology Society," in Curran, *Faithful Dissent,* 282–84.

15. National Catholic News Service, March 12, 1986, 10.

16. Curran, *Faithful Dissent,* 284–85.

17. *Catholic Standard,* July 10, 1986, 7.

18. In 1997 the Vatican excommunicated Tissa Balasuriya, O.M.I., of Sri Lanka for his theological positions, but in 1998 Balasuriya was reconciled with the church. In 2005 the CDF declared that Fr. Roger Haight, S.J., because of doctrinal errors in his book on Jesus, cannot teach Catholic theology until he changes his positions.

19. "Intervista a Josef Ratzinger," *30 Giorni* (May 1986): 10–11.

20. Richard A. McCormick, *The Critical Calling: Reflections on Moral Dilemmas since Vatican II* (Washington, D.C.: Georgetown University Press, 1989), 125–29.

21. Kenneth L. Briggs, *Holy Siege: The Year That Shook Catholic America* (San Francisco: Harper, 1992), 8.

Notes to Chapter 6

1. For a more detailed discussion, with all the appropriate references, see Charles E. Curran, *Catholic Higher Education, Theology, and Academic Freedom* (Notre Dame: University of Notre Dame Press, 1990), 210–44, and *The Living*

Tradition of Moral Theology (Notre Dame: University of Notre Dame Press, 1992), 217–39. In keeping with the nature of this narrative, this chapter will not give endnotes for the material that is found in greater depth in these two sources.

2. Kenneth L. Briggs, *Holy Siege: The Year That Shook Catholic America* (San Francisco: Harper, 1992), 58.

3. For both addresses and for many other essays discussing the case, see William W. May, ed., *Vatican Authority and American Catholic Dissent: The Curran Case and Its Consequences* (New York: Crossroad, 1987).

4. "Report to the Chancellor from the Ad Hoc Committee of the Academic Senate of the Catholic University of America in the Matter of Professor Charles E. Curran, October 9, 1987," in author's possession. This report is cited by page number parenthetically in the text.

5. William J. Byron, S.J., "At Catholic U. the Issue Is Religious, Not Academic Freedom," *Washington Post*, Outlook Section, June 5, 1988.

6. Committee on Academic Freedom and Tenure, "Academic Freedom and Tenure: The Catholic University of America," *Academe* 75 (September–October 1989): 27–38.

7. The five students were Julia Fleming, Kevin Forrester, Rose Gorman, Frederick Hayes, and Johann Klodzen.

Notes to Chapter 7

1. Charles E. Curran, *Faithful Dissent* (Kansas City, Mo.: Sheed and Ward, 1986), 286.

2. For the most complete published account of what occurred before and after my going to Auburn, see Committee A on Academic Freedom and Tenure, "Academic Freedom and Tenure: Auburn University: A Supplementary Report on a Censured Administration," *Academe* 77 (May–June 1991): 34–40. In my account of these events I am also relying on my correspondence, official minutes and documents of the Auburn University senate, and articles from newspapers in the area.

3. *Montgomery Advertiser*, November 21, 1990, A1.

4. Ibid., November 29, 1990, A6.

5. University Senate's ad hoc Investigating Committee, "Report on the Issue of Dr. Charles Curran," in author's possession.

6. *Montgomery Advertiser,* November 21, 1990, A1, A10.

7. Ibid., December 11, 1990, A1, A12.

8. *Atlanta Constitution,* September 11, 1990, A1, A14.

9. Letters to the Editor, *Montgomery Advertiser,* October 7, 1990.

10. See *Chronicle of Higher Education,* December 19, 2003, A29.

11. Committee A, "Auburn University: A Supplementary Report," 34–40.

12. "Report of Committee A," *Academe* 79 (September–October 1993): 38–39.

Notes to Chapter 8

1. Richard P. McBrien, *Catholicism,* rev. ed. (San Francisco: HarperCollins, 1994), 9–12; Andrew M. Greeley, *The Catholic Myth: The Behavior and Beliefs of American Catholics* (New York: Charles Scribner's Sons, 1990), 36–64.

2. For a Catholic critique of Karl Barth and the differences between Barth and the Catholic theologian Hans Urs von Balthasar on this point, see Christopher Steck, *The Ethical Thought of Hans Urs von Balthasar* (New York: Crossroad, 2001), 58–122.

3. Jaroslav Pelikan, *The Vindication of Tradition* (New Haven: Yale University Press, 1984).

4. For a contemporary ecumenical discussion of scripture and tradition, see Daniel F. Martensen, Harold C. Skillrud, and Francis J. Stafford, eds., *Scripture and Tradition: Lutherans and Catholics in Dialogue,* vol. 9 (Minneapolis: Augsburg Fortress, 1996).

5. Margaret O'Gara, "Lutherans and Catholics: Ending an Old Argument," *Commonweal* 127 (January 14, 2000): 8–9.

6. Donald L. Gelpi, *The Gracing of Human Experience: Rethinking the Relationship between Nature and Grace* (Collegeville, Minn.: Liturgical, 2001).

7. James M. Gustafson, "Charles Curran: Ecumenical Theologian Par Excellence," in *A Call to Fidelity: On the Moral Theology of Charles E. Curran,* ed. James J. Walter, Timothy E. O'Connell, and Thomas A. Shannon (Washington, D.C.: Georgetown University Press, 2002), 211–34.

8. Thomas Aquinas, *Summa theologiae, Ia IIae* q. 94, a. 4.

9. For the insistence on an intrinsic morality in Thomas Aquinas and in the Catholic tradition, see John Mahoney, *The Making of Moral Theology: A Study of the Roman Catholic Tradition* (Oxford: Clarendon Press, 1989), 224–58.

10. Aquinas, *Summa theologiae, Ia IIae* q. 90.

11. Ibid., qq. 93–96.

12. Ibid., q. 120, a. 1.

13. Charles E. Curran, *Contemporary Problems in Moral Theology* (Notre Dame: Fides Press, 1970), 189–224.

14. Charles E. Curran, *Tensions in Moral Theology* (Notre Dame: University of Notre Dame Press, 1988), 87–109.

15. Charles E. Curran, *A New Look at Christian Morality* (Notre Dame: Fides Press, 1968), 201–21.

16. Josephus Fuchs, *De Castitate et ordine sexuali* (Roma: Editrice Università Gregoriana, 1959), 109; see also Sixtus Cartechini, *De Valore notarum theologicarum et de criteriis ad eas dignoscendas* (Roma: Editrice Università Gregoriana, 1951), 99–100; Marcellinus Zalba, *Theologiae moralis summa* (Madrid: Biblioteca de autores Cristianos, 1952), 2:340–41.

17. David Hollenbach, Review of *Catholic Social Teaching, 1891–Present: A Historical, Theological, and Ethical Analysis,* by Charles E. Curran, *Theological Studies* 64 (2003): 437–38.

18. Ernst Troeltsch, *The Social Teaching of the Christian Church* (New York: Harper Torchbook, 1960), 2:691–990.

19. Ibid., 2:691–729, 991–1013.

20. John T. Noonan Jr., *A Church That Can and Cannot Change* (Notre Dame: University of Notre Dame Press, 2005), 17–123.

21. For commentaries on Grisez's approach, see Robert P. George, ed., *Natural Law and Moral Inquiry: Ethics, Metaphysics, and Politics in the Work of Germain Grisez* (Washington, D.C.: Georgetown University Press, 1998).

22. See Bernard Hoose, *Proportionalism: The American Debate and Its European Roots* (Washington, D.C.: Georgetown University Press, 1987); Paulinus Ikechukwu Odozor, *Richard A. McCormick and the Renewal of Moral Theology* (Notre Dame: University of Notre Dame Press, 1995).

23. James Hitchcock, "The Fellowship of Catholic Scholars: Bowing Out of the New Class," in *Being Right: Conservative Catholics in America,* ed. Mary

Jo Weaver and R. Scott Appleby (Bloomington: University of Indiana Press, 1995), 186–210.

24. George Weigel, "The Neoconservative Difference: A Proposal for the Renewal of Church and Society," in Weaver and Appleby, *Being Right,* 138–62.

25. See William D. Miller, *A Harsh and Dreadful Love: Dorothy Day and the Catholic Worker Movement* (Garden City, N.Y.: Image, 1974); Mel Piehl, *Breaking Bread: The Catholic Worker and the Origin of Catholic Radicalism in America* (Philadelphia: Temple University Press, 1982); Michael L. Budde and Robert W. Brimlow, eds., *The Church as Counterculture* (Albany, N.Y.: State University of New York Press, 2000).

26. Walter, O' Connell, and Shannon, *Call to Fidelity.*

Notes to Chapter 9

1. Charles E. Curran, "Where Have the Dominant Theologians Gone?" *National Catholic Reporter,* February 4, 2005, 16.

2. Charles E. Curran, *Catholic Moral Theology in Dialogue* (Notre Dame: Fides Press, 1972), 24–64.

3. For a symposium celebrating the many aspects of Noonan's scholarly achievements, see "Founding Symposium: God, the Person, History, and the Law: Themes from the Work of Judge John T. Noonan, Jr.," *University of St. Thomas Law Journal* 1 (fall 2003): 1–779.

4. Curran, *Catholic Moral Theology in Dialogue,* 125–35.

5. See ibid., 1–23; Charles E. Curran, *Ongoing Revision: Studies in Moral Theology* (Notre Dame: Fides Press, 1975), 1–36.

6. See Charles E. Curran, *The Moral Theology of Pope John Paul II* (Washington, D.C.: Georgetown University Press, 2005), 120–23.

7. See Charles E. Curran, *Critical Concerns in Moral Theology* (Notre Dame: University of Notre Dame Press, 1984), 123–70; Charles E. Curran, *Toward an American Catholic Moral Theology* (Notre Dame: University of Notre Dame Press, 1987), 174–93; Charles E. Curran, *Tensions in Moral Theology* (Notre Dame: University of Notre Dame Press, 1988), 110–18.

8. James M. Gustafson, *Protestant and Roman Catholic Ethics: Prospects for Rapprochement* (Chicago: University of Chicago Press, 1978), xi.

9. Ibid.; James M. Gustafson, "Charles E. Curran: Ecumenical Moral Theological Par Excellence," in *A Call to Fidelity: On the Moral Theology of Charles E. Curran*, ed. James J. Walter, Timothy E. O'Connell, and Thomas A. Shannon (Washington, D.C.: Georgetown University Press, 2002), 211.

10. Gustafson, "Charles E. Curran," 232.

11. R. Scott Appleby, "American Ecclesiastical Review," in *Religious Periodicals of the United States*, ed. Charles H. Lippy (Westport, Conn.: Greenwood Press, 1986), 21–25; Bernard Noone, "Homiletic and Pastoral Review," ibid., 245–49.

12. Philip Gleason, *Contending with Modernity: Catholic Higher Education in the Twentieth Century* (New York: Oxford University Press, 1995), 258–59.

13. Catholic University of America, School of Religious Studies, *A Century of Religious Studies: Faculty and Dissertations* (Washington, D.C.: Catholic University of America, School of Religious Studies, 1989).

14. Reverend Hunter Guthrie, "Presidential Address," in *Tradition and Prospect: The Inauguration of the Very Rev. Hunter Guthrie, S.J., as Thirty-Fifth President of Georgetown University, April 30 and May 1, 1949* (Washington, D.C.: Georgetown University Press, 1949), 70–74.

15. Patrick W. Carey, "Catholic Theology in Historical Perspective," in *American Catholic Traditions: Resources for Renewal*, ed. Sandra Yocum Mize and William L. Portier (Maryknoll, N.Y.: Orbis, 1997), 243–59.

16. Andrew M. Greeley, *The Changing Catholic College* (Chicago: Aldine, 1967), 105–34.

17. John Tracy Ellis, "American Catholics and the Intellectual Life," *Thought* 30 (1955–56): 351–88.

18. Rosemary Rodgers, *A History of the College Theology Society* (Villanova, Pa.: College Theology Society/Horizons, 1983), 11–12; Gerard S. Sloyan, "Present at the Sidelines of the Creation," *Horizons* 31 (2004): 88–93; Sandra Yocum Mize, "On Writing a History of the College Theology Society," *Horizons* 31 (2004): 94–104.

19. Carey, "Catholic Theology in Historical Perspective," 259–61.

20. James F. Keenan, ed., *Catholic Ethicists on HIV/AIDS Prevention* (New York: Continuum, 2000). This book contains essays by Catholic theologians from all over the world.

21. See James A. Coriden, "Moral Theology and Academic Freedom: The New Context," in Walter, O'Connell, and Shannon, *Call to Fidelity*, 77–94.

22. Larry Witham, *Curran vs. Catholic University: A Story of Authority and Freedom in Conflict* (Riverdale, Md.: Edington-Rand, 1991).

23. Curran, *Critical Concerns in Moral Theology*, 171–99.

24. Charles E. Curran, *Transition and Tradition in Moral Theology* (Notre Dame: University of Notre Dame Press, 1979), 139–70.

25. Curran, *Toward an American Catholic Moral Theology*, 93–118.

26. For my most developed discussion of the common good, see Curran, *Tensions in Moral Theology*, 119–37.

27. For the article in which I address this subject most fully, see Charles E. Curran, "Churches and Human Rights: From Hostility/Reluctance to Acceptability," *Milltown Studies* 42 (1998): 30–58.

28. Curran, *Critical Concerns in Moral Theology*, 123–70; Curran, *Toward an American Catholic Moral Theology*, 20–51; Curran, *Tensions in Moral Theology*, 138–61.

Notes to Chapter 10

1. For a comprehensive treatment of these issues of sexuality, see Charles E. Curran and Richard A. McCormick, eds., *Readings in Moral Theology No. 8: Dialogue about Catholic Sexual Teaching* (New York: Paulist Press, 1993).

2. Pope John Paul II, "Ordinatio sacerdotalis," *Origins* 24 (1994): 49–52.

3. Karl Rahner, "The Church of Sinners," *Cross Currents* 1 (spring 1951): 64–74. This article first appeared in German in *Stimmen der Zeit* 52 (1947): 163–77.

4. Pope John Paul II, "Tertio millenio adveniente," pars. 33–36, *Origins* 24 (1994): 410–11; Pope John Paul II, "Incarnationis mysterium," par. 11, *Origins* 28 (1998): 450–51; Pope John Paul II, "Jubilee Characteristic: The Purification of Memory," *Origins* 29 (2000): 649–50. For an analysis of the papal teaching, see John Ford, "John Paul II Asks for Forgiveness," *Ecumenical Trends* 27 (December 1998): 173–75; Francis A. Sullivan, "The Papal Apology," *America* 182 (April 8, 2000): 17–22; Analine H. Kaliban, "The Catholic Church's Public Confession: Theological and Ethical Implications," *Annual of the Society of Christian Ethics* 21 (2001): 175–89.

5. For a good commentary on Mark, see Francis J. Moloney, *The Gospel of Mark: A Commentary* (Peabody, Mass.: Hendrickson, 2002).

6. For more on this controversy, see Frederick M. Jones, *Alphonsus de Liguori: The Saint of Bourbon Naples, 1696–1787* (Westminster, Md.: Christian Classics, 1992), 264–66, 424–26.

7. Bernard Sesboüé, "Le 'Sensus Fidelium' en morale à la lumière de Vatican II," *Le Supplément* 181 (June 1992): 153–66.

8. James A. Coriden, "The Canonical Doctrine of Reception," *Jurist* 50 (1990): 58–82; the entire issue of the *Jurist* 57, no. 2 (1997) is devoted to the issue of reception.

9. Charles E. Curran, *The Crisis in Priestly Ministry* (Notre Dame: Fides Press, 1972), 82–89.

10. Yves M.-J. Congar, *Journal d'un théologien: 1946–1956,* annotated by Etienne Fouilloux (Paris: Cerf, 2001); Yves M.-J. Congar, *Mon journal du concile,* annotated by Éric Mahieu (Paris: Cerf, 2002).

11. Yves M.-J. Congar, "Preface: Appels et cheminements: 1929–63," in *Chrétiens en dialogue* (Paris: Cerf, 1964), ix–lxiv; Yves M.-J. Congar, "A mes frères pretres," *La vie spirituelle* 113 (1965): 501–20.

12. Curran, *Crisis in Priestly Ministry,* 87.

13. Ibid., 89–96.

14. This saying, often attributed to Augustine, is from Rupert Meldenius, a seventeenth-century Lutheran theologian. Philip Schaff, *History of the Christian Church,* 2d ed. (New York: Charles Scribner's Sons, 1911), 6:650–53.

15. John Tracy Ellis, "The Formation of the American Priest," in *The Catholic Priest in the United States: Historical Investigations,* ed. John Tracy Ellis (Collegeville, Minn.: Saint John's University Press, 1971), 65.

16. Thomas Bouquillon, "Moral Theology at the End of the Nineteenth Century," *Catholic University Bulletin* 5 (1899): 267.

17. See, for example, John P. Kenny, *Principles of Medical Ethics,* 2d ed. (Westminster, Md.: Newman, 1961); John F. Cronin, *Social Principles and Economic Life,* 2d ed. (Milwaukee: Bruce Publishing, 1964).

18. Charles E. Curran, *The Living Tradition of Catholic Moral Theology* (Notre Dame: University of Notre Dame Press, 1992), 134–59.

19. For my analysis and criticism of proposals for a global ethic, see Charles E. Curran, "The Global Ethic," *Ecumenist* 37 (spring 2000): 6–10.

20. Congar, *Chrétiens en dialogue,* lvi–lvii.

Published Works of Charles E. Curran

Books

Invincible Ignorance of the Natural Law According to St. Alphonsus. Rome: Academia Alfonsiana, 1961.

The Prevention of Conception after Rape: An Historical Theological Study. Rome: Pontificia Universitas Gregoriana, 1961.

Christian Morality Today: The Renewal of Moral Theology. Notre Dame: Fides Press, 1966.

A New Look at Christian Morality. Notre Dame: Fides Press, 1968.

Contemporary Problems in Moral Theology. Notre Dame: Fides Press, 1970.

Medicine and Morals. Washington, D.C.: Corpus, 1970.

Catholic Moral Theology in Dialogue. Notre Dame: Fides Press, 1972. Paperback edition, Notre Dame: University of Notre Dame Press, 1976.

The Crisis in Priestly Ministry. Notre Dame: Fides Press, 1972.

Politics, Medicine, and Christian Ethics: A Dialogue with Paul Ramsey. Philadelphia: Fortress, 1973.

Blueprints for Moral Living. Chicago: Claretian, 1974.

New Perspectives in Moral Theology. Notre Dame: Fides Press, 1974. Paperback edition, Notre Dame: University of Notre Dame Press, 1976.

Ongoing Revision: Studies in Moral Theology. Notre Dame: Fides Press, 1975. Reprinted in paperback as *Ongoing Revision in Moral Theology.* Notre Dame: Fides/Claretian, 1975.

Themes in Fundamental Moral Theology. Notre Dame: University of Notre Dame Press, 1977.

Issues in Sexual and Medical Ethics. Notre Dame: University of Notre Dame Press, 1978.

Transition and Tradition in Moral Theology. Notre Dame: University of Notre Dame Press, 1979.

American Catholic Social Ethics: Twentieth-Century Approaches. Notre Dame: University of Notre Dame Press, 1982.

Moral Theology: A Continuing Journey. Notre Dame: University of Notre Dame Press, 1982.

Critical Concerns in Moral Theology. Notre Dame: University of Notre Dame Press, 1984.

Directions in Catholic Social Ethics. Notre Dame: University of Notre Dame Press, 1985.

Directions in Fundamental Moral Theology. Notre Dame: University of Notre Dame Press, 1985.

Faithful Dissent. Kansas City, Mo.: Sheed and Ward, 1986.

Toward an American Catholic Moral Theology. Notre Dame: University of Notre Dame Press, 1987.

Sexualität und Ethik. Frankfurt: Athenäum, 1988.

Tensions in Moral Theology. Notre Dame: University of Notre Dame Press, 1988.

Catholic Higher Education, Theology, and Academic Freedom. Notre Dame: University of Notre Dame Press, 1990.

The Living Tradition of Catholic Moral Theology. Notre Dame: University of Notre Dame Press, 1992.

The Church and Morality: An Ecumenical and Catholic Approach. Minneapolis: Fortress, 1993.

History and Contemporary Issues: Studies in Moral Theology. New York: Continuum, 1996.

The Origins of Moral Theology in the United States: Three Different Approaches. Washington, D.C.: Georgetown University Press, 1997.

The Catholic Moral Tradition Today: A Synthesis. Washington, D.C.: Georgetown University Press, 1999.

Moral Theology at the End of the Century. Milwaukee: Marquette University Press, 1999.

Catholic Social Teaching, 1891–Present: A Historical, Theological, and Ethical Analysis. Washington, D.C.: Georgetown University Press, 2002.

The Moral Theology of Pope John Paul II. Washington, D.C.: Georgetown University Press, 2005.

Cowritten Books

Curran, Charles E., and Robert E. Hunt, with John F. Hunt and Terrence R. Connelly. *Dissent In and For the Church: Theologians and Humanae Vitae.* New York: Sheed and Ward, 1969.

Hunt, John F., and Terrence R. Connelly, with Charles E. Curran, Robert E. Hunt, and Robert K. Webb. *The Responsibility of Dissent: The Church and Academic Freedom.* New York: Sheed and Ward, 1969.

Books Edited

Absolutes in Moral Theology? Washington, D.C.: Corpus, 1968.

Contraception: Authority and Dissent. New York: Herder and Herder, 1969.

Curran, Charles E., and George J. Dyer, eds., *Shared Responsibility in the Local Church.* Mundelin, Ill.: Catholic Theological Society, 1970.

Moral Theology: Challenges for the Future; Essays in Honor of Richard A. McCormick. New York: Paulist Press, 1990.

Coeditor and editor of the series Readings in Moral Theology, published by Paulist Press. Volumes 1–8 and 10–11 coedited with Richard A. McCormick.

Readings in Moral Theology No. 1: Moral Norms and Catholic Tradition. 1979.

Readings in Moral Theology No. 2: The Distinctiveness of Christian Ethics. 1980.

Readings in Moral Theology No. 3: The Magisterium and Morality. 1982.

Readings in Moral Theology No. 4: The Use of Scripture in Moral Theology. 1984.

Readings in Moral Theology No. 5: Official Catholic Social Teaching. 1986.

Readings in Moral Theology No. 6: Dissent in the Church. 1988.

Readings in Moral Theology No. 7: Natural Law and Theology. 1991.

Readings in Moral Theology No. 8: Dialogue about Catholic Sexual Teaching. 1993.

Feminist Ethics and the Catholic Moral Tradition: Readings in Moral Theology No. 9. 1996. Ed. Charles E. Curran, Margaret A. Farley, and Richard A. McCormick.

John Paul II and Moral Theology: Readings in Moral Theology No. 10. 1998.

The Historical Development of Fundamental Moral Theology in the United States: Readings in Moral Theology No 11. 1999.

The Catholic Church, Morality, and Politics: Readings in Moral Theology No. 12. 2001. Ed. Charles E. Curran and Leslie Griffin.

Change in Official Catholic Moral Teachings: Readings in Moral Theology No. 13. 2003. Ed. Charles E. Curran.

Conscience: Readings in Moral Theology No. 14. 2004. Ed. Charles E. Curran.

About the Author

Charles E. Curran, a Roman Catholic priest of the Diocese of Rochester, New York, is Elizabeth Scurlock University Professor of Human Values at Southern Methodist University. He was the first recipient of the John Courtney Murray Award for Theology and has served as president of the Catholic Theological Society of America, the Society of Christian Ethics, and the American Theological Society. In 2003, Curran received the Presidential Award of the College Theology Society for a lifetime of scholarly achievements in moral theology, and in 2005, Call to Action—a reform movement of 25,000 Catholics—presented him with its leadership award. He is the author of *The Moral Theology of Pope John Paul II* and *Catholic Social Teaching, 1891–Present,* both published by Georgetown University Press.

Index